D1432777

...nder, 1922-
... Captain James Cook
... 1st U.S. ed. -- New

... of plates : ill. ;

S
(

The Last Voyage
of
Captain James Cook

The Last Voyage
of
Captain James Cook

Richard Hough

WILLIAM MORROW AND COMPANY, INC.

NEW YORK 1979

Library of Congress Catalog Card Number 79-63210

ISBN 0-688-03413-6

Printed in the United States of America.

First U.S. Edition

1 2 3 4 5 6 7 8 9 10

Contents

Illustrations

Author's note

GENERALLY THROUGHOUT THIS book I have used present-day spelling of islands, place names etc. except where the naming by Cook and his officers is relevant. In the case of the Hawaiian islands, by contrast with the Society and Friendly Islands, he accepted the local rendering, with numerous variations in spelling. Among the original journals, documents, logs and diaries, the spelling, punctuation and sentence construction are highly personal and inconsistent. Some of the best educated officers (James Burney for one) were the worst spellers. Spelling ability was not rated highly at this time. I have smoothed out inconsistencies and corrected spelling and punctuation to modern practice. Anyone wishing to refer to the original spelling may consult either the relevant MSS. or the late Professor Beaglehole's prodigious works to whom every Cook student will for ever be in debt. Similarly, any reader wishing to trace the source reference to quotations in this book will find many of them in the Beaglehole-edited Journals, which I have used in conjunction with the original MSS. in this country, Australia and New Zealand.

My thanks must be recorded to the Librarians and their Staff at the National Maritime Museum Library, Greenwich, the London Library, the Royal United Services Institution Library, the Naval Library, the British Library, the City of Auckland Public Library, the Alexander Turnbull Library, Wellington, the Dixson and Mitchell Libraries at Sydney, the Whitby Library; and to the Staff at the Public Record Office, Chancery Lane and Kew.

I wish to thank Dr Eliot Slater, C.B.E., M.A., M.D. and Dr Nicholas Rea, M.D. for advice on Cook's medical condition; Geoffrey Graham, M.A. of the Whitby Literary and Philosophical Society; Miss Suzanne Mourot; Anthony Murray-Oliver; Canon Alun Morris, C.B.E.; Professor Christopher Lloyd; Stephen Higginbottom, F.B.H.I. on horology; Douglas Matthews for an impeccable index; and my ever-patient, ever-admirable typist, Mrs Kloegman.

My thanks are also due to the pilots of light aircraft, float-planes and land planes, as well as helmsmen of motor launches, who took me to several awkward places, from Bruni Island off Tasmania to Alaska, which I wished to see and photograph.

ACKNOWLEDGEMENTS FOR ILLUSTRATIONS

The portraits of Captain James Cook, Sir Hugh Palliser and the Earl of Sandwich; the drawings of Adventure Bay, Queen Charlotte's Sound and Nootka Sound; the Zoffany painting of the murder, and the drawing of the sloops in Arctic ice, are all reproduced by permission of the Trustees of the National Maritime Museum.

The drawing of the *Resolution* and of Prince William Sound are reproduced by courtesy of the Trustees of the British Library.

The National Library of Australia was kind enough to allow me to reproduce the portrait of John Gore.

I am grateful to the Governor-General of New Zealand for allowing me to reproduce the portrait of Captain Charles Clerke which hangs in Government House, Wellington.

The photographs are my own copyright.

RICHARD HOUGH

I

Dinner for four

IT HAD BEEN a heavy, damp day, with fresh breezes from the south, conditions which James Cook observed as if he were still searching fruitlessly for Bouvet Island in the South Atlantic, a rare and irritating failure of exactly twelve months before. Cook noted weather as a deer registers scent, through every conscious moment of every day and night; if he was writing his journal in Mile End Row, or was on the quarter-deck of the *Resolution*. He predicted imminent heavy rain before dusk fell over London at the end of this unpleasant Thursday. And on the morrow, 9 January 1776, with winds veering and freshening, there would be bright winter sunshine, but always with the threat of black skies and squalls.

Cook was right on both counts. The rain began to fall on the stone cobbles of Admiralty yard before his carriage was admitted through the Adams' screen, and the horses drew it along the carriageway to the pillared façade. And the sun, which was to break through at last on the following morning, would reflect the state of his spirits and the imminent change in his fortunes, just as the predicted squalls were harbingers of danger.

James Cook was to dine with his patron and one-time commander, Rear-Admiral Sir Hugh Palliser, Comptroller of the Royal Navy; the First Lord of the Admiralty, the Earl of Sandwich; and Philip Stephens, the Admiralty Secretary. He would dine well, still a comforting consideration in spite of being off shipboard rations for more than six months. The subject for discussion was close to his heart, and yet was a painful one. It was another voyage to the Pacific in order to add to the knowledge of that vast ocean, to chart the coastline of New Albion (North America's western seaboard), and to unravel one of the last great geographical mysteries.

But Cook was not to be the commander. His old friend and lieutenant, Charles Clerke, was the most likely candidate for leading this expedition of 1776. James Cook's duties were limited to those of an adviser—consultant and adviser on a superior level, but a non-participant. Mutually, regretfully, that had been the decision. The most celebrated explorer-scientist of his day had accepted a profitable sinecure appointment at the Royal Hospital, Greenwich, not quite pensioned off but at 47 years relegated to honourable semi-retirement, like a veteran First Rate ship-of-the-line laid up at the end of an arduous war. He remained, as he was demonstrating this afternoon, a fount of unparalleled wisdom and experience of the Pacific Ocean.

Cook paced briskly—no rolling sailor's gait—across the yard from the carriage to the door leading to Admiralty House, dressed in blue frock coat with spare gold trimmings, white breeches and waistcoat, and carrying his tricorne hat in spite of the rain. The watchman recognized the tall, slightly stooping six-foot-two figure as he stepped from his carriage. He saw a heavy, crag-like head, long tied-back steel-grey hair and eyebrows, and deep-set, responsible eyes that were sharp in judgment and perception of danger. The nose, unashamedly big, matched the heavy-boned impression of the purposeful body; mouth and chin together almost as one strong and uncompromising unit.

Because of the captain's pace, the watchman saw all this only briefly. Perhaps he thought as their eyes met, 'There's a taut hand—and no tricks'd get past *him*.' Certainly he could not have escaped the breath of greatness as the big man passed by, for no one could be insensitive to that. It was more likely that he failed to recognize how tired the man was.

Cook paused to sign the visitors' book, and proceeded to the

First Lord's drawing room. The three men arose from their seats as Cook was shown in. They had observed the germination of his greatness, and its growth to maturity. They had perforce seen it in sudden leaps at the end of long voyages, as a father sees his son anew at the end of boarding school terms: the new firmer demeanour, the new confident voice, the new assertive expression.

Palliser had known him longest, since Cook had been 27, and he as his commander five years older. As he looked now at his protégé and dear friend, who was quite at ease in the exalted company, Palliser contemplated the evening ahead uneasily. Was it right, was it wise even, to lay this man open to the temptation that was soon to be presented to him?

John Montagu, Fourth Earl of Sandwich, had no such doubts. He had known Cook since the conclusion of the navigator's first Pacific voyage in 1771, which had coincided with the beginning of the earl's third period of office at the Admiralty. As a shrewd and experienced judge of men, he had quickly recognized the outstanding qualities of the lieutenant promoted from the lower deck, and gave all his support to the new star of five years ago who had now become a planet in the naval firmament, outshining every fighting admiral, for all their glittering honours and mountainous prize money.

And Stephens? It was to Philip Stephens's credit that he had put forward Cook's name to Palliser as commander of the first voyage, the first step towards fame. One of the smallest consequences of that expedition was the naming by Cook of a New Zealand cape after him. Stephens had been sponsored by the great George Anson, with whom he had shared the adventures and hazards of his circumnavigation: first his secretary, then the Admiralty's assistant secretary, now Secretary of the Admiralty. He was a sturdy, sensible, modest, well-organized man, and this was reflected in his appearance; whereas Sandwich's long, fallen-in aristocratic face and heavy eyelids told of a dissolute life: night-long gambling while eating only the new dish he had invented to save time, and named. Much drink to make up. Numerous visits to the notorious Hell-Fire Club. His mistress, the singer Martha Ray, living with him openly at the Admiralty, until she was to be shot dead on the steps of Covent Garden three years later.

As for Palliser, whatever anxiety he might be feeling, the face that Cook knew so well was, as always, full of good puckish humour, smiling often yet reflecting profound intelligence.

Dinner at 4.30 followed the exchange of personal and general talk—on the subjects of the warm, damp, unseasonable weather, the progress of Cook's journal, the health of Mrs Cook, who, like most sailors' wives, was advanced in pregnancy exactly as long as her husband had been home, the health of the king, the troubles in America. The conversation for the most part followed the predictable subjects of the progress of the refit of the *Resolution*, Cook's ship on his last voyage, and the modifications to the second ship, the *Discovery*, which had been purchased a month earlier, the alterations being approved only the previous day.

The subject of the instruments for the voyage was on the agenda, too, and the chronometers the two ships were to carry. The respective merits of a Kendall, a Harrison or an Arnold was always a subject for technical debate.

But later it became clear to Cook that the selection of the expedition's officers was the leading object of the dinner—the qualities and deficiencies of those who had served with Cook on his last voyage: Cooper, Kempe, Tobias Furneaux, who had commanded the second ship, and Charles Clerke himself. Was that popular, cheerful, hell-for-leather officer, Clerke, the right man to command such a long, arduous and important expedition? He was, it was argued, experienced in the Pacific. Would the weight of responsibility lead to a growth in his stature and leadership qualities, as it should do? Or would his waggish style and his inevitable consorting with the native women lead to loss of respect by his men?

As Cook knew so well, and to his cost, a commander's duties on a voyage of discovery were not only onerous but were borne alone, or should be. Every day, at every awakening, the responsibilities bore down implacably: decisions to be made, weather to be judged, danger to be assessed, state of the ships, provisions and water to be checked, defaulters to be punished, good men praised. The weight was always there, week after week, month after month; for the last voyage over three years.

Would the gregarious Clerke, who liked nothing better than yarning over a bottle, conduct himself with the detachment as well as the dignity of a great commander? And did he have the weight and steadiness, the judgment and stamina?

Cook admired and loved the man. And yet? At one stage of the evening, the doubts were aired more freely by Palliser, Stephens and Sandwich. The poison began its work on Cook, as if the wine had been laced. And then at one moment, cunningly timed by Sandwich, the inevitable happened. Cook suddenly stood up at the table, eyeing the three men in turn and said, 'I will myself undertake the direction of this enterprise if I am so commanded.'

The other three at once arose to their feet, pouring out their thanks and congratulations, charging their glasses and toasting his health and success again and again. Palliser, a compassionate man as well as a realist, attempted and temporarily succeeded in stifling his own feelings of guilt and anxiety. They had all played on the navigator's vanity, his sense of duty and enjoyment of power and responsibility. He was drugged with the lust for voyaging, and he was bound to succumb. But Hugh Palliser, who knew his protégé better even than Cook's wife Elizabeth, also recognized how weary Cook still was from the unbroken strain of command for more than eleven hundred days and nights of the last voyage. If he were fit, there was no one to equal the man for the task that lay ahead, but was it asking too much to risk his own life along with those of his men, to despatch him to the other side of the world for another two years or more?

The formalities followed swiftly and decisively. Sandwich had an audience of King George III, who had met and greatly admired Cook and took a deep interest in all voyages of discovery. He warmly approved of the appointment.

Cook returned to the Admiralty on Saturday morning to write out the acceptance of his appointment, adding a typically cautious rider that he hoped upon his return that he would be restored to his appointment at the Hospital. On the same day he made his way to Deptford and the docked *Resolution*, and hoisted his pendant, the formal confirmation of the dramatic turn of events in his life. At the Admiralty the order was issued which was to have such profound repercussions: '*Resolution* and *Discovery* to be sheathed and filled, and fitted for voyage to remote parts. . .'

The choice of the *Endeavour* for the first Pacific voyage, and the *Resolution* for the second voyage, with her consort the *Adventure*, were Cook's own, and were the result of his experience as a young apprentice seaman back in the 1750s. The vessels he had sailed in were typically practical Yorkshire vessels, Whitby 'cats', stout and strong and capacious, shallow of draught, light of rig and easily worked with a small crew, not too large to be beached and repaired or careened, and if they struck ground, could sit on it as stoutly as any fat cat until the tide ebbed.

Sensible James Cook wanted no nippy frigate, nor ship-of-the-line as advocated by those misguided enough to believe that safety lay in size, nor East India Company ships, nor three-decked West India ships, 'nor indeed any other but North-Country-built ships such as are built for the coal trade'—a trade he had worked in, off and on, for more than a decade of his life.

A collier, in fact, a plebeian cat, renamed sloop for decency in His Majesty's service. The *Endeavour* had proved herself on the first voyage, the *Resolution* on the second voyage. Cook had first seen and examined her at Whitby in 1771, a cat of 462 tons, three-masted, stout as a publican's wife, 110 feet long on the lower deck, a fraction over 30 feet in the beam, built at Whitby by Fishburns in 1770.

Her consort, *Discovery*, was similar but smaller, of 295 tons, purchased from William Herbert of Scarborough. A good, solid cat that was to prove the faster sailer, and better able to claw off a lee shore.

Cook was fully aware that his was the greatest age for romance and science since the Elizabethans'. He had seen the two march side by side comfortably and triumphantly in the person of Joseph Banks on his first voyage: Banks, like a schoolboy with a fanatical hobby, tripping over his own legs and his instruments as he raced ashore to study the plants, identify the birds, measure the trees and plant his seeds.

Cook remembered Banks and his party, a nuisance though they often were, ceasing to talk only in order to write up their notes or make detail drawings. Nothing could ever again quite equal that first great voyage, the transit of Venus voyage, when they had observed from their protected and 'taboo-ed' area on Matavai Bay, Tahiti, the passage of the planet across the face of the sun.

Cook's mind was constantly stimulated by the presence on board of these learned enthusiasts. But he had always been less trustful of the romantic side of their natures. This nonsense of the great southern continent! Cook flattered himself that he had an open mind, a practical Yorkshire mind. He had always entertained grave doubts about the existence of the so-called *Terra australis incognita.* As a gifted cartographer himself, what offended him more was that there were even charts of it, showing it was a huge land mass occupying half the Pacific Ocean between Cape Horn and New Holland (Australia), complete with mountains and rivers and headlands to balance the weight of all that northern land mass!

It seemed remarkable to Cook that men with such developed intellects—Banks himself for example—could believe such nonsense, simply because it had been accepted for centuries and they were incapable of envisaging an ocean as vast and as empty as the Pacific. And even now, in 1776, after the deep Antarctic penetrations he had made like dagger thrusts on his charts, which had killed this myth, there were still those who remained unconvinced. Like Alexander Dalrymple, the famous scientist and navigator who had so badly wanted to command the *Endeavour* back in 1768, and had never forgiven Cook for being appointed in his place.

And now it was the North-West Passage, the 'free and open passage' between north Atlantic and north Pacific. This was the second great mystery he was enjoined to solve. It, too, had been charted, as early as 1592, by the Spaniard Juan de Fuca, despatched by the viceroy in Mexico to search for the Strait of

Anian. He had found it, too, sailed clean through it in twenty days, observing a land rich in gold and silver, then out into the Atlantic. What a voyage!

Cook, the hard-headed, mightily experienced navigator, did not give a fig for this account, this fairy tale. People believed what they wanted to believe, and romanticism seemed always to prevail. If the Strait of Anian did not exist, there would be another. There must be. And it could be discovered, for certain in the summer, when the icebergs from the rivers would have melted. Seawater did not freeze. The Royal Society said so. And now that control of Canada had been wrested from France, to discover and then to control this short-cut to the Orient would add immense new riches and power to Britain, which already possessed one-eighth of the earth's land surface. A £20,000 prize was the reward for its discovery—perhaps half a million in today's money. But a successful passage north of the American continent would also mark a voyage as great as any since Columbus's time, and bring everlasting fame and riches to its commander.

Cook flatly rejected as a myth the Strait of Anian's existence. He had read of the numerous abortive and often fatal attempts of the past two centuries. Certainly he did not share the Admiralty's imaginary picture, neatly painted with the alternate brushstrokes of the romantic and practical schools: the triumphant meeting in the North-West Passage of Cook's *Resolution* from the Pacific, and the expedition, commanded by his old shipmate, Richard Pickersgill, they were despatching from the Atlantic to coincide with his penetration from the Pacific.

But, Cook had argued to himself at length, his present fame and financial security stemmed as much from the destruction of myths as from the discoveries in New Zealand, New South Wales and the Pacific Islands he had charted. The north Pacific was new to him, the coast of New Albion almost entirely uncharted north of California, and if he succeeded in penetrating through the strait discovered by the Russian Vitus Bering, who could tell? It was not impossible. . . .

He had not realized how powerful was the longing to be away, to feel the stout decks of the *Resolution* beneath his feet again, to see the lift of strange shores upon the horizon and to mark and chart islands and headlands—not until that moment when he had stood up to settle all doubts as to who would command this expedition, the most ambitious of them all.

Within days of the appointment he was writing to a friend that he hoped to be away in April. Certainly it should not be much later than that month if he was to reach the west coast of America by the following April allowing for mishaps and for refreshing the crews and replenishing the supplies. Instead, on 2 April James Boswell met Cook for the first time when they dined at the house of a mutual friend. The diarist noted: 'It was curious to see Cook, a grave steady man, and his wife, a decent plump [she was now eight months pregnant] Englishwoman, and think that he was preparing to sail round the world.'

Grave and steady, as Boswell had observed. Patient, persevering, accomplished, and now self-confident, too. The self-confidence had been vital to his success and had grown with it. It was the self-confidence of a man with a measured pace and keen intelligence, accustomed to good fortune. For Cook was that blessed creature, a man to whom good luck had become a habit so that now, at 47, he accepted it almost as a right.

Since early childhood he had been fortunate in the people he met and the time he met them. At Marton-in-Cleveland, the village schoolmistress had early recognized his bright mind, and she taught him to read without payment. Working on the land, in a shop, and at length as an apprentice at sea, his special talents were recognized by the right people at the right time, bringing him preferment. Within weeks of joining the navy, he had Palliser as his commanding officer; and how much he owed to that spirited and influential officer! And there had been others in the navy who had seen to it that his talents as a hydrographer, cartographer and navigator were fully exploited, men like Lord Colville and Admiral Thomas Graves, an officer to be reckoned with before his woeful action off Chesapeake Bay twenty years later, which had led to victory for the Americans in the War of Independence. And now the sovereign himself, King George III, one of his most ardent admirers.

A good wife had come his way when he was in need of her, and fine children had followed. Only 'the gift of fortune' of 'the well-favoured man' could have taken James Cook from a clay-built two-room hut in the hardness of North Yorkshire to world recognition. And once again in 1776—or so it seemed to Cook—good luck and good health were his.

He had in the past been fortunate, and shrewd, in his choice of officers and midshipmen—the young gentlemen.

The most important amongst the many tasks that now faced him was the selection of officers for the *Resolution*, and for the *Discovery*, in conjunction with Clerke. This was nominally the responsibility of Secretary Stephens, working closely with the First Lord. But Cook's influence was so powerful that if he wrote, as he frequently did, 'I beg you will move their Lordships' to make an appointment, it was almost invariably complied with. There was a great deal of competition among young officers for a billet under Cook, and he had the ready assistance of the manning board and Stephens at the Admiralty in making his choice.

Cook did not know whether Charles Clerke had learned how close he had come to commanding the expedition. Unlike Dalrymple, he would not in the least have resented yielding to his old friend. Instead Clerke was now to be second-in-command and commander of the *Discovery*. The two men worked well together, the flippant, waggish lieutenant from Braintree in Essex and the steady Yorkshire captain. Clerke, bright-eyed, fair with a ruddy complexion, was an inspired seaman when, as one of his contemporaries qualified, 'a certain line of action is chalked out to him and then no man is readier to pursue it than himself'. Nor did he have any aptitude for surveying or drawing. But his men loved him. In the past he had often overstepped the accepted limits of familiarity with his subordinates, but Cook had witnessed his maturing and steadying over the years. He thought he would do well.

Clerke was 32, and he came from a family of modest but by no means slender means, the seat being Weathersfield Hall. Unlike Cook, he had been in the navy since boyhood, and good fortune had followed him in his career, too. He had seen more action than Cook. In one fight with a French 74 he had been stationed in the mizzen top when the mast was shot away. All were drowned except Clerke, who managed to save himself in the rigging.

Cook had selected him as mate in the *Endeavour* on his first voyage for his cheerful manner and because he had just completed the circumnavigation with Wallis, and therefore knew Tahiti and much of the Pacific. His excitement at the discovery of Tahiti, and his exuberant behaviour with the women there, had been witnessed joyfully by all the *Dolphin*'s company. 'Clerke is a right good officer,' wrote a shipmate in the *Resolution* on Cook's second voyage. 'At drinking and whoring he is as good as the best of them.'

Clerke's generous nature had led him to stand as guarantor for his improvident brother's debts. Cook did not know of this, nor that this brother, a fellow naval officer, had just sailed for the East Indies.

John Gore, an American and the *Resolution*'s first lieutenant, was another highly experienced Pacific sailor, who had crossed that ocean with Byron before joining Clerke in the *Dolphin* and crossing it all over again. He had none of Cook's inspiration and second sense as a navigator but he was as steady and error-free as his captain and possessed a cheerful spirit always ready to see the bright side. A steady optimist. There was never a cross word between the two men, and a nervous seaman could have doubled Cape Horn in a full gale with them without a single pulse of fear.

Gore, fair-skinned with close-set pale eyes and thinning red hair, was the oldest officer on the voyage second to Cook. He had none of Clerke's reputation as a libertine but was believed to have a mistress and a child born out of wedlock tucked away. He had been with Banks on a trip to Iceland when it had proved impossible for that scientist to accompany Cook again on his second voyage, and in later correspondence there had been references to a lady called Nancy (or perhaps just his 'nancy', as sailors' fancies were often called) and to Banks promising to look after 'a young one' in the event of Gore's death.

In even stronger contrast to Clerke was William Bligh, whom Cook had selected for the important role as master of the *Resolution*. There would be no 'drinking and whoring' with

Bligh. Lord Sandwich had recommended this 22-year-old man for his exceptional proficiency as a navigator and cartographer, qualities which the First Lord knew would be appreciated by the commander; and like Cook, this master had entered the navy through the lower deck.

Cook saw a man of medium height, six inches shorter than himself, with a sharp chin, sharp nose and thin mouth which did not readily form into a smile. Keen, close-set blue eyes shone out from a rather pale face. He spoke incisively and self-confidently. Cook was not immediately sure that he—or perhaps anyone else—was going to become a close friend of this intense young Devonian. But he agreed with Sandwich that he would make no navigational errors and inspire respect among the men.

James King, the *Resolution*'s second lieutenant, was an officer of very different qualities and character from Bligh, a refined intellectual, son of a parson, friend of Edmund Burke the statesman and philosopher and of Thomas Hornsby the astronomer, who recommended him to Cook. King was a gentle, fastidious, hypochondriacal and kindly man who might be regarded as effeminate by the ruder members of the *Resolution*'s company—of which there were many—but who was to be a great solace and close companion to Cook during the difficult months ahead.

As Cook rapidly built up his team it became clear that the *Resolution* would be sailing with a remarkably rich yet disparate company of officers and men. Some were to die or return unloved by their companions. Others were to gain esteem and develop close friendships that would lead to other voyages together.

Bligh himself was to sail on another expedition, this time in command, with two of the *Discovery*'s company, the kindly and enthusiastic gardener from Kew, David Nelson, and the stalwart gunner William Peckover. The *Resolution*'s surgeon and observant amateur natural historian and ethnologist William Anderson—a Scot liked by all and admired for his exceptional intelligence—embarked with the seeds of a fatal disease within him. Nor was he the only one.

Another bright star, observant, clever, companionable and

also son of a churchman, was one of Anderson's mates, David Samwell. He was a Welshman from Nantglyn, and inevitably a poet. He was more than an amateur, too. He had a wide reputation, not least for being the only competent poet, in English and Welsh, who had enjoyed a sea passage to Greenland and back. His comments in the admirable journal he kept, on the day to day affairs of the *Resolution*, of events ashore and of his fellow sailors, were, next to Cook's, to be the most valuable of all.

Anderson and Samwell, surgeon and his assistant, were two of the most popular men in the *Resolution*. Without doubt, the most unpopular was the third lieutenant, John Williamson, an Irishman and a disastrous appointment. Like all unpopular men, over a period of time in the same company, his unlikable characteristics became self-nourishing and evergrowing.

The famous musicologist, Dr Charles Burney had persuaded Sandwich and Cook to take on the previous voyage his young son James ('Jem'), who had entered the navy at ten and shown unusual spirit and promise. He had sailed as an A.B. in Cook's second ship, the *Adventure*, and been promoted lieutenant en route. His sister Fanny Burney described Jem as 'honest, generous, sensible, unpolished; . . .very careless, and possessed of an uncommon share of good nature; full of humour, mirth and jollity; ever delighted at mirth in others.' Jem Burney having returned earlier in the *Adventure* was serving in the frigate *Cerberus* on the American station while Cook was on his way home from his second expedition. Fanny wrote telling him that another Pacific voyage was planned but that it would not leave until Cook returned. 'There is nothing that Jem so earnestly desires as to be of the party,' she wrote. 'It is just possible that [he] may be returned in time.' He did return in time and Cook made him Clerke's first lieutenant. Jem Burney would have preferred to have served directly under Cook in the *Resolution*, especially as his close friend Molesworth Phillips was lieutenant of marines.

Phillips was described as 'a fine made, tall, stout, active, manly-looking young fellow as you shall see'. He had a good military record, but as the voyage proceeded it became evident that he was 'a bone idle fellow' quite unsuited to maintaining discipline and any sort of standard amongst his men. This came to be regarded as something of a joke amongst his fellow officers, except by Cook, and of course by Bligh, who said that 'he never was of any real service the whole voyage, or did anything but eat and sleep'.

Phillips commanded in the *Resolution* a sergeant, two corporals, 15 privates and a drummer—there were 12 more marines in the *Discovery*.

Phillips' sergeant of marines, Samuel Gibson, was very different from most of his service and rank. He was still in his teens when he was appointed as a private in the *Endeavour* on Cook's first voyage. He and another private deserted at Tahiti having 'strongly attached themselves' to two girls, but he was easily recovered and duly flogged. His love affair had the more satisfactory result of leading him to learn Tahitian. This was a great asset in itself, but he also saved Cook's life in a critical affair with some Maoris, so he had no difficulty in signing on for the second voyage, when he was promoted corporal. Cook had a great affection for him, and Gibson hero-worshipped his captain.

One of Gibson's corporals was an original character, too. John Ledyard was a 24-year-old American from Groton, Connecticut, with a lust for adventure. He was tall, powerful, handsome and of a singularly attractive disposition. He had half trained as a missionary to the Red Indians, grown impatient with the discipline, and shipped as a sailor. On a voyage to the Mediterranean he tried unsuccessfully to desert into a British regiment, itself an unusual thing to do: there was a strong touch of the original in John Ledyard. He eventually worked his passage to Plymouth, walked to London, and charmed Cook into letting him join as a marine.

There were other Americans in the *Resolution* and *Discovery*, the *Resolution*'s bosun William Ewin from Pennsylvania, the seaman Benjamin Whitton from Boston, George Stewart from Charleston and several more, seven in all. There were also several Germans and a nomadic Dutchman, Heinrich Zimmermann, who tells us in a book he published after his return that he was a belt-maker but had adopted other trades, too, while working in Geneva, Paris, Lyons and London. He does not appear to have been over-modest, either, claiming that it was 'the natural courage of a native of the Palatinate' that led to his adoption of a seafaring life.

Cook could pick and choose among the numerous midshipmen who would give their right arm to sail with him, and he selected well. They were a lively and bright lot of youngsters, some of them only fifteen, and included several destined for greatness, including James Trevenen, and Edward Riou and George Vancouver in the *Discovery*.

As for the seamen, 'the people', a few of them stand out from the grey ranks, among them George Gilbert, son of Bligh's predecessor as the *Resolution*'s master on the last voyage. Young Gilbert was an amiable fellow with a great devotion for Cook, and with a keen eye for all that he saw, which makes his neglected journal especially interesting.

Then there was William Watman, an 'old' man of 44, 'belov'd by his fellow, for his good and benevolent disposition'. He had been a marine for 21 years and had served with Cook in the *Resolution* as an A.B. on the second voyage. It occasionally happened that a commander took a special fancy to one of his seamen, which need cause no resentment. A warm affection grew between these two men with the same humble origins and of nearly the same age. When Cook had accepted the governorship at Greenwich Hospital he obtained a post for Watman, too—the captain and seaman retiring together after a lifetime at sea, at the end of a long and hazardous voyage. When Watman heard that Cook was embarking once more on a voyage, he begged to be allowed a berth, and Cook at length agreed. For Cook, the old marine was a talisman of good fortune and success.

Most of the seamen were no better and no worse than in any other Royal Navy vessel, mainly illiterate, opinionated yet ignorant, mercurial in temperament yet deeply suspicious of change in routine and especially in their food. They were a tough, lascivious, mainly foul-mouthed lot, often violent and hot-tempered yet capable of sturdy loyalty. With few exceptions the *Resolution*'s seamen admired and respected Cook, while those of the *Discovery* naturally admired him more distantly, reserving a real affection for their own Charles Clerke. Their view was a short one, their respect for law and duty conditioned entirely by fear of punishment, which they accepted stoically when it was administered. Cook might be 'a taut hand' at sea but did not often have to resort to the lash.

If the lower deck was commonplace, the supernumeraries carried in both ships were exceptional. Neither in numbers nor quality were the scientists the equal of Banks and his party on the first voyage, but they added colour and, together with Anderson and King and the bright midshipmen, were to give Cook all the interest and stimulus he would need. John Webber was the official artist, 'Draughtsman and landscape painter' as he was formally styled. An accomplished landscape painter and son of a Swiss sculptor, he was to prove a prize beyond calculation. He drew swiftly, prolifically and skilfully so that, visually, this was to be the best-recorded of all Cook's voyages. The amateur painter William Ellis, the surgeon's second mate in the *Discovery*, added numerous delicate water colours to Webber's output, and he was especially talented with birds.

Then there was William Bayly, the astronomer who had sailed with Cook before; serious, industrious, a good companion for Cook although he was to sail in the *Discovery*. He attracted teasing and took it hard like so many in science who start without advantages. Like Cook, his father was a farmhand whose son's talents were somehow recognized, and when Cook was observing the transit of Venus in Tahiti, Bayly was watching it from the North Cape.

And there was Omai. Without doubt, this Polynesian with his quaint affectations and beguiling ways was the most immediately sensational consequence of Cook's second voyage. He had at his own request been brought to England in Cook's second ship, the *Adventure*, to become the toast of society, the most sought-after house guest, the personification of 'the noble savage'. He was nothing of the kind, and Cook was one of the few people who retained a level judgment of the young man, while retaining a somewhat proprietorial affection for him.

Like some precocious performing animal, Omai was dressed up in fashionable suits, taught to handle a stick stylishly, to play cards expertly, to comport himself correctly at the dining table, and, after a fashion, to talk English. His pronunciation was naturally deplorable and his vocabulary limited, but he could sometimes make himself understood. When he was received by the king and he cried out, 'How do, King Tosh', George III did not take offence.

Fanny Burney, on the other hand, found that 'George' was one of the words he could pronounce correctly. Hers is the best picture of Omai as seen by the dazzled London establishment. Banks had taken him to the House of Lords to listen to King George make his speech from the throne, and brought him to the Burneys' house for dinner. When she came downstairs, Fanny 'found Omai seated on the great chair, and my brother [Jem] next to him, and talking Otaheite as fast as possible. . . . Jem introduced me, and told him I was another sister. He rose, and made a very fine bow, and then seated himself again. . . . He had on a suit of Manchester velvet, lined with white satten, a *bag*, lace ruffles, and a very handsome sword which the king had given to him. He is tall and very well made, much darker than I expected to see him, but has a pleasing countenance.'

She qualified this, however, by describing him as '*by no means* handsome' and noted his hands being heavily tattooed. She was surprised to find his table manners almost extravagantly polite and noted his possession of 'an uncommon share of observation'. Contrasting him and his behaviour with a boor of her acquaintance, she remarked that Omai, 'with no tutor but Nature, changes after he is grown up, his dress, his way of life, his diet, his country and his friends;—and appears in a *new world* like a man who had all his life studied *the Graces*.'

James Boswell, dining on another occasion with Omai and a notable peer of the realm, described his manners as genteel, and, in the poor light, observed that 'there was so little of the savage in Omai, that I was afraid to speak to either, lest I should mistake one for the other'.

Fanny Burney's extravagant conclusion was that 'he seems to shame Education, for his manners are so graceful, and he is so polite, attentive and easy, that you would have thought he came from some foreign Court. You will think that I speak in a *high* style; but I assure you there was but one opinion about him.'

Alas! that was not so. Increasingly as time went by Banks and Sandwich, who were chiefly responsible for his well-being, became exasperated with his behaviour. For example, when he discovered that his suit was of English velvet and not the fashionable Genoese, he was very angry and abused Banks for his parsimony. He frequently behaved like a spoilt schoolboy. Samwell found him 'like all ignorant people very superstitious' and quickly aroused to anger if contradicted.

However, the fashionable intelligentsia continued to heap praise upon him, and there is no doubt that he had the same engaging characteristics as a precocious child. Sir Joshua Reynolds and others painted him, he learned quite quickly to cope with his sword and other social niceties, he even learned to skate, of all things, though he never could manage to ride properly. He tried to learn to read but it was soon clear that he did not possess the necessary powers of sustained concentration.

Omai remained pleased with himself throughout his long sojourn in England, and, unlike Bougainville's 'savage', who died on the way home, his health remained splendid, partly, no doubt, thanks to the king, who sensibly suggested early on that he should be inoculated, which no one else seemed to have considered. When he was told he was going home with Captain Cook ('Toot'), Omai appeared pleased at the prospect and set about collecting his considerable luggage—crockery and kichenware and 'an electrical machine' to impress his friends, a jack-in-the-box, a 'kind of serpent that darts out of a cylindrical case when the lid is removed' to divert them, a globe to show them his travels, a hand-organ for evening music, port wine to serve at the end of a Polynesian dinner, an immense Bible with coloured engravings to preserve his new-found Christian principles, a collection of tin soldiers to fight miniature battles, a coat of mail and complete suit of medieval armour to defend himself in real battles and a number of muskets with ball and powder to annihilate his enemies.

Cook accepted stoically this considerable extra cargo, which also included bed, table, chairs and any number of toys. He disapproved of the firearms, however, but was overruled by the Board on this delicate point. Omai fancied himself with a gun and had acquired a considerable bag at a number of shoots on some of the greatest estates in the land, although farmyard poultry were treated by him as ripe game, too, and no one seemed able to blunt his enthusiasm.

So much for the expedition's personnel, a total company of 112 in the *Resolution* and 70 in the *Discovery*; as richly varied a complement as could be found, from boys in their mid-teens who would be grown men when they next saw the shores of England, to grave artists and scientists, boozers and wenchers already with 'the venereals' when they came on board, a dour ship's master who was to suffer more numerous and more notorious mutinies than any officer in naval history, the most famous explorer and navigator in the world, and an engaging, exasperating, excitable Polynesian native bent on setting himself up in the flashiest establishment in all the Society Islands.

These men accepted that they would be living at close quarters for many months, that they would endure together the inevitable dangers of a long voyage. But even the worst alarmist could not have predicted the critical events that lay ahead on the other side of the world, in the Arctic and sub-Antarctic, nor that they would be away for more than four years.

The ships' cargoes, which were to make life on board even more crushingly uncomfortable for everyone, were equally diverse and unusual. For Cook's second voyage additional and lavishly equipped cabins had been built onto the *Resolution*'s upper deck for Banks and his greatly enlarged party. This caused the ship to be virtually unmanageable in any sort of a sea. Banks, informed that he would have to accept regular accommodation, sulked and said in that case he would not go. For the third voyage, however, Cook had even more awkward and unmanageable company—livestock in such variety and numbers that the ship became like the ark and it was a wonder that she could be navigated at all.

The king, 'Farmer George', had set his heart on turning Tahiti into good English-style farmland. His interest in the Pacific increased with every voyage, but the pictures brought home of the natives' narrow view of agriculture gave him concern and fired him with the wish to reform their ways. Naturally growing palms and breadfruit, yams and wild pigs, and a modest fishing industry, was not his idea of a properly balanced agricultural economy. The fact that the natives already enjoyed an excellent and abundant diet was by the way, for George III was possessed of an idealistic vision of Tahiti and its satellite islands divided by hedges and neat fences into fields of corn or grazing livestock — proper English livestock.

So, generously, he presented Cook with the nucleus of a good mixed Tahitian farm for a start, the *Resolution* alone being expected to accommodate a bull, two cows with their calves, a large number of sheep and rabbits, a mare and a stallion, numerous pigs, and a vast quantity of fodder. All these were in addition to the ship's goats — milk for the officers — hens and cock and the free-running cats and dogs that formed the usual complement of the crew's pets. And a magnificent peacock and hen from the king's friend the Earl of Bessborough, Viscount Duncannon, Baron Ponsonby of Sysonby, Lord of the Admiralty.

In a vessel as small as the *Resolution* this menagerie created problems not only of space, leading to the construction of pens and cages on the already cluttered decks, but of hygiene, and Cook's standards were very high in this department. The fodder had to be stowed and much additional water — that most precious of all commodities on shipboard — to be carried in casks.

Then there were great quantities of seeds for this new arable grazing land — grass seed, wheat, barley, mustard, all to be kept dry and secure from rats and mice.

Another unusual additional load was the tools and toys 'to cultivate a friendship with the natives' of many lands. On a long voyage these trifles and trinkets and more practical objects were a form of currency. A dozen axes took up a great deal less space than the provisions for which it was hoped they could be traded, and fresh provisions at that. Nevertheless the *Resolution*'s 200 axes, about half a ton of nails (always popular), 24 dozen common knives, 20 dozen fish hooks, files and saws and scissors, looking glasses and countless beads, vast quantities of red feathers (all the rage in Tahiti), old clothes and old sheets, 26 items in all, took up much valuable space in the sloop's hold.

The exceptional nature of the cruise, embracing so many variations in climate, also called for special equipment and special clothing for the *Resolution*'s crew, for example 'A pair of Fearnought Trowsers and a Jacket for each Man and four or five good Watch Coats'. Then Bayly's instruments—an astronomical clock, special compasses and barometers, theodolites and thermometers, marine barometers and telescopes, a large tent observatory and several smaller tents, and the precious £10,000 Kendall 'Watch Machine', 'to be returned at the end of the voyage in the best condition possible'. (See note on Page 259.)

All these items, many of them awkward ones requiring special stowing, were additional to the great quantity of victuals, clothing, arms and so on required for a prolonged circumnavigation. The *Resolution* had to be prepared to fight off an attack by another armed vessel or hordes of savages, to reconnoitre by small boats and bring on board dozens of fresh water casks, tons of timber and coal for fuel, to anchor in deep or shallow water, and to keep its company healthy and fed for months on end from its own resources. Room had to be found for 40 bushels of white bay salt, 3400 pounds of best muscovado sugar, 30 quarters of best wheat, 50 barrels of powder for the muskets and the 12 four-pounder cannons, and the dozen each of swivel guns and musquetoons, 580 pounds of beef for salting down, 700 pairs of trousers, 800 pairs of shoes, 340 caps, 440 shirts, 1800 gallons of spirits, vast quantities of wine and beer.

The victualling problem had been complicated by Cook because of his assiduous attention to the health of his men. The scourge of disease at sea increased with the length of the voyages. It had first taken serious toll of crews during the early Portuguese voyages sponsored by Henry the Navigator in the 15th century, scurvy being by far the most lethal ailment. The prolonged debilitating effect of this vitamin C deficiency disease caused many shipwrecks, and more men were drowned as an indirect consequence than directly from the scurvy itself. In time it came to be an accepted price for the profits of long-distance exploration and trading, and little effort was made to find a cure. Cook and some of his sailors could recall the return of Commodore George Anson from his offensive circumnavigation in 1744 with half a million pounds of Spanish treasure but 1300 dead from disease and four from enemy action.

Dr James Lind, the foremost nautical physician, had published his *Treatise of the Scurvy* in 1753, but remarkably little notice was taken of its accurate findings and certain cure by the administration of orange or lemon juice. Whether or not Cook absorbed the lessons of this book and later works before he embarked on his first Pacific voyage, he was the first to rate the health of his men as one of the highest priorities. Any captain could have attained Cook's health standards. His subsequent fame as a great humanitarian as well as a great navigator rested not on his dietary innovation but on his application of all that was known about diet at sea in the mid-18th century. To vary the traditional diet of salt pork and beef, duff pudding, ship's biscuit, dried peas, vinegar and oil, Cook included among his provisions meat essence called portable soup, decoction of malt, and oranges and lemons.

But that was only a start. The smartness of Cook's ships did not end with the gleaming upper decks and brasswork. Below decks they were aired daily, healthfully 'smoked' two or three times a week when conditions permitted, blankets, hammocks and clothing hung out in all but the foulest weather, the crew were kept as clean as rough seamen could be kept clean and the ship's casks of fresh water were refilled at every opportunity. Every landing became an exercise in dietary experimentation, with Cook exhorting his men to sample the berries and root and leaf vegetables, and bullying them to take a walk, to 'smell the fresh earth and herbage' and loosen their limbs.

The seamen hated it all. They hated the novel food and the insistence on changing their clothes; and walking ashore was traditionally confined to an eager search for the nearest willing woman. When he ordered the cook to 'cause great quantities of green stuff to be boiled amongst the pea soup and wheat and care not whether they were bitter or sweet', they would 'curse him heartily and wish for God's sake that he might be obliged to eat some damn stuff mixed with his broth as long as he lived'.

By contrast, Cook's view was that, in spite of the 'murmurings against the man that first invented it, the moment they see their superiors set a value upon it, it becomes the finest stuff in the world and the inventor an honest fellow'. And one of his men noted the benefits that would accrue from pleasing their commander, 'for they knew it was a great recommendation to be seen coming on board from a pleasure jaunt with a handkerchief full of greens'.

The benefits of this regime were startling, as even the most hidebound old sailor had to concede. On that first voyage, the *Endeavour* had reached Tahiti without a single death from sickness, and the smallest suspected early signs of scurvy were cured at once with a dose of lemon juice. Bougainville on anchoring in Matavai Bay shortly before him had 34 down with the scurvy.

Cook's concern with the health of his men increased with every voyage. He considered it a personal affront for one of his men to be taken sick. Apart from humanitarian considerations, the benefits of always having a full complement were immense. But the elaborate victualling added one more complication, one more worry for a commander who, in preparing for this third voyage, had so much else on his mind.

A further grave anxiety was the state of the *Resolution*. She had been little more than a year old when he had selected her in November 1771. Since then she had sailed to the Pacific, made immense sweeps across that ocean and deep into the Antarctic, and come safely home after just three years of exploration. The tough little 'cat' was in sound condition but in great need of a major refit. The *Resolution* was taken in hand at Deptford in September 1775 to prepare her for the new extensive voyage already being planned. Cook saw nothing of her until the following February. She was with the navy yard authorities, who were ultimately the responsibility of Palliser. Knowing as he did the depth of corruption and slackness at navy yards, Cook had always personally followed every stage of the fitting out of his ships in the past. When he first visited her after agreeing to take on the command, his examination was perfunctory and he never was able to supervise the vital work of caulking, replacing weak masts and spars, cleaning and checking the copper bottom of the ship as he had done before earlier voyages.

After this visit he returned to Mile End Row, announced that he would be away by April, and continued his demanding work on the journal of his last voyage.

In the preliminaries and preparations for this new voyage there are similarities with the earlier expeditions and significant differences. Concern for his wife if he should fail to return preceded all his voyages, even the shorter ones to Newfoundland when, four years in succession, he made the successful surveying voyages which had led to his selection as commander of the *Endeavour*. Besides the tenderness he always showed towards Elizabeth, the sense of duty he felt for his growing family was as instinctive as the duty towards his men at sea which the merchant service and navy had trained him to feel.

In the early days of their marriage, Cook had made whatever small provision he could for Elizabeth before embarking. The threat of the poor house for your wife and family at home was the best formula for survival at sea. Opposite the Cooks' house in Mile End Row a plaque was set into the side of the largest of a number of buildings. Its ominous legend ran: 'Alms House. 28 decay'd Masters and Commanders of ships, or Widows of such are maintain'd by the Corporation of Trinity House. 1695.' There they were, these fortunate few, in their charity dwelling. But what of the hundred of others? Whenever Cook was at home, the alms houses were a constant reminder—as if he needed it—of the hazards of life at sea and the misery into which his dependents might at any time be thrown.

These risks were discussed between Elizabeth and James. But, to Cook's heartfelt relief, official provision was made by Sandwich for his wife's security in case he should not return, a liberal allowance which 'set my heart at rest and filled it with gratitude to my noble benefactor'. As a good Yorkshireman, Cook was frank and open about his calling. On the eve of this voyage, although he was too sensible and tender to refer to them to his wife, he was aware of real doubts about the likelihood of his safe return. He referred in letters to friends to the dangers of trying to force the North-West Passage. 'The attempt must be hazardous,' he wrote, 'and must be made with great caution.' This is not the Cook of 1768 and 1772. Nor is 'If it please God to spare me till I reach the place for discoveries', for Cook was not a religious man and only rarely held divine service on board his ships. To his old friend and employer, John Walker, he uncharacteristically refers to the new voyage as 'perhaps dangerous' and mentions that he will be fortunate 'to get safe home'. There seem to be premonitions of his fate in these sentiments.

Then there was a sharp distinction between the treatment accorded to Cook before his second and before his third voyage. After the first (1768–71) in which he had sailed round New Zealand, charting the coastline of North Island and South Island, and exploring the east coast of Australia from Point Hicks to Cape York, he received due professional credit. But it had been Banks who took all the glory, and to the public it was Banks's voyage. Banks himself, while acknowledging privately his debt to Cook, gladly accepted the lionizing.

But nothing and nobody could deprive Cook of the credit and glory of the second great Pacific expedition in which he had ranged in great sweeps across that ocean, charting the islands of Tierra del Fuego to the east, Easter Island, the Marquesas and the New Hebrides to the west. As the first man to sail into the Antarctic alone, Cook's place was engraved in the annals of exploration. On his return he was confirmed in the rank of post-captain. Even Banks came out of his sulks to give praise. He did more than that. He was instrumental in having Cook made a Fellow of the Royal Society, the highest scientific accolade.

Captain James Cook, of Mile-end a gentleman skilful in astronomy, & the successful conductor of two important voyages for the discovery of unknown countries, by which geography and natural history have been greatly advantaged & improved. . . .

Thus ran his nomination, and his election was inevitable. Almost every name of note in the fields of science and medicine appeared among the signatures, and Cook was duly elected in February 1776. A paper above his name on the health of seamen appeared in the Royal Society's *Philosophical Transactions*, and he read another on 'The Tides of the South Seas'. His portrait was painted by Nathaniel Dance. He was sought as a guest at the best dinner tables. James Boswell, after dining with him, called upon him at Mile End, and was minded to come on the next voyage as a passenger. Dr Johnson rightly thought the idea ridiculous.

In the course of an audience of King George, Cook discussed at length the last voyage and his plans for the next. It was at this meeting that the monarch offered the livestock and fodder from his own farms that were to prove such a burden on the voyage. Cook was awarded Sir Godfrey Copley's Gold Medal for his paper describing methods of maintaining good health, the highest of all scientific honours. He was recognized in the street and in the fashionable coffee houses he frequented. The preparation of his journal, which finally ran to two massive volumes of 774 pages, was in itself a great labour as writing did not come naturally to him, and there must be no errors—none at all. Frequent visits to country estates, with Elizabeth in an advanced state of pregnancy, imposed their own strain too.

It was no wonder that he had little time to spare for supervising the refitting of his ships, something to which he had given the most minute attention in the past. And it was no wonder that the tiredness of the man was even more evident in May, when Elizabeth gave birth to another boy on the 23rd, than it had been earlier to Hugh Palliser, after whom the infant was named. The fact that Cook was still in England in May when he should have left in April in order to catch the Arctic in the following summer was both inauspicious and uncharacteristic of the man. And many more weeks were to pass before the *Resolution* could sail.

*

Down at Deptford, the entering of men, the fitting out and the taking in of stores, dragged on through May. The *Resolution* sailed down river to Long Reach at last on 30 May, but she was still not ready to depart. Nor was the junketing yet over. Sandwich and Palliser representing the Admiralty, senior Fellows of the Royal Society and 'several other noblemen and gentlemen' were welcomed on board on 8 June, being saluted with 17 guns and three cheers. Dinner included Westmorland ham, pigeon pie and strawberries. In their turn, Cook and his officers were dined at The Gun inn by the Speaker of the House of Commons, an unscrupulous lawyer called Sir Fletcher Norton, or 'Sir Bull-face Double Fee'.

Cook made his way for the last time to his house in Mile End to spend two more weeks with his family. Every day the weather was warm and sunny—beautiful mellow June weather—and little Hugh was outside on the lawn at the back of the house for much of the time. Cook worked valiantly to add polish to his stiff narrative, and wrote copiously to his friends, to his father, and to Walker and others he knew at Whitby.

Early on the morning of 24 June, another warm, cloudless day, Omai arrived in Sandwich's carriage. Fortunately, his vast and heterogeneous luggage was already stowed on board the *Resolution*, and he had with him only a few cases. There was much bowing and smiling to Mrs 'Toot', much admiring of little Hugh. Then Cook embraced his wife and climbed into the carriage beside the man he had been ordered by the Admiralty 'to land at such of the South Sea islands as he may desire'.

There was a brief fluttering of handkerchiefs, and the house was at once shut from Cook's view as the carriage turned the corner into Sydney Street towards the river.

The two men—the 47-year-old navigator and the young Polynesian—could by now communicate quite fluently. The subject of their conversation as the carriage clattered over the cobbles towards the landing stage, where the boat that was to take them down river awaited them, can be identified by a note Cook made later. 'Omai left London with a mixture of regret and joy,' he wrote. 'In speaking of England and such persons as had honoured him with their protection and friendship he would be very low spirited and with difficulty refrain from tears; but turn the conversation to his native country and his eyes would sparkle with joy.'

The *Resolution* sailed from the Nore the next day. The weather had broken, the wind had got up and there were 'some flying black clouds'. The sloop anchored off Deal in order to take on board two boats which had been built there, and a crowd gathered on the shore. The object of their curiosity was less the most famous ship and the most famous navigator of the day than the most famous Polynesian. They were disappointed, for Omai neither went ashore nor even appeared upon deck.

Assisted by favourable winds, the *Resolution* sailed into Plymouth Sound on 30 June, to collect her last fresh victuals and water and fodder, and to receive her marines and the final secret orders which were not to be opened until they were at sea. Cook had now a bare twelve months to sail via the Cape to New Zealand, thence to Tahiti and another 4500 miles to the American Pacific Coast, following it north through the Bering Strait and into the Arctic. Allowing for unfavourable weather, for taking in supplies and resting the crews and settling in Omai, the expedition was going to be hard pressed to keep to its timetable.

But now a totally unpredictable crisis loomed, an event which was destined to have a fatal effect upon the progress of the voyage yet again, and upon its final outcome.

On 13 June, Clerke, already on board and in command of the *Discovery*, had been summoned by the King's Bench to stand for the debts of his improvident and absent brother. He at once wrote to Stephens, 'Some of my own private affairs of the utmost importance to me require my attention to them in Town.' Could Lieutenant Burney take over temporary command and sail the ship to Plymouth? he enquired. Stephens agreed, but then Clerke was unceremoniously dumped into the King's Bench prison at the order of the Justices. It was an ugly place to be 'fairly cast away', as Clerke ruefully put it, damp and dreadfully unhealthy. Nor did any of his influential friends, including Sandwich and the Speaker of the House of Commons, have any success in getting him released.

'There's a fatality attends my every undertaking,' the normally perky Clerke wrote ominously and prophetically to Banks. He also divulged confidentially to him that, at the first opportunity, he was going to take the law into his own hands. 'I'm resolved to decamp without beat of drum,' he told him, 'and, if I can, out sail the Israelites, get to sea and make every return in my power.'

At Plymouth Cook fretted at the delay. Ten days after his arrival, and still with no word of his friend, he wrote to Clerke in prison ordering him to put to sea 'without a moment's loss of time' after he secured his release, 'to follow me to the Cape of Good Hope'. On 12 July the *Resolution* stood out to sea, just a year short of a few days since she had sailed past the Sound from her last historic cruise. In London it was a thundery day with much lightning. Gibbon's *Decline and Fall* was just in the bookshops.

Three more weeks were to pass before Clerke succeeded in extricating himself from the coils of 'the Israelites'. He raced down to Plymouth, urging on the stage all the way, and took belated command of his ship. He was bursting with his old high spirits, triumphant in his freedom, confident of catching up his commander. 'Huzza my boys, heave away,' he exclaimed. 'I shall get hold of him I fear not.' Then he ordered a mild flogging of one recalcitrant seaman to show he would stand for no nonsense.

He remained in the Sound for one day only, dealing with some cases of smallpox in his ship. All but two of his men had 'suffered this distemper' and 'as the contagion can go no farther I think I may venture to go on. I shall immediately get under weigh,' he reported to Stephens.

But the dreadful and unknown truth was that in his lungs there lurked, young and fresh from that unhealthy London prison, a far worse contagion.

2

Sunshine and desolation

CAPTAIN COOK'S THIRD voyage, which was to discover and chart so much of the future United States coastline, neatly coincided with the course of the American War of Independence. As the *Resolution* stood out alone from Plymouth Sound on 12 July 1776, America was in effect just eight days old, Congress having adopted the Declaration of Independence the previous week. When she anchored in the Thames again final victory at Yorktown was only 12 months away.

Cook saw plenty of evidence of the troubles in the colonies while he lay at anchor in the Sound impatiently awaiting the arrival of Clerke. On 6 July a massive convoy of transports—62 ships in all—sought shelter there from a strong south-west wind. On board was a complete division of Hessian troops, with their horses, bound for the war.

The eyes of the world were turned towards the rebellion in North America, and there was much speculation in the newspapers. But Cook's departure was of world importance, too, and widely reported. In Spain there was a measure of real concern, and the viceroy of Mexico was ordered to seize and imprison him if he should come within his domain. The Spanish government still liked to pretend to itself and proclaim, in a now muted voice, that the Pacific Ocean belonged to Spain. The French, too, were concerned. While observing with satisfaction the troubles Britain was facing in North America, they knew that this new expedition might result in the discovery and acquisition of rich new lands and rich new markets for trading to add to the vast territories France had recently lost to perfidious Albion.

Britain was in a state of peace—uneasy peace as always—with both these European nations. But paradoxically her rebellious American colonists, as if subconsciously aware of the rich fruits it might bring to them, gave Cook's expedition its blessing and every encouragement. Lord Sandwich had earlier 'made every endeavour to persuade the Executive Government of the American States to offer Cook protection'. The Americans had been 'laudably anxious' to help, which Banks considered 'a happy omen of protection to science in future wars'.

Later on the voyage, Benjamin Franklin, confident that Cook would soon be sailing triumphantly through the North-West Passage, went further by issuing an order to all American armed ships prohibiting them from interfering with 'that most celebrated navigator and discoverer, Captain Cook'. More, they should 'treat Captain Cook and his people with all civility and kindness, affording them as common friends to mankind'.

The truth was, though Cook was unaware of it when he broke the seal of his secret instructions, that the world already knew, or would shortly know, his destination. No one had believed the story that had been put about that he was returning once more to the Pacific to reinstate Omai on his chosen island and chart a few more islands; and official confirmation of the suspicions of foreign envoys in London appeared in the respected pages of the *Gentleman's Magazine* a few days after Cook put to sea. Captain Cook, it divulged to its readers, 'is to attempt a northerly passage home'. That was more than the sailors were to know for another 14 months.

The secret instructions defined clearly this attempt in the summer of 1777 'to search for, and to explore, such rivers or inlets as may appear to be of a considerable extent and pointing towards Hudson's or Baffin's Bays'. Failing that, the expedition was to winter at the Russian port of St Peter and St Paul in Kamchatka, and then in the spring to force its way as far north as would be required 'in further search of a north east or north west passage from the Pacific Ocean into the Atlantic Ocean. . . .'

Apart from the Dutch colony at the Cape of Good Hope, and the Russian outpost, both belonging to friendly nations, Cook was instructed to be circumspect, to avoid touching 'upon any part of the Spanish dominions on the western continent of America, unless driven thither by some unavoidable accident, in which case you are to stay no longer there than shall be absolutely necessary, and to be very careful not to give any umbrage or offence to any of the inhabitants or subjects of His Catholic Majesty'. All of which was in stark contrast with Francis Drake's instructions 200 years earlier.

The instructions offered nothing to Cook that he did not know already, but he did note the necessity of keeping to the timetable that was already threatened by his late departure. He was enjoined to leave Cape Town by the end of October if possible; to search for some islands to the south but without spending too much time in doing so; to touch at New Zealand if necessary, but to arrange to leave Tahiti—after settling in Omai—by the beginning of February 1777, 'then proceed in as direct a course as you can to the Coast of New Albion, endeavouring to fall in with it in the latitude of 45° north [just south of present day Astoria]; and taking care, in your way thither, not to lose any time in search of new lands. . . .'

Urgency, then, was the keynote, with the only proviso that the people must be properly refreshed.

Within a few days two facts became evident that were to dog their progress, delay them and add to the strains of command as well as the patience of the sailors. The first was that the *Resolution* had not been thoroughly refitted in spite of the immensely long time she had been in the hands of the shipwrights at Deptford. The result of Cook's absence from Deptford in the past weeks was evident in the first heavy rain when the poorly caulked decks let in water. Swearing at the condition of their ship at the very outset of a long voyage, the men set to at the pumps. Their tempers were already stretched by the presence of the livestock which, with their smells, seemed to be everywhere about the crowded decks of the ship. It was worse in rough weather, their cries of alarm adding a mournful note to the sounds of creaking spars and timbers and the screaming of the wind.

For Cook the more serious problem with the stock was that a quick calculation showed that there was nothing like enough fodder to last them to Cape Town. They would have to call at Madeira or Tenerife to replenish supplies, another time-wasting business. The Admiralty, in its formal style, had informed him that the ship 'had been fitted out in all respects proper to proceed'. It was not. Nor had they, it was becoming clear, even 'taken on board the necessary stores and provisions for the voyage which was as much as we could stow and the best of every kind that could be got', as Cook himself claimed. At Deptford Cook had recorded his thanks to Sandwich, Palliser and the whole Board of Admiralty for 'the extraordinary attention they had all along paid' to the equipment. It was already beginning to appear that it was the inattention that was extraordinary.

Cook decided on Tenerife rather than Madeira, one more sacrifice to the king's livestock, the fodder being better, the wine being worse—much worse—at this island. Cook anchored the *Resolution* half a mile off the shore at Santa Cruz and ordered a boat hoisted out to take him ashore. Anderson was among those who accompanied him, eager to learn and record all he could of the botany of the island. In the role of doctor, he also laid special emphasis on the curative effect of the healthy air on people suffering from tuberculosis, recommending that they should be sent here instead of the more common sanatoria at Lisbon and Montpelier. Besides, 'a certain grape growing here, is reckoned an infallible remedy for such diseases'.

That seasoned traveller, Omai, was less impressed by the island, remarking that the inhabitants were rather Polynesian in appearance and not so well mannered as the English.

There was a French frigate offshore making astronomical observations, an activity that always intrigued Cook. When an officer came on board to ask him if he wanted for anything, they had a good scientific discussion.

Spanish boats were chartered to replenish the ship's fresh water supplies and bring out grain and hay for the livestock, and wine and fresh fruit, vegetables and meat for the crew. It was all conducted at a leisurely pace, with much friendly interchange with the island's authorities, and three more days passed before the *Resolution* stood out from the Santa Cruz roadstead and steered south-west by south into the Atlantic on Sunday 4 August.

All through that week the *Resolution* made steady progress, favoured by moderate following breezes, rolling gently and no longer leaking after makeshift caulking. The days were misty and hot, the nights clear. They had plenty of fresh fruit and meat in their diet, and the livestock were less of a nuisance in these more moderate seas. Cook ensured that his men kept to his high standards of hygiene and cleanliness, and on the Tuesday and Friday the ship was washed thoroughly below decks and then smoked. Anderson noted a dolphin and flying fish and later some bonitos and a turtle. A sense of contented lethargy overcame the ship's officers and company—all except Bligh, who, ever industrious, worked on drawings he had made at Tenerife.

As the week drew to an end of Saturday evening, they were approaching the Cape Verde islands. It had been the hottest day since leaving Tenerife, and Anderson came on deck at 11 p.m. to enjoy the cooler air and to watch the little island of Bonavista slip by on the starboard quarter before turning in. The island had first been sighted two hours earlier, and the *Resolution* bore away to the south-east and then east. Now, in Anderson's eyes, the land appeared uncomfortably close in the clear night. 'I thought something like breakers appeared at a distance ahead,' he recalled later, and, thoroughly alarmed, he wondered if he should warn his captain, who was keeping the watch.

At that moment Cook appeared at his side and saw what had alarmed the surgeon. Instantly he yelled to the helmsman, 'Hard astarboard!' And then, 'Brace the yards sharp up!' The watch were quick off the mark, racing up the ratlines to the yards, many of them adding to the clamour by repeating 'Hard astarboard!' again and again. Roused from their hammocks by the clamour, the other watches appeared on deck, Bligh among them. The ship's master was horrified at their situation. How could his commander have brought the vessel within half a league of exposed and foaming rocks with all the vastness of the Atlantic about them?

Cook admitted that their situation was 'very alarming', and for ten minutes it appeared that they had little hope of weathering the breakers. Slowly the tubby cat came round parallel to the rocks although still moving even nearer to them in the heavy, implacable swell. 'At last, however, we cleared the large range,' Anderson noted, 'and also a single place over which the sea broke that seemed to threaten danger after passing the other.'

Bligh had not sailed with Cook before but he knew his unsurpassed reputation, and he was amazed at this occurrence. The trust of the whole ship's company suffered a severe shock. Anderson recalled episodes on the last voyage, occasions when Cook's navigation had demonstrated a sublime quality, when his sensitive navigational antennae warned of some ferocious lee shore long before the eyes and ears of any other veteran sailor could recognize the danger ahead. Or periods of sheer terror when the *Resolution* had sailed blindly yet safely in the dark through a maze of reefs and islets as if guided by St Christopher himself. What was the comment of one of the *Resolution*'s seamen? 'When no one else had a suspicion of danger, he often came up on deck and changed the course of the ship because land was near . . . he was always right.' Anderson remembered the *Resolution* threading between the islands of Tierra del Fuego at the end of 1774, and working through thick fog and ice deep in the Antarctic. When Cook was taken ill and his life despaired of and Anderson had helped tend him, they wondered if they could survive without him. He had been father to them all. And now . . . ?

'To bring a ship into so alarming a situation as we were in at this time,' Anderson noted, 'without being able to give satisfactory reason for it certainly deserves the severest reprehension.' He was a surgeon, not a sailor, but, he reasonably asked, 'Why hazard anything by falling in with the land at night which might be done in the day?' He remembered that they had been in this identical situation exactly four years earlier in the *Resolution* off the island of Bonavista, and they had wisely shortened sail until daylight. This time there was not even a lookout posted, 'or the breakers could not have been discovered first from the quarter'. And, he might have added, by chance and by the ship's surgeon at that.

It was indeed an astonishing business that a ship equipped with the most up-to-date navigation equipment in the world, commanded by the most famous navigator—himself on watch—should have come within an ace of total destruction on a calm clear night.

But that was not the end of it. On the following day, in broad daylight, Cook misidentified one of the islands in the Cape Verde group and brought the *Resolution* close to some more breakers, succeeding, less critically this time, in close hauling and passing to windward of them. 'The error was so gross,' exclaimed Anderson in amazement, 'that it might well excite the indignation or perhaps the laughter of those but indifferently versed in naval affairs. I am sure no apology can be offered for such mistakes as it would seem they are the result of negligence.'

'Saw breakers on our bows,' was Gore's only laconic observation. The American was not only a great optimist; any crisis was always underplayed.

Cook had left instructions with the *Discovery* to look for him at the little port of Praya in case he should make an exceptionally speedy passage south, but they found only two Dutch Indiamen and a small brig at anchor there. The *Discovery*, in fact, was still only ten days out from Plymouth.

After these crises, the voyage to the south proceeded without further incident. The men picked oakum, 'exercised the great guns' and the small arms. They lit a fire in the bread room when it became damp. In a calm they hoisted out a boat and fished. A harpoon was lost in a porpoise.

For a while it remained hot and steamy during the day. The seams in the sloop opened up and when it rained the water poured in again. 'There was hardly a man who could lie dry in his bed,' Cook recorded in mortification. 'The officers in the gunroom were all driven out of their cabins.' They shouted and cursed, searching for a dry place to rest. More seriously the rain got into the sail rooms, ruining much of their spare canvas. Cook cursed the negligent shipwrights, and ordered the caulkers to work as soon as the weather improved.

Crossing the line provided a distraction during those long and mainly uneventful weeks. The traditional ducking at that time was hilarity approaching savagery. Anderson thought Cook ought to have suppressed the 'absurd custom'. Clerke, three weeks later, did so, characteristically giving the men a double tot of rum instead. All through September there was little for Anderson to note, but he kept a punctilious journal as always, recording the temperature six times a day, the barometric pressure, the weather, the state of the sea and their position. A single puffin qualified for an entry, and a curious form of petrel was closely described. Anderson, too, cursed the ship's leaks, and with special feeling, for the health of the men was his responsibility.

At last, on the afternoon of 17 October, the cry of land was heard, and as the day wore on the unmistakable configuration of Table Mountain and the hills about it arose on the horizon. To the ship's master, who had never seen the end of this mighty continent, it was an impressive sight which sent Bligh at once to his drawing board. For the captain, it was his fourth visit. He appreciated the value of Table Bay as a place to recuperate and replenish and he always had a high regard for the efficiency of the Dutch administration. 'There are few people who are more obliging to strangers than the Dutch in general at this place,' he wrote during his last visit.

Cook stood off and on during the night and succeeded in manoeuvring the *Resolution* into the bay the following afternoon. The Admiralty had told him not to remain here for too long, time being of the essence, and to leave instructions for Clerke to rendezvous with him elsewhere rather than risk losing the Arctic summer. But Cook showed no sign of any urgency. After the formalities and the exchange of salutes (11 guns) and other courtesies with Joachim van Plettenberg, the governor, Cook ordered the ship's officers ashore, along with tents for their accommodation, and all the livestock, the seamen coming ashore to refresh themselves and see the sights in groups of ten. With the governor's consent, Cook set up a veritable colony within a colony on the shores of the cape and in the shadow of Table Mountain. Bayly brought his astronomical instruments ashore, too, and established his observatory. It appeared to the Cape colonists that they were settling in for a long spell.

No one appreciated this new regime more than Anderson, who began his fervent botanizing within minutes of landing, and Omai, who strutted about the streets of Cape Town in his finery as if he owned the place, a brown-skinned anachronism among the Dutch.

As for Cook, he busied himself arranging for the purchase of fresh supplies of food, spirit and fodder for the *Resolution*, and for the *Discovery*, too, when she arrived. The baking of great supplies of ship's biscuit was always a long-drawn-out business. By contrast with 1775 and his other earlier visits to the Cape, events did not run smoothly, and his conclusions about the place and the people were this time harsh instead of enthusiastically favourable. There was, for instance, the business of the sheep. These rams and ewes, from King George's prize herds, were carefully penned at night alongside the tents, but some dogs were let loose among them killing four and scattering the rest. At daylight none could at first be found. Six were finally caught, one of them badly savaged, but some of the finest rams and ewes were completely lost. Most were later recovered by offering rewards to 'the meanest and lowest scoundrels in the place', the police having proved useless.

Then to Cook's annoyance he discovered that the bakers he had commissioned to prepare the *Discovery*'s biscuit had failed to start work until the sloop arrived, which meant further delay.

On learning that a French ship that had been driven ashore nearby had been plundered by the colonists, seemingly with police connivance, Cook expressed himself forcefully and wrote in his journal, 'The Dutch in this affair strictly adhered to the maxim they have laid down at this place which is to get as much by strangers as they possibly can without ever considering whether the means are justifiable or not.'

This comment was typical of the new note of petulance in his journal, besides being a reversal of his opinion on earlier voyages, when tolerance of others' shortcomings was almost invariably evident.

The arrival of Clerke in the *Discovery* at last on 10 November, received with three cheers and 13 guns by the *Resolution*, raised everyone's spirits, although by this time the whole expedition should have been away, heading east across the Indian Ocean. Clerke had lost his corporal of marines overboard on the way, and the *Discovery* was in as great a need of caulking as the *Resolution*. But this perky officer's first priority on arrival was to order six half-hogsheads of brandy, and three puncheons of wine the next day.

While all this work was being carried out, Anderson and Nelson and four others hired a wagon and took a trip inland. The botanizing was disappointing as there were few flowers and insects were scarce too at this season. It was nevertheless a delightful if bumpy trip to the little town—30 houses—of Stellenbosch, with its surrounding vineyards and orchards. Anderson was impressed by the neatness and thriving appearance of the hinterland. A farmer invited them all into his house, and 'entertained us with the greatest hospitality', Anderson recounted, 'and in a manner very different from what we expected. He received us with music and a band also played while we dined, which considering the situation of the place might be reckoned elegant. He showed us his wine cellars, his orchards and vineyards, all which I must own inspired me with a wish to know in what manner these industrious people could raise such plenty in a spot where I believe no other European nation would have attempted to settle.'

If the collecting of flowers had been disappointing, Cook had no difficulty in adding to his already large contingent of livestock. To the dismay of many of the ship's company, he purchased more cattle, sheep, goats, poultry and rabbits. Two stallions and mares were ferried out to the anchored *Resolution* and hauled protestingly on board. They were for Omai to breed from, and, according to Cook, he 'consented with rapture to give up his cabin' for them. Even Cook now used the term 'a complete ark' in referring to the *Resolution*. He reported all this in his last letter to Sandwich before sailing, certain in the knowledge that the news would be passed to the king and that he would savour it with delight as a further strengthening of his idealistic vision of Polynesian husbandry.

Cook added that Omai enjoyed 'a good state of health and great flow of spirits', and sent his best respects to Sandwich and other noblemen, 'and to a great many more, ladies as well as gentlemen, whose names I cannot insert because they would fill up this sheet of paper'. And the North-West Passage? In case Sandwich might think he had lost sight of 'the great object of the voyage', just as he had lost a month in time, Cook assured him that 'my endeavours shall not be wanting'.

To Clerke, Cook passed his secret sealed instructions, with orders not to open them without authority unless the ships became separated for long or the *Resolution* was lost.

On 23 November, the men began striking camp on shore, dismantling the observatory, tenderly carrying to the boats Bayly's priceless instruments. Calculations showed that the 'watch' was losing just over two seconds a day, more than they had hoped for but manageable and simple to correct.

On the last day of the month the two sloops came to sail with a light breeze, weighed, and slipped slowly out of Table Bay. They presented a fine and moving sight to those who witnessed their departure. Everyone was filled with a sense of contentment and excitement for what lay ahead. They had been living well at the Cape, with fresh meat, fresh bread and unlimited fruit every day, and physically were in good shape to face the rigours of the long haul east in high southerly latitudes.

The only exceptions were two men of the *Resolution* and Cook's friend, William Watman, who was showing signs of weakness. Cook regretted now that he had yielded to the old man's pleas at Greenwich, and regretted again that he had not taken the opportunity of sending him back from the Cape on a homeward bound English ship. He knew he would not forgive himself if the seaman's loyalty resulted in his death.

It was good for the two sloops to be together at sea for the first time. It was not only for practical reasons that, since Cook's first voyage, there were two vessels in the expedition. The sight of another set of sails, another hull beating through the seas close

James Cook
painted by Nathaniel Dance before the last voyage.

Sir Hugh Palliser, *(above left)*, Cook's patron and Comptroller of the Navy, later court-martialled for apparent lack of courage.

The Fourth Earl of Sandwich *(above, right)*, First Lord of the Admiralty when Cook embarked in 1776, an aristocrat of mixed accomplishment, gambler, womanizer, drinker, inventor of the sandwich, painted by Gainsborough.

Captain Charles Clerke *(left)*, commander of the *Discovery*, wag and lusty extrovert, who escaped from debtor's jail to join Cook.

James ('Jem') Burney,
son of the great musicologist
and brother of Fanny Burney.

The jaunty Polynesian, Omai,
brought to London on the previous journey.

The veteran American, John Gore.

James King,
aesthete and *bête noire* of William Bligh.

Four of the expedition's colourful company.

The sloop *Resolution*,
a fine Whitby-built 'cat' that sailed with many unknown grave
defects, drawn by the expedition's official artist, John Webber.

Adventure Bay, Bruni Island, off the southern coast of Tasmania, drawn by William Ellis from the ships' watering place. It is little changed today.

Cape Farewell, New Zealand.

Ship Cove, Queen Charlotte's Sound, New Zealand, drawn by Webber in 1777 *(above)*, and photographed by the author in 1977 *(below)*.

Matavai Bay, Tahiti, today *(above)*, and with Moorea in the
distance *(below)*.

Fare Harbour, Huahiné, where a home for Omai was built by Cook's men.

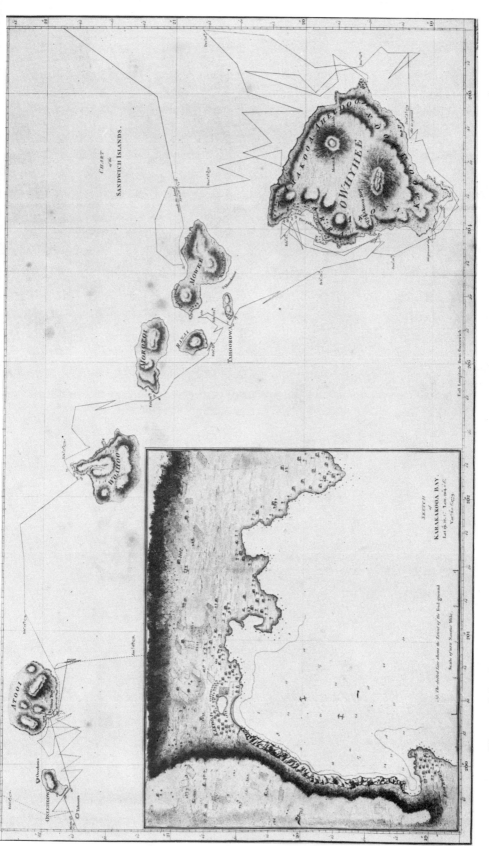

Chart of the Sandwich Islands, with inset of Karakakoa (Kealakekua) Bay, from the published Journal.

Nootka Sound, Vancouver Island *(above)*, where Cook sought to repair his ships and prepare for the Arctic.

Prince William Sound, Alaska *(left)*, Gore thought this might lead to a passage.

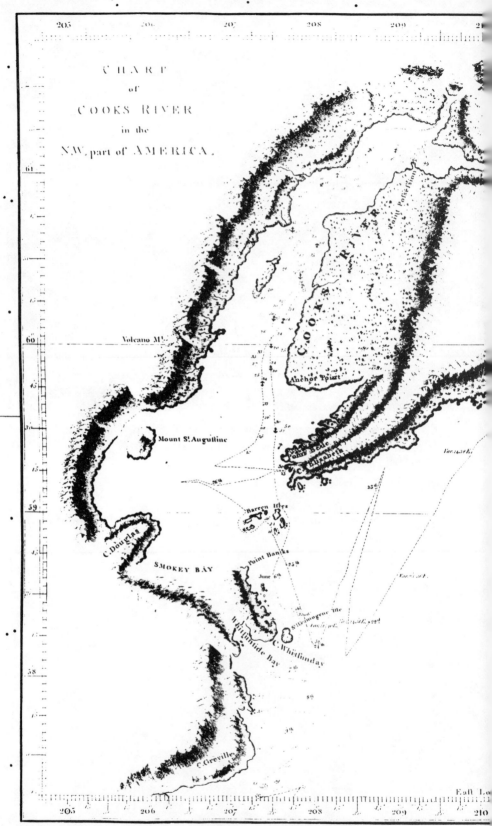

Chart of Cook Inlet, Alaska, from the published Journal.

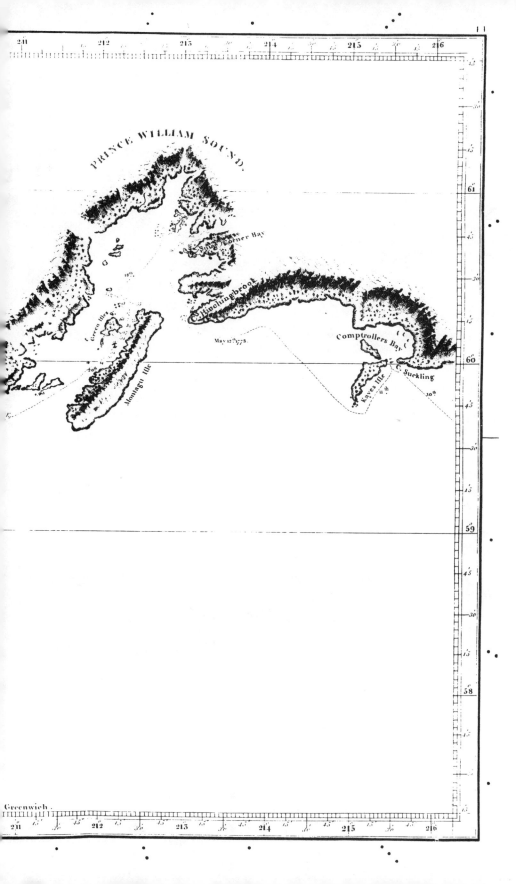

PRINCE WILLIAM SOUND.

Snug Corner Bay

Hinchingbrook

Comptrollers Bay.

May 12th 778.

C. Suckling

Green Illes

Montagu Ille

Kayes Ille

Turnagain 'River', Cook Inlet, near present-day Anchorage, where the hopes of even the most sanguine were dashed.

A safe anchorage at last *(below)*. The two sloops at anchor in Kealakekua Bay, looking north-west towards the rocks where Cook fell.

The *Resolution* and *Discovery* in the Arctic ice. This is as far as they
sailed into the North-West Passage.

The murder. John Zoffany's painting is probably the least fanciful, although it does not reveal

by, the knowledge that there were friends not far off as allies in the constant struggle with the elements—all these factors added greatly to the feeling of strength and purpose. The sea was never lonely with another vessel in sight, however remote from civilization you might be.

All those who had been on the last expedition—Anderson, Burney, Gore and the others, and Clerke and Cook, too—remembered the sense of deprival when the two vessels had become separated. From that time, ill luck had dogged the *Adventure* like a recurring nightmare. The wind had never seemed favourable. She became crank and leaked and, with her provisions bad, had limped back home early.

A separation could easily occur again, in fog or storm. Cook and Clerke had made proper provision for the contingency, with a rendezvous in Queen Charlotte's Sound, New Zealand.

From the time when the mountains of the Cape slipped below the horizon, the temperature began to fall. The men exchanged their petticoat trousers for thick, lined Fearnoughts, and their thin, sometimes threadbare or patched jackets for wool-lined Magellan coats with fixed hoods that could be secured tightly beneath the chin. Anderson, in 'gloomy weather', noted 'penguins and a Port Egmont hen'. High seas and falling thermometers caused great suffering among the stock, especially Omai's horses, who were thrown about dreadfully. One of Phillips's slacker marines was given six lashes for fighting, for drunkenness and neglect of duty.

French explorers had been in these seas before them, Yves-Joseph de Kerguelen-Trémarec and Marc-Joseph Marion de Fresne and his second-in-command, Julien-Marie Crozet, leaving French names on raw and unproductive islands. Marion went on to be killed and eaten, along with a number of his men, in New Zealand. His discovery, called then (it is Marion Island today) Terre d'Espérance, was sighted on 12 December. Cook wrote of barren mountains topped with snow, and even the best glasses failed to reveal vegetation.

They had unsuccessfully searched for Kerguelen's island on the last voyage. With their ever-increasing world trade, the British were always on the look-out for refreshment bases, secure anchorages where a ship might put in to rest her crew, and find wood and water and fresh food too. Cape Town was, of course, ideal, and the British were to relieve the Dutch of this colony in a few years time. But one of Cook's duties on his voyages was to locate and survey suitable anchorages for the comfort and safety of future voyagers. It was considered that Kerguelen might offer these facilities, although inevitably the French, and many Englishmen, too, judged it to be a fragment of *Terra australis incognita.*

Kerguelen is the last and utterly dispensable fragment of Africa, hurled by a mighty throw more than two thousand miles south-east from the Cape of Good Hope down to the 50th parallel. There is nothing more all the way to Australia. Anderson spotted the first of its fragments at six o'clock on the morning of Christmas eve. They had been sailing on a zig-zag course for several days, with look-outs posted, and here at last was their reward. Another islet came into view soon after, with a high rocky peak, then another, no more that a fist thrust out of the cold sea.

All the officers and midshipmen came up from below on the *Discovery*—how well named for this moment!—and the *Resolution.* Kerguelen itself was just momentarily visible as a massive shape bearing south-east before the fog shut it off again. A Frenchman may have been here once but he had made no survey, brought back no chart. Cook was going to do both. This was the work for which they were intended and so well equipped to fulfil. There were many sketchbooks out, but Bligh's drawings were to be the official and by far the best ones. The practised hands of this serious, plump, pale-faced warrant officer began to work fast on the parchment as he sat at his board, and seamen stood admiringly a little behind him, watching the strokes of his pen.

Clerke in the *Discovery* took one look and commented, 'Nature seems to have designed this land solely for the use of sealions, seals, penguins and sea fowl.'

They passed within half a league of the rock fist, and Cook said it was to be called Bligh's Cap for that was what it most resembled and the master deserved that little honour anyway.

There would be more. Other names celebrated more lofty personages as the *Resolution* worked down the east coast of the island, taking bearings and soundings—Cumberland Bay and Cape for the noble duke, Point Pringle for the President of the Royal Society, and Cape Sandwich and Port Palliser for Cook's patrons and to honour the Admiralty.

But the more they saw of the island, its gaunt and un-productive hills leading from the rocky shoreline to the snow-line and lacking all sign of vegetation, the less of an honour it seemed to have one's name bestowed upon any part of it. The fog cleared to mist and returned to fog. The wind howled. Thomas Edgar, the normally cheerful master of the *Discovery*, who always got on so well with Clerke, complained of 'the melancholy croaking of innumerable penguins'. Here at the ultimate limit of Africa was the ultimate limit in dreariness. Cook normally respected the names given by those who had preceded him and Kerguelen's Cape St Louis was allowed to remain on Bligh's chart. But it had to be Island of Desolation. Nothing else would do.

That evening the sloops anchored off a sheltered bay behind Cape St Louis, which Bligh sounded in a boat and reported 'safe and commodious with good anchorage at every part, and great plenty of fresh water, seals, penguins and other birds on the shore but not a stick of wood'. Cook made nothing of Christmas morning, no divine service, no rest for his crews. 'Never before had experienced Christmas day so little noticed', was one seaman's melancholy comment. Then it suddenly seemed as if the Lord did not intend them to forget. As they ventured into the inlet, there loomed through the damp mist a great tower-like arched rock, in the shape of a Gothic church window, heavily perforated about the edge. There could be no more appropriate ecclesiastical sentinel for what inevitably was named Christmas Harbour. Bligh made a drawing of it.

Cook took a boat to the beach. 'I ascended the first ridge of rocks,' he reported, 'which rise in a kind of amphitheatre one above another, in order to have a view of the country, but before I got up there there came on so thick a fog that I could hardly find my way down again.' A few tufts of tussock grass had been found and the men were cutting it with sickles—scarcely enough for the ewes. Others were clubbing the few seals for their oil, and a group of sailors were knocking down the tame little rockhopper penguins, who had no reason until now to fear man, for the sport as if in a fair's skittle booth. Cook did not bother to rebuke them though he did not much like it. Anderson hated it and said so. The two ships' masters were sounding and the monotonous cries of the leadsmen blended with the shrieks of the penguins. '10, 12, 16, 12.' It was a Godforsaken Christmas Day.

The next day was all water. It poured with rain, the damp fog was thicker than ever, and the crews laboured with the casks, filling them from a bubbling freshet, although 'the sides of the hills bounding the harbour seemed to be covered with a sheet of water', the commander recorded.

On the 27th Cook relented and gave his men a day off. It was still raining and there was little for them to do but wander about the countryside which 'they found barren and desolate in the highest degree', and to commit more carnage. The penguins, Anderson noted, were already beginning to flinch away at the approach of man. In the evening, Cook had the fires lit on board to provide cheer and try to dry out the ships. The weather cleared at last; and like a belated celebratory chorus there came 'some small birds to serenade us,' Anderson noted, 'as if to convince us that cheerfulness was the portion of the contented in the most desolate situation. Their notes were most exquisite. . . .'

One of the men had earlier found a quart bottle wired to a projecting rock and containing a sheet of parchment. The writing, in Latin, Anderson translated inadequately, 'Under Lewis XVth King of the Gauls and the Duke of Boynes secretary to the maritime affairs to the King in the years 1772 and 1773.' So the French had been here twice, and wanted to prove it. Not to be outdone, Cook had written on the reverse, 'Naves Resolution & Discovery de Rege magnæ Brittaniæ Decr 1776'. Then he ordered a cairn to be built in a prominent position, the lead-capped bottle buried within it, and the union flag hoisted on a small staff. This gave everyone immense satisfaction, even the Americans in the ships, though it had no legal relevance until a British settlement was established. (It is French today and almost all Cook's names have gone.)

Busy days of charting the west coast of the island followed with both Cook and Bligh hard at their most satisfying work. Of the two, Cook had the greater experience, many times over, but Bligh was by no means only the pupil. They worked in mutual harmony, each respecting the other as if nature had destined them for this occupation and no other. The fog came and went, it rained and rained, and briefly cleared. A gale got up as they sought shelter and they had to strike the top-gallant yards. Bligh sounded up inlets, and Cook went ashore again, finding the country even more desolate here than about Christmas Harbour. It was not cold, and he was puzzled that there was no sign of any life—trees, shrubs, crustaceans, plants, fauna or land birds. Anderson found some more land birds but very few. Worse than that, this place was even killing off their own remaining livestock. Some goats had died on the long hard haul from the Cape, but in the few days off this coast many more of the young goats and three of the heifers had died though never short of fodder.

With the new year they were thankful to be clear of the Island of Desolation, steering east with the happier prospect of New Holland and New Zealand ahead, land that was familiar and comprehensible. Cook had the *Resolution* smoked again. It was like a purge after Kerguelen.

3

Strange anchorages

IT WAS NEARLY seven years earlier, on 19 April 1770 at 6 a.m., when Cook had first sighted the coast of Australia. The man who had cried 'Land!' was Lieutenant Zachary Hicks, 31 years old, born in Stepney, east London, second lieutenant of the *Endeavour*. He was suffering from tuberculosis at the time, survived the subsequent holocaust at Batavia which carried away by dysentery so many of the men Cook had preserved from the hazards and diseases associated with long voyages, but had expired shortly before the ship reached home. The young, rakish master's mate, Charles Clerke, had taken over his duties.

Cook had then stood north and up the coast of the land he later named New South Wales, and in four months charted its entire length, more or less accurately and missing little, in the most daring and accomplished single act of survey in maritime history.

The navigator had never claimed more than to have made known to the world the shape of the eastern side of this great subcontinent—and at the time Banks took the credit anyway. The Dutch navigator Abel Janszoon Tasman had sailed along the west and south coasts of Australia on his voyage of 1642, rightly naming it New Holland, and had explored the Gulf of Carpentaria and much of the northern coast two years later. Even before him, other Dutch traders had touched the western and northern coasts, and the Englishman William Dampier had been here in the 1690s too. Australia stood, a great land mass awaiting occupation and exploitation, only sketchily known but enough for mariners to point to a chart and say, 'There it is'.

Cook had never been back to New South Wales, nor had he intended to on this voyage. But at Van Diemen's Land, Tasman's name for the south-east corner of New Holland (neither he nor Cook ever found the passage between Tasmania and the mainland), the *Adventure* under Furneaux in April 1773 had found a perfect bay for resting and refitting, wooding and watering. It had not been mentioned in Cook's instructions as a stopping place for this voyage. Such was the urgency of his itinerary that the Admiralty had envisaged his sailing clear from the Cape to Tahiti—some 11,000 miles—without rest, or perhaps halting briefly at New Zealand if it should prove necessary.

Such a voyage would have placed an insupportable strain on Cook and his men under any circumstances. With the king's stock on board, augmented by further animals at Cape Town, this non-stop leg could not possibly be contemplated. With the deaths of more goats, sheep and cattle—some said it was Kerguelen's wretched grass spoiled by penguin droppings that was killing them, not the weather or confinement—and now fearful of arriving at Tahiti with no livestock at all, Cook gave Clerke an earlier rendezvous than New Zealand, Furneaux's Adventure Bay, named after his ship. It was in these same southern Indian Ocean waters that Cook's two ships had lost one another on the last voyage; and now when thick fog came down, sometimes for days on end so that you could scarcely see prow from poop, there was a great risk of one losing the other again. Regularly the signal guns cracked out, sometimes anxiously distant, as Cook and Clerke endeavoured to remain in touch, shouting and halloing into the freezing, choking fog when they came too close. The *Resolution* also continued to leak in spite of all that the caulkers had strived to do at the Cape, and in a squall three weeks after leaving Kerguelen, the fore topmast and main top-gallant mast were carried away.

Swearing renewed vengeance on the Deptford shipwrights,

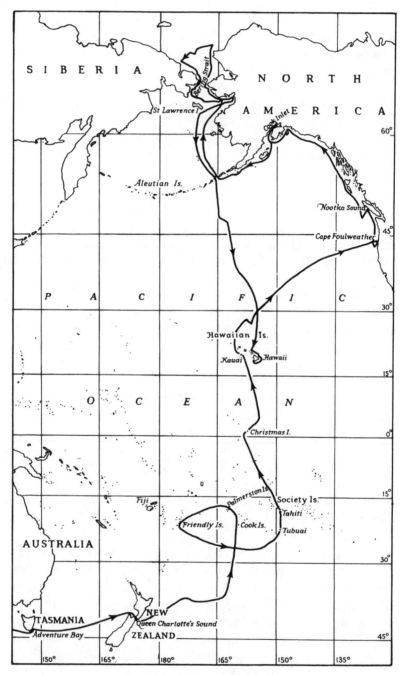

Cook's last voyage in the Pacific.

the men struggled to cut them free. Lieutenant King commented that it was in part their need to make up time that was the cause of the accident, by carrying all sail possible; but it was poor workmanship in dock which had led to much of their delay. And now another day was lost to clearing up the wreckage and stepping a new topmast—they had no spare main top-gallant.

Adventure Bay, Tasmania, is a weary sailor's dream, an oasis in a desert of hostile headlands and cliffs and dangerous lee shores of this southern coastline. Jem Burney loved it—loved the climate and the country—'exceeding pleasant'.

It is as if the hand of some master architect had taken a compass and marked out of this ragged, inhospitable coast a near-circle with the open part so placed as to attract no unwanted winds or seas. Having excavated this lagoon, he must have ordered a great quantity of shelving white sand, cut here and there by babbling brooks; and behind that perfect beach, and climbing up the gentle slopes, an unlimited quantity of timber, sweet-scented and admirably suitable for spars and for ships' stoves. Here, until they came, even man was not vile, just shy, primitive and withdrawn.

Cook closed the coast of Tasmania just a month after sighting Kerguelen. It was a fine clear morning, with mellow mid-summer temperatures, and by contrast with that other island's desolation, the coast was richly wooded, and the smoke of many fires spiralling up into the blue sky told of a rich, inhabited interior.

Bligh made one of his sensitive and stunningly accurate drawings of a part of the southern coast to assist future navigators searching for Adventure Bay, and began his chart of the approach to their anchorage.

'A gentle breeze,' said Anderson, 'came from the southward, which increasing carried us into Adventure Bay where we anchored at 4 o'clock.' It was 26 January. Even the breeze was accommodating here. Cook ordered grass-cutting and timber-felling. Anderson and Nelson were soon ashore, botanizing away with their customary zeal, noting only two types of tree—both, in fact, eucalyptus.

Bayly embarked in a boat with his tent observatory and

instruments like a country fair stallholder settling himself in. Cook was quick ashore, too, with Clerke. Jem Burney told them that they had not caught sight of any natives last time, so shy were they. Cook was taking no chances, not after what had happened to one of the *Adventure*'s boat crews later on that voyage. He told Clerke to send a party of four of his marines with the grass cutting and wooding parties. Sergeant Kich selected Moody, Herriott, Poole and William Broom. The marines thought this delectable beach called for a celebration and stole the bottles of spirit intended for everyone. The serious drinking began early. Later they were found paralytically drunk on the beach, and they had to be thrown like sacks into the boat and hauled unceremoniously on board again. Cook ordered the bosun to give them a dozen lashes the next morning. Neither the miscreants nor anyone else thought this unjust.

Having surveyed the limited fauna and flora of the bay, Anderson the naturalist became an equally eager anthropologist, accompanied by David Nelson, Bayly, Cook wearing a striped jacket, and Omai, as usual armed with one of his muskets—a mixed exploratory party from Scotland, London, Somerset, Yorkshire and Polynesia. Evidently the natives were much less shy this time, emerging tentatively from the thick forest in groups. The first party they met consisted of eight men and a boy. Later, women appeared, reassured and with no sign of shyness. Anderson described them as rather smaller than most natives, dull black but not as dark as African negroes, nor with broad lips, and noses full rather than flat. He found their eyes gave 'a frank, cheerful cast to the whole countenance'; their bodies well proportioned though with rather full bellies. Their favourite standing posture was with their upper part leaning back, with one hand behind grasping the other arm. Their harsh woolly hair was 'clotted or divided into small parcels, and like their beards abundantly smeared with a greasy red dye'. They were without any decoration and stark naked, and Anderson, who had seen the native tribes of Tierra del Fuego on the last voyage, compared the length of kangaroo's skin with the sealskin that the Fuegian women wore to support their children on their backs, which actually emphasized their nakedness.

The first man of the party was holding a short pointed stick which suggested that Cook's caution may have been justified. But he was instructed by signs from the others to lower his weapon, such as it was, and the whole party gave themselves up to turning over and handling the knives and handkerchiefs Anderson and Cook offered them, giving no evidence of delight or gratitude. Soon they began nosing around for more. To the white men it was pilfering, to these natives it was as natural as dogs searching for titbits.

Bread was refused so Anderson produced some fish they had caught in the bay. They turned aside in horror and disgust as a white man might from a bowl of intestines. Anderson could not know that their strange code forbade eating fish, the one plentiful food, though they could spear them for fun. What on earth did they eat, then? Anderson puzzled. Later, they found piles of shells, indicating that they lived mostly on crustaceans, although it seemed that they also consumed birds when opportunity offered. It could not have done so often for the rough spear the man had been carrying appeared to be their only weapon, and when he set up a target at a mere 20 yards Samwell said he threw it 'in the same manner that the rabble in England throw at cocks'.

This was too good an opportunity for Omai to miss. He would show them one of the wonders of civilization. He brought up his musket, took aim at the target and fired. The natives fled like starlings into the forest, holding their hands over their ears, and never admired his marksmanship.

Later in the day, Cook left a boar and a sow deep in the woods close by a stream, hoping that they might survive, turn wild and multiply, and thus provide these pathetic savages with a better diet. They met the natives again, now recovered from their fright, and Cook gave them some beads. Again they kept them but there was little response until one of them fingered Cook's striped jacket, indicating that he would like it. Cook at once slipped it off and gave it to him.

It took a lot to achieve any sort of response from these primitive and passive people except occasional infectious giggles. They seemed cheerful enough, tranquil in temperament, with few strains of jealousy or anger. Anderson the philosopher surmised that the reason for their equanimity was that they had so little to lose or care for, like the Fuegians or the Easter Islanders; but unlike the richly endowed natives of the Marquesas islands whom they had found so turbulent. Their huts were of the most primitive kind, and all they seemed to possess was the ability to make fire, gather crustaceans and procreate.

Anderson also noted how completely submissive they were, the women allowing themselves to be 'examined without the least appearance of bashfulness'. As for the men standing about them, watching with little interest such unprecedented scenes in their dull lives as fully clothed men filling cask after cask with water or digging up plants and writing notes, they would merely, as Anderson recorded, 'play with their penis as a child would with any bauble or a man twirl about the key of his watch while conversing with you'. Quite without self-consciousness, Clerke observed, 'these people in the most natural action are without the least restraint and have much less idea of decency than a dog, pouring forth their streams whether sitting, walking or talking without any preparation or guidance or even appearing sensible of what they are doing, not in the least interested whether it trickles down their own thighs or sprinkles the person next to them'. Then they would lie down and go straight to sleep on the sand in the great heat of the mid-day sun.

The aborigines appeared neither to resent nor much to appreciate the sudden appearance in their land of these 200 or so white people who emerged from the great ships anchored in their bay. The high spot of the visit for the aborigines was brief but did serve to reveal to Anderson and Cook that they possessed a spark of life in spite of their seeming passivity. An unarmed and unescorted watering party filling casks at the stream with buckets and funnels at the northern end of the bay was surprised by the sudden descent from the forest of a number of natives. Their intentions were, as always, quite innocent; but numerous acts of native hostility, here and elsewhere on Cook's earlier voyages, were always in the men's minds when they were ashore. Now this watering party panicked when they saw the naked painted savages advancing on them, and dropped their casks and ran. According to Bayly, this afforded the natives the utmost delight and they 'began to jump and halloo', running after them in the greatest good spirits, even teasingly seizing the boat's gunwale as if to draw it higher up the beach.

The happiness was short-lived. One of the watering party seized a musket from the bottom of the boat and fired it into the air. As at Omai's target practice, the natives at once fled twittering in distress, holding their hands over their ears.

David Samwell's favourite character was a little hunchback, like a demented deformed clown, who leaped about with joy and high spirits in contrast with so many of the men. He was Omai's fancy, too, the Polynesian decorating the Melanesian negritoid with a length of white cloth, cut Tahitian style, about his hunched shoulders. It was Omai's one riotous success.

Inevitably, as Cook had learned from his previous voyages, there was trouble with the women—and, appropriately, it originated in Clerke's sloop rather than his own. Cook himself was invariably celibate on his long cruises, like Bligh, and not all his officers enjoyed the native women when opportunity occurred. But very few of the seamen abstained, and many thought of little else when land was sighted, and were hell-bent for the shore and the women as soon as they could.

Cook tried to contain this lust as far as he was able, strove in every way he could to keep those of his men with 'the venereals' away from the natives, but reluctantly bowed to the inevitable when the women were obviously willing and the men had not seen one for weeks. In the event, there was nothing he could have done to prevent contact when, as had so often occurred in the past, the Polynesian girls had swarmed on board, forcing their bodies on the men in their eagerness, and loudly showing how much they despised Cook himself and others who refused to submit.

In places with which he was unfamiliar, Cook recognized the grave dangers of his crew interfering with the women without the encouragement of the men. In Adventure Bay he learned that a number of Clerke's crew on leave ashore had tried to seduce the women—unwashed, lice-covered, painted and 'fragrant of noisome smells' as they were—with generous offers of gifts, and 'had been rejected with great disdain'. An elderly aborigine, observing these approaches, fiercely ordered all the women and children off the beach. So much for the white men's patronizing attitude towards the 'naked savages'!

As for the more responsible members of the expedition, besides Nelson's and Anderson's botanizing and anthropologizing, Bligh predictably was sounding the bay and its entrance and making drawings and charts. He did not have time to discover they were on an island and not on Van Diemen's Land as he inscribed his chart—an island off an island off Australia: Bruni Island as it is now called, and little changed.

Ellis was ashore to draw a creditable panorama of the bay above the point where the best stream enters the sea. A small monument marks the spot where he sat at Resolution Creek.

Gore was off shooting whenever opportunity occurred. He was less interested in ethnology. He commented economically that the natives were of 'a cheerful, inoffensive disposition'.

At first Cook had given every sign that their stay here would be relaxed and prolonged, as at Cape Town, in spite of the fact that only recently he had still been determined to proceed non-stop to New Zealand from Kerguelen, with Queen Charlotte's Sound as the two ships' rendezvous should they be separated. Bayly was already ashore on that first day, labouring on the elaborate business of setting up his observatory. The wooding and watering parties revealed no sign of urgency in their work. Then, on that same evening, Cook sent for Bayly. 'I have altered my mind,' the captain told him. 'I intend to sail for New Zealand as soon as possible.' And he asked Bayly to dismantle his observatory and bring it back on board.

They had arrived on Sunday 26 January. Three days passed at this paradise on Adventure Bay, and there was speculation that they were going to by-pass New Zealand entirely after all and thus make up some of their lost time.

Early on the morning of the 30th, with the wooding and watering still far from completion, Cook ordered anchors weighed, and the two sloops stood out east, past the torn coastline of the Tasman Peninsula. They were heading for New

Zealand after all. Cook justified his call here by claiming that the winds were so light they had lost little distance. Then why, Bligh might well have asked, had not the commander ordered more energetic use to be made of the time to provide their accursed livestock with enough fodder to see them direct to Tahiti? It had not at first seemed grass of high quality or quantity, but a more diligent search would have found the ample supply on Penguin Island at the entrance to the bay at once and not on their last afternoon, Cook belatedly chivvying along the grass cutters.

This was only one of the numerous questions, and complaints, Bligh recorded on a voyage the irascible ship's master found increasingly unsatisfactory. He knew, as all the officers knew, that Cook had never in the past waited in port for a fair wind. One of the reasons for his success as a navigator was his previously invariable practice of putting to sea in calm weather to look for a fair wind. And how often he had found one, too!

The passage to New Zealand was swift, occupying less than 12 days, with some heavy swells and much rain. The only mishap was the *Discovery*'s loss of another marine on the night of 6–7 February. George Moody, one of Clerke's four drunks who had received a dozen lashes, had evidently overdone it again and fallen overboard. Otherwise all were well, as indeed they should be, with the exception of able seaman Watman, although both Clerke in the *Discovery* and Anderson in the *Resolution* found themselves feeling the cold and coughing frequently.

The two sloops remained in sight of one another through each day, and at 4 p.m. on the afternoon of 10 February high land was seen ahead. Cook recognized Rocks Point, which he had charted in March 1770 during his stunning, non-stop survey of the whole New Zealand coastline in the *Endeavour*. Cape Farewell, marking the north-west extremity of New Zealand's south island, was to the north. He was 45 miles out in his landfall, an inaccuracy forgivable enough in many navigators but unsatisfactory by his high standards on former voyages.

Early the next morning the heavy dark cliffs of the cape which Cook had named as he departed New Zealand shores on his first voyage were already to the south. Soon, with a fine breeze from the north-west, the two sloops were among the multitudes of rocky islands, spits, headlands and deep inlets, which mark the spectacular fractured northern coastline of South Island. These were waters Cook knew well and had, in part, surveyed.

Jem Burney knew them well, too, and observed again the thickly wooded slopes of the hills and the deep sandy coves, this time with some unease. He had not been back since that terrible December day more than three years ago when he had been ordered to search for the *Adventure*'s missing cutter, despatched with its crew to cut grass.

Besides the launch's crew, Burney had had ten marines under his command. All day he had sailed up and down Queen Charlotte's Sound, studying every cove with his glass, calling out and firing volleys of musket fire as a signal. A dreadful air of fear and doom hung over these waters, which had always until now seemed so happy and friendly, and when he landed on one beach to search the huts of a settlement there were gestures of defiance from some of the men before flight. One of the Maori warriors was carrying a large bundle of spears down to a beach. 'Seeing I looked very earnestly at him,' Burney recounted later, 'he put them on the ground and walked about with seeming unconcern.'

Burney felt certain that some dreadful catastrophe had occurred. He offered a looking glass and a large nail to one group who seemed particularly fearful, hoping for news. He received none.

Farther along the shores of the sound on the east side, almost opposite and only seven miles from their anchorage, Burney saw there was a very large double canoe drawn up on the beach, with two men and a dog beside it. On seeing the launch, the men fled into the woods. His suspicions aroused again, the young lieutenant went ashore at the spot and examined the inside of the canoe. There, unmistakably, was a piece of the cutter's gunwale, and near it some shoes, one pair identifiable as belonging to Midshipman Tom Woodhouse. Then one of his seamen approached Burney carrying a chunk of meat, suggesting it was some of the salt beef the cutter's crew had taken as emergency rations. Jem Burney smelt it and decided it was not salt but fresh meat. Someone else suggested it might be the flesh of a dog, and Burney agreed.

They were wrong. Others of the party had found baskets, their tops tied down. They cut them open, and the full horror of the discovery swept over them in a sickening wave. They were handling the flesh and bones—a forearm here, a calf there—of their shipmates, some of it roasted, some raw. In other of the baskets was roasted fern root, the Maoris' favourite vegetable to accompany the planned feast of human flesh.

Further search of the area yielded more shoes, a hand tattooed 'T.H.'—Thomas Hill had had the tattoo etched at Tahiti. A black head, belonging to the captain's negro servant, James Swilley.

Carrying these grotesque remnants, Burney ordered the party back into the launch, and with the light now falling, sailed round a point into Grass Cove. It was as if some great celebration was about to take place there—Burney likened it to a fair. Drawn up on the beach were three big double canoes and a single one. Beyond, and all the way up the hill upon which a fire was burning, were natives. They might have been waiting for the curtain to rise on a great drama. Those lower down were retreating but shouting towards the launch, waving it in for the show to begin.

By this time the launch crew's horror had changed to fierce anger and a need for vengeance. Burney ordered a musket to be fired at one of the canoes in case an ambush was concealed on the beach. No Maori sprang from it, and as the launch was pulled in closer, the marines stood and fired a volley into the crowd. It had no effect as far as they could see in the poor light, and after reloading, the marines fired again, and then again and again, scattering the crowd on the lower slopes and causing them to retreat into the forest, screaming—all but two old stout men who remained unruffled by the panic about them until they recognized that they were quite alone. 'Then they walked away with great composure and deliberation, their pride not suffering them to run,' Burney wrote in his report.

Burney went ashore with the marines to face a new nightmare

in the dusk. The bundles of grass confirmed that this was where John Rowe, the young Devonian master's mate, had brought the cutting party, and where he and the rest had been butchered. The sight that met Burney's eyes was so awful he could not bear to describe it in detail later. 'Such a shocking scene,' he managed to write, 'of carnage and barbarity as can never be mentioned or thought of but with horror.'

Peter Fannin, the *Adventure*'s wise master, who had stayed behind to guard the launch, ran across the beach towards his lieutenant when he heard threatening sounds of the Maoris gathering as if for a mass attack. His warning words held back Burney, who was beside himself with rage after what he described as his stupefaction at their further discovery had passed.

What could they hope to accomplish against such numbers? Burney shouted at his men to smash up the canoes before they left, and they did so with vigour, their blows echoed by the rising chorus of mass fury from the unseen hordes on the wooded hillside.

The launch's crew put out into the sound in a hurry. The onset of darkness matched the increasing weight of menace and fear in the sound. The fire on the hill above Grass Cove had died, but in its place at a distance of three or four miles along the shore a huge Valhalla-like fire flared up, formed into the shape of an oval reaching from the top of the hill to the shore.

One of the launch's crew thought he heard the sound of a voice in the darkness and Burney ordered them to rest on their oars for a moment to listen. They called out in chorus, 'But to little purpose,' wrote Burney, 'the poor souls were far enough out of hearing.'

It was a sombre evening in the *Adventure*, an evening none would forget, the long separation from the *Resolution* serving to add to their melancholy. What little of the victims that had been retrieved was committed to the deep, wrapped in a hammock and thrown into the waters of this bloody sound, weighed down with ballast and shot: just a couple of hands, the second identified as young Rowe's by a scar, a few other bits, and the great black severed head.

*

Of all those who had been involved in the tragedy of the *Adventure* and were now returning to the scene, Omai had been among the most shocked—a younger, un-Europeanized, still unspoilt Omai. He had regarded these Maoris as his friends and cousins, fellow Polynesians with a near-common tongue, and he saw their barbarity as a reflection on himself and his race. Had he not been talking freely with them that very day? Bayly, too, had been shattered when Jem Burney, Fannin and the rest had come alongside the *Adventure* close to midnight; and George Vancouver's friend Midshipman Richard Hergest; Alex Dewar the *Resolution*'s clerk; and the master's mate William Lanyon. Now, three and a quarter years later, as the *Resolution* and *Discovery* worked across Blind Bay, doubled Cape Stephens and Point Jackson and headed up Queen Charlotte's Sound again, these men were filled with memories—of the talk of vengeance through the night, of the commander's decision that it would be profitless, of the departure out of the sullen cove, past Long Island and out into Cook Strait to put as many leagues between themselves and Grass Cove as quickly as possible. No one had been the same after that event.

At 10 a.m. on 12 February in a flat calm, the *Resolution* was towed by her boats into Ship Cove and anchored in her old station alongside the *Discovery*. A silence hung over the sound, as if the Maori tribes who lived so densely in the forests all about them were holding their breath in expectation of imminent disaster. After the cables had raced noisily through the hawse holes, Anderson was aware only of a 'perpetual and universal chirping in the woods which I never heard before in this place'. Might it be the natives breaking into hushed, excited chatter? Later he found it came only from great numbers of cicadas speeding between the trees.

Ship Cove is not the most sheltered anchorage in Queen Charlotte's Sound, and sometimes in the past Cook had experienced difficulties there in sudden stormy weather. Its first advantage was its stream, which flows down, pure and swift, from the high hills at all times. Then it has a fine and accessible beach with enough flat land above the high water mark for setting up an encampment and safely exercising men and beasts. Cook had once comfortably careened the *Endeavour* here. Then its situation quite close to the entrance to the sound saved the long and tiresome working up to more sheltered but more distant coves.

By now Cook knew the sound well, and still, better than any other, preferred Ship Cove with its deep wooded valley curving up to the right, its beach of brown flat pebbles and clean sand. He and all his men on every visit relished the purity of the cool stream water after weeks of the filthy stale cask stuff.

William Bligh, here for the first time, experienced none of the associations with doom shared by Jem Burney and the others who had last been here in the *Adventure*. After supervising the anchoring of the *Resolution* he was able to look about him at ease, with one eye as a surveyor, the other as an artist. In both capacities he savoured what he saw, determining to improve upon the crude drawing of Ship Cove and the hills made on the *Endeavour* voyage, noting the characteristic and spectacular fern trees that rose up so gracefully among the beech, rimu, miro and other hard timber. More distantly, on the far side of the sound and on the two large islands in its centre, stains indicated where the Maoris had made their fires.

For the present there was no other sign of the inhabitants; nor did Bligh much care. Certainly not a breath of fear touched this dour, business-like figure.

It was a beautiful clear warm day, and the people were soon stripping and sweating as they pulled ashore with the tents and tools, Bayly's instruments and the surviving stock. By dinner time in the mid-afternoon a little community had grown up in a cleared area beside the stream, its similarity to an English village unmistakable: grazing cattle and sheep, chickens and geese pecking curiously in their new freedom, the horses being exercised on the green, the rising smoke and smell of cooking. Like good English villagers, they even had their vegetable patch, planted on their last visit, though now neglected and in need of attention after their long absence. If there was no inn, a brewery was already in production, and the spruce beer it provided was soon flowing.

The brewing of beer was a practice Cook had started when working on his Newfoundland survey, as a promoter of good health and a preventive measure against scurvy. It was made by cutting off the green tops of the spruce pine, boiling them and adding liquid malt (which he kept always in stock) and sugar. It was one of the few innovations actually welcomed by the seamen, and it was described as 'a very tasty and healthful drink'. Here at Ship Cove they used the rimu, which was equally effective.

Inevitably the natives began to emerge, tentatively and nervously, singing their song of peace and waving a white cloth. It appeared to Cook that the Maoris' only explanation for the arrival of the white men in such strength was to exact revenge for the murder of the *Adventure*'s boat crew. But as the day wore on several canoes packed with armed men also approached the *Resolution*. Cook came on deck to greet them, but although among them he recognized a man with whom he had once been on the friendliest of terms, he could not persuade them to come near.

Gilbert reflected the sharper reaction of the lower deck, who were in favour of repressive methods against recalcitrant natives, in commenting, 'I think nothing can be a greater proof of their treachery than their suspecting it in us.'

The sight of Omai on the *Resolution*'s deck appeared at first to inflame their fear. Omai, so different from the others, was the one man from the *Adventure* whom they could at once recognize; no doubt he was here to direct the purpose of the expedition, the *utu*, the act of revenge. But Omai spoke their language, or near enough to be understood, and at Cook's instruction he did all he could, by gestures, words of reassurance and waving his dainty white London handkerchief, to reduce their fear.

They came on board in ones and twos, in stark contrast to the abandoned assaults of earlier visits, scarcely believing that 'Toote' would not exact *utu* upon them; and later making clear their disdain for his failure to do so. Among those whom Cook recognized was Tiarooa, son of a chieftain killed in battle, only a 14-year-old before and now a stalwart youth to whom Omai appeared to be giving special attention.

More Maoris followed, drawn by curiosity and the urge to trade, carrying fish and taking nails and fish hooks and priceless axes in exchange. Phillips had his marines' muskets loaded with ball, posted on board and on shore. Ships' boats on grass-cutting trips up the sound carried marines and the crews were armed too. Gilbert was among those who visited Grass Cove, sickle in one hand, musket and cutlass always beside him. Looking about uneasily he recognized that 'no place could be more favourable for such intentions as the wood was so thick that the natives could approach close to them before they were discovered. We saw 4 or 5 of them,' he recounted, 'who seeing our number were afraid to come near us till we made them to understand we had no intention to hurt them.'

Cook was determined to learn the truth behind the Grass Cove attack, and there was no shyness among the Maoris about telling him as soon as they knew they were safe from *utu*. The difficulty was to distinguish between the various accounts. But, thanks to Omai, Cook reckoned that the story he took away with him was as accurate as it would ever be. Neither to him, nor to Jem Burney, was the explanation a surprise. Rowe was known to have been sharp in his comments on the 'savages' and an advocate of more violent measures against thieving. He and his party had anchored the cutter off Grass Cove, had waded ashore leaving the Negro servant, with all the arms except Rowe's musket, on board as guard. They had worked hard in the heat to collect the bundles Burney had found the next day. Then they had made a fire and were settling down to their dinner of salt beef and ship's biscuit and—no doubt—liberal spirits.

The natives had appeared in some numbers, drawn by the hope of trade, or failing that some successful pilfering. Their demands for biscuit were rebuffed. Their forays became more daring, some biscuit was stolen, the party angrily and noisily attempted to drive them off. Other natives waded out to the cutter in search of loot, were attacked gallantly by the Negro, who shouted for help. On shore, Rowe seized his musket, fired and killed a Maori. Another shot fatally injured a second. Then the natives ran amok in a fever of revenge. The odds were hopeless, and in a few seconds all the party had been clubbed to death.

What followed was as natural as the burying of enemy dead in the Western world. To eat your enemy ensured his eternal damnation. Cook had learned all about that on his first visit here, when a mimed demonstration with old human bones, and other episodes, had excited his disgust. In the certainty of their superiority the Europeans in their early visits to New Zealand believed—but not for long—that they, as white strangers, must be immune from such barbarous practices. It was Rowe's hotheaded arrogance that had led to the end of his party.

Besides the careful security measures established by Cook, he was surprised yet satisfied to observe that his men this time would have nothing to do with the women, even those sailors who (in Samwell's elegant Welsh choice of words) 'are never known to be peculiarly nice in the choice of their paramours'. They were soon making their appearance, on shipboard and ashore, lavish in their daubed red paint like some Rowlandson caricature of a Portsmouth whore, ready with their favours for a nail or two. It was unprecedented, but there were no takers. Not cannibals.

As the expedition settled in at Queen Charlotte's Sound, living well off the fruit—'a sort of plum'—and wonderfully varied fish with mainly perfect summer weather, there remained those who were perplexed by their commander's seeming disregard for their original timetable. The officers who knew that by this time they should have been somewhere in the uncharted seas of the north Pacific and heading towards New Albion were mystified by Cook's inaction. Those who had been with Cook in the *Endeavour* recalled his strict adherance to the timetable designed to fetch them up at Tahiti for the transit of Venus observations.

Now Cook seemed content for his two sloops to remain idly at anchor, and Bligh was the only officer who busied himself improving the earlier incomplete and not altogether accurate charts of the sound. For most of the crews day followed day occupied in the light routine tasks of cutting grass or timber and working on shipboard. But the atmosphere both on board the sloops and ashore had an unreal and uneasy nature and was quite unlike the relaxed atmosphere at Adventure Bay, in spite of the domestic character of their encampment. Everyone was aware of the unpredictability of these Maori tribes, who fought so bitterly among themselves and were without a steady ethic in their lives. Samwell, a temperate commentator, regarded them as 'the most barbarous and vindictive race of men on the face of the globe'. Anderson the anthropologist gave more elaborate and considered thought. But he too noted their 'mistrustful temper', their dishonesty and hysterical response. While recognizing that war was their chief occupation, he had a low opinion of their bravery, their warlike spirit 'to be looked upon rather as an effect of a furious disposition than great courage'.

It was this mercurial quality of the inhabitants that made these waters so uneasy. As soon as the encampment had been established ashore and the Maoris knew that they were safe from *utu*, families landed from canoes with their arms and the frames of their transportable dwellings, and within hours, tearing down the undergrowth for thatch, had created a tight-packed neighbouring village. There was no way of stopping them. When there was no space remaining, others moved into the adjoining coves and the islands offshore until there were many hundreds of Maoris surrounding the expedition, Cook estimated two-thirds of the entire population of Queen Charlotte's Sound. Given a coordinated plan and the readiness to face losses, they could have overwhelmed the lightly defended ships and shore establishment at any time.

But they seemed amiably enough disposed towards Cook's men, bringing fish and curios and carvings in exchange for nails and trinkets and, most prized of all, axes. Anderson noted their colouring, from black to olive tinge, their less than perfect physique (with notable exceptions), their broad teeth, full lips and noses, their black, strong straight hair elaborately cut and piled and tied, the open expressions of the young, the tendency to sullenness of the mature males. He also examined closely their simple cloth garments made from flax and the decorations of birds' feathers, or the skin of dogs, which were everywhere; and the elaborate personal decorations of ochre and pearl and feathers besides the tattooing and painting which they especially fancied.

As the voyagers had noticed on previous visits, fires would spring up unpredictably from the forests and there would be chanting and sudden shouts in the night. David Samwell, sleeping ashore in a tent, recorded in one sentence the two extremes of mood to which the cove subjected them. 'As we were every night disturbed by the mournful cries of distress, so we were every morning most agreeably delighted by the harmony of the birds that echoed through the surrounding woods, man alone even in these regions being the prey of misery and despair.' Perhaps it was not so much like an English village after all.

On board the *Resolution* no event revealed more clearly the quaint morality of these Maoris than the appearance of Kahura, the very chieftain who had killed Rowe and brought on the massacre at Grass Cove. The natives already in the ship, as usual trading hard, urged Cook to kill him at once, according to the traditions of *utu*, and no doubt to ingratiate themselves with the commander. Opinion among the seamen, although publicly unspoken, was the same. Why wait?

Omai was the most outraged. 'There is Kahura, till him,' he urged his captain. 'Why do you not till him? If a man tills another in England he is hanged. This man has tilled ten. . . .'

Cook refused and instead asked Omai to question Kahura: why had he killed Captain Furneaux's people?

Kahura answered silently by folding his arms and hanging his head in submission and shame.

'Tell him he will not be killed,' Cook ordered; and the outraged Omai did as he was told.

At once a transformation came over the chieftain, and he had ready a cock-and-bull story about unfair trading on the part of Rowe. Now he was full of fearless cockiness, and observing one of Webber's portraits of a Maori hanging in the cabin indicated through Omai that he, too, wished to be drawn for posterity. Webber was duly summoned and Kahura was a model sitter, unmoving until the artist had completed his likeness.

Captain Clerke supported Cook's merciful policy, as did

most of the better educated officers. Violence would have served no purpose at all, he commented. At the same time, this discriminating and fastidious commander, who had sailed among the Polynesians for more than a decade, shared David Samwell's low rating of the Maoris and their trustworthiness. 'There are few indians,' he wrote, 'in whom I would wish to put a perfect confidence, but of all I ever met with these should be last, for I firmly believe them very capable of the most perfidious and most cruel treachery.'

That day ended harmoniously. But no one, from Cook himself down to the most illiterate seaman, felt able to relax in this place, just as—according to Cook—'the New Zealanders must live under perpetual apprehension of being destroyed by each other'. Once there was nearly a repetition on a larger scale of the Grass Cove catastrophe. It began with a sudden flare-up ashore between Sergeant Gibson of the marines, who had saved Cook's life before in New Zealand, and a chief. It was a constant nightmare keeping the light-fingered natives from the tents, and Bayly's observatory in particular, and there had been numerous incidents before. This time it was more serious. Thrown into a typical paroxysm of fury, the chief shouted abuse and threats of vengeance at the water's edge, repaired to his canoe and was paddled urgently to the other side of the cove, the sound of his voice gradually fading. There he collected his warriors, and a veritable flotilla of war canoes began speeding across the sound in the direction of a grass-cutting party labouring on an island.

Fortunately the incident had been observed from the *Resolution*, the alarm was raised, and Cook ordered the pinnace with marines in pursuit. They were just in time. The war party diverged from its course and the pinnace took up extra guard until the party could board their own boat and return.

As preparations were at last made to depart, to the relief of almost everyone of the expedition, it became evident that Omai had reached an agreement with Tiarooa that this fatherless chieftain's son would accompany him as personal servant to Tahiti. Cook had humoured Omai by seeming to agree to this proposed arrangement. But as the time came for dismantling the encampment he began to realize that Omai meant it seriously, and was very firm on the subject. Faced with this resolve, Cook made enquiries of the boy's mother and other relations to make sure that they did not object, urging them to understand that he would never return. She wept aloud, according to tender-hearted Clerke, 'singing a song in a very melancholy cadence'. But the mother soon recovered from her grief, evidently proud of her son's destiny. The newly elected Tiarooa at the last minute objected that the son of a warrior of his rank must himself have a personal servant.

And so it came about that the *Resolution*, after her 11-day-long sojourn, sailed out of Queen Charlotte's Sound with New Zealand's first migrants to the Society Islands on board, 9-year-old Koa and his master, 17-year-old Tiarooa: both boys for the present in a lively, chatty mood, and excited at this prospect of adventure; while Omai regarded them with satisfied indulgence.

In his turn, Cook left behind some rabbits, which in the fullness of time had an effect on the economy of this land that he could never have predicted. And also a pair of goats, several descendants of which, it has recently been made known, may have been identified close to the area where their ancestors were set free in 1777.

4

'Savouring of cruelty'

BY ANY CALCULATION, James Cook had been a navigator blessed by favourable breezes. Considering the extent of his great voyages, the number of times he was held up by adverse winds was very few. It was not all Cook luck. His voyages in the south Pacific had given him the opportunity of studying the pattern of the winds through the seasons, and a man of his skill, experience and capacity of observation noted more than any of his contemporaries, with the possible exception of his own ship's master on this voyage, William Bligh. But time and again, sailing serenely through the traditionally ferocious waters of Cape Horn, saved by a hairsbreadth by 'a small air of wind' when drifting onto Great Barrier Reef coral, good fortune blessed his vessels with fair winds.

At this critical time in February 1777, weeks behind in a timetable not yet beyond salvation, Cook's luck broke.

The omens for the passage to Tahiti were poor from the beginning when 'adverse airs' prevented the expedition even from leaving Queen Charlotte's Sound, and it took 48 hours to pass Cape Palliser on the north-east corner of South Island. Like a weathercock in a passing front, the wind veered and backed, sometimes brisk, sometimes dying to a calm. He knew the route he had to follow to reach Tahiti, by the westerly trades, then in a wide curve to the north to about 20° to catch the south-easterlies that would take him into the Society Islands from the east. But the westerlies were so elusive it was as if the timeless pattern of the Pacific winds had been broken to deceive him.

To match Cook's distress, the New Zealand boys were seasick, grief-stricken and homesick beyond consolation. 'They wept both in public and in private,' Cook observed sadly, 'and made their lamentations in a kind of song, which so far as we could understand it, was in praise of their country they should never see more.' Who could blame them? Then, just when it seemed as if they might be cheering up, little Koa would dart off miserably to the chains and lie there, lamenting and singing in a soft voice until Tiarooa came to his side like an elder brother to console him; only to become infected again with grief himself, and add his voice to the melancholy melody.

Cook did what he could for them. He even ordered precious red cloth to be made into jackets, a prize for a chieftain worth countless hogs, unnumbered women. They had little effect on the boys' spirits. Later they perked up, suddenly and unpredictably in typical Polynesian style. Koa showed his natural high spirits, which the people found very engaging, and he was treated with the affectionate attention of a pet. Steadier, more thoughtful, Tiarooa was liked and respected, too.

The sloops continued their undesired course to the north all through March. Anxiety about the livestock ran parallel in Cook's troubled mind with the loss of the northern summer. He ordered sheep killed to save fodder and to break the routine of salt meat. His worry brushed off on the ship's company and boredom and irritability led to petty thefts of food, deplorable but commonplace on long voyages. He failed to discover the thieves, and when his men failed too, he cut everyone's meat allowance. The men refused the allowance entirely; Cook was sparked to anger, threatened to extend the reduced allowance and described their act as 'a mutinous proceeding'. It was almost unprecedented for him to be in such conflict with his men, and he made no note of the episode in his journal as if to forget it ever happened.

This deviation from the intended course, this trend to the north, 'these nasty light breezes,' Clerke complained, 'which render this passage exceedingly tedious,' led to the discovery of a group of islands.

It was remarkable how navigators, like Byron for one, could sweep across the Pacific and miss so much, while Cook's ships seemed to be drawn to land as if by magnetic navigational attraction. In the midst of these miseries, it happened again. At 10 a.m. on 29 March a cry from the masthead of the *Discovery* told of an island bearing north-east. Edgar was given the privilege of charting and naming it, and he did so after his sloop. Today it is called Mangaia in the southern Cook Group. It brought them no benefit, and some anxiety, when they so sorely needed refreshment for their stock.

As Cook bore up for the west side the white spread of surf along the reef confirmed the impossibility of a landing. It was the first time Bligh had seen a Pacific coral isle, and he studied it through a glass with professional interest. Neither the shore nor the people appeared hospitable. The natives were on the reef in hundreds, he could see, brandishing their spears and clubs.

Prospects were no more favourable on the western or northern coasts of the stubby little island. Not to be frustrated, Cook ordered a boat to be lowered from each sloop, and with Omai as interpreter, along with his youthful and now more cheerful escort, and a few marines for protection, departed to search for a landing place.

Here was the Cook of old again, fearless in the face of mass native hostility — fearless to the point of rashness you could say, but a fine example to all the expedition.

A canoe came alongside almost at once, and a native stepped into the boat without invitation or more ado. Ask him where there is a landing place, Cook ordered Omai; and they were directed, but where a canoe could make light of the surf and the reef, a ship's boat faced disaster. Within a few minutes it appeared they might be facing disaster anyway as a multitude of natives swam out, climbing into the boat, thieving with typical Polynesian relentlessness and threatening to upset them.

With his men beating them off, Cook ordered the boat back, carrying only their original guide, who followed Cook up the gangway on board the *Resolution* after some persuasion, and with little interest in the strange sights—the towering masts and yards, the staring white men, the animals everywhere. Cook took him down to his cabin with Omai in the hope of eliciting some information.

The only positive response made by this native was to a wandering goat, which he stumbled over on leaving Cook's cabin; an incident which reveals how intimately the sloop's company lived with its livestock.

'What bird is that?' he demanded of Omai. This made a fine joke, especially as he kept repeating the question to the seamen on deck. Cook, in a petulant aside, exclaimed at the ignorance of a people who could not distinguish between flying and walking. (In fact the Polynesian *manu* means bird only in the Tahitian islands, and elsewhere bears the wider meaning of animal *or* bird.) The portrait Webber drew of this intrepid native, a knife stuck through a hole in his ear, was the only benefit they gained from this island, and Cook then stood north, now desperate for fodder.

They sighted land again the next day, closed it slowly in light airs, and judged it to be some 15 miles in circumference, with a smaller satellite, like Moorea to Tahiti. This was Atiu, and to Cook's consternation it appeared as strongly fortified by nature as Mangaia, the timeless boom of the surf against the reef audible at a great distance like a continuous deep drum roll. But at least the natives appeared to be less hostile, dexterously manipulating their canoes over the reef and paddling out over the heavy swell to the sloops.

One native, identifiable as a chief by his corpulent belly, sent a tree branch ahead of him as a sign of peace, and Omai again proved his usefulness by going through the business of welcoming him on board, a ceremony that was like some caricature of Royal Navy custom. Short harsh sentences were uttered by the chief and echoed by Omai, and each in turn tore off a leaf from the branch until both appeared satisfied at the goodwill of the other. The chief was then presented with a looking glass, some red cloth (always a favourite), some nails and a hatchet, and he in turn invited a party ashore.

Cook selected Jem Burney from the *Discovery*, and Anderson

and Gore from the *Resolution*, with Omai and his boys, along with a rich assortment of trinkets and tools in the hope of acquiring some plantain shoots for the livestock.

Escorted by a strong contingent of canoes, the three well-protected ships' boats were rowed towards the reef, but again there appeared to be no way through. Finally, Gore determined to accept the natives' invitation into their canoes, and moreover, 'to create a greater confidence in the Indians,' as Anderson put it, 'we determined to go unarmed and run the hazard of being treated well or ill'. Or almost unarmed, for he secreted in the canoe, a wrapped-up pistol which was later stolen and recovered only with difficulty.

It turned out to be a hot, strenuous and sometimes alarming day for the visitors. The reef was negotiated by leaping onto it from the canoes between the breakers, dragging them over and into the lagoon and re-embarking before the next roller. Ashore, they were introduced in turn to the three chiefs who ruled the island, all of them more or less grossly fat, with 'serious but not severe countenances', adorned with red feathers and fanning themselves.

These great men they saluted with proper deference, and at once found themselves being entertained by a dance of complexity and exact timing performed by the islands' chosen beauties—olive-skinned, full featured, black hair flowing in ringlets, 'rather stout than slender,' the surgeon reported approvingly, adding, 'Their waist and limbs were elegantly formed, for as they had only a piece of blazed cloth fastened about the upper part of the belly, which scarcely fell down as low as the knees in many, we had an opportunity of observing every part.'

This entertainment was succeeded by a thunderous war chant and pageant, with much banging of clubs, a simulated battle and pursuit. It seemed to Anderson and Burney, when they managed to exchange a few words after being separated by the press of the crowd, that this might be an overture to hostile action against them. The natives were brazenly picking their pockets and nipping what they could lay their hands upon, including Jem Burney's small sheathed bayonet. When they attempted to make their way to the shore, they were halted and ordered back.

Omai himself was most alarmed by the turn of events, especially after he had spotted a party digging an oven. Nor was he much reassured when they answered his reasonable and obvious inquiry with an indignant denial. Only later did it become clear that it was a pig they were preparing for.

No actual threats were made to the members of the party. It just made them uneasy that any attempt to move was frustrated, and the heat as the crowd pressed round them, examining them in silent curiosity and picking at their clothes and possessions, for hour after hour was desperately fatiguing. Demands for a canoe were met with disapproving refusal. But when they asked for something to eat, it was provided in abundance. Only Gore remained stoically undismayed by all the fuss and press. He cheerfully referred to the chief as 'His Majesty' and commented after in surprise, 'I had not the least apprehension of danger.' His only concern was that this was not much of a place for fishing or shooting.

Omai confided to Anderson at a rare moment when they were able to communicate that it was the custom in these parts to entertain strangers, whether or not they liked it, for two or three days. At the same time, Omai impressed upon their hosts the god-like power of the white men's ships and guns by sprinkling some gunpoweder from a musket cartridge he happened to have on him, and igniting it. There! In a trice the whole island could be blown to pieces!

Whether it was this that signalled the end, or a growing sense of boredom now that their curiosity was satisfied and there was nothing more to filch from them, they could not tell. But as the sun was about to set after a humid day in the 80s, when Gore, whose cheerful optimism had long since dissolved, absolutely refused to remain for the night as required and demanded a canoe, they were released. With a few sprigs of plantain which had been cut for them, they were taken back to their ships.

Samwell, the philosopher, thought that the natives were guilty of no more than the gratification of their curiosity, 'for they were as much pleased and astonished with looking at them as the rabble rout in England [not Wales, of course] are with seeing a collection of wild beasts at a country fair'. But then he had not experienced the discomfort and unease of the shore party.

Cook, in his anxiety for their safety, had closed the island during the day, keeping a glass on the shore, reassured only by the fact that other islanders kept coming out to the ships in search of trade.

Clerke was equally gratified to have Jem Burney back safely on board as darkness fell. He had had his share of thieving, too. A native had left his return too late, and finding the fellow uneasy at remaining on board the *Discovery* all night, Clerke invited him to take supper in his cabin, when he seemed happy, no doubt cheered up by Clerke's excellent French wine. Extending his hospitality further, Clerke had a bed made up for him in· his own cabin. During the night, his guest took every small removable object from the cabin, securing them about his person, most of them concealed but enough unconcealed as a denial of any hint at stealth.

Later, after Clerke had retrieved from the over-decorated scoundrel his personal possessions, his guest seized a pair of new trousers the ship's tailor was working on and leapt overboard with them.

Thievery and frustration! It was 4 April. Cook should by now have been on the coast of New Albion at 45° north or higher, not 20° south on the other side of the Pacific, with starving cattle and Omai on board, and not a breath of wind to fill the sails.

Cook's luck changed over the following days, but not by much, not enough to cause him to reverse a decision he had now reached. He succeeded in getting a party ashore on another uninhabited island of this group. With a nice appreciation of the importance of honest behaviour, Lieutenant Gore left a hatchet and some nails to what he calculated was the full value of the provisions. There was nothing like creating a good impression.

If only the next island had been uninhabited too! It was not, though it should have been because Cook had discovered it on an earlier voyage and found no one here. It was now peopled by a 'wretched and roguish' lot who became threatening if frustrated

in their thievery, threw stones, beat one sailor, attempted to
kidnap Bayly's servant, John Lett. Tiarooa and Koa, with their
bellicose upbringing, were amazed at the white men's for-
bearance. All these miracle weapons, and never a one used!

This was Harvey's Island, named after one of Bligh's mates.
Palmerston, a group of lovely little islets, without a native to be
found, was a vast improvement, which was as well as Cook was
on the point of having to destroy his remaining cattle. Shore
parties laboured all day collecting scurvy grass, coconuts, young
leaves and shoots—anything edible. Even when there were no
interpreting duties for Omai, as here, he proved his worth time
and again. His skill at fishing and baking had not been blunted
by his slack, spoilt existence away from home. In no time he had
caught with a scoop net enough fish for the whole shore party,
with more over for the sloops, and then cooked it. 'With him we
fared sumptuously,' said Burney.

Omai spent the night on shore and expressed himself
delighted with Palmerston, named after the second Viscount, a
Lord of the Admiralty. 'I come back here to live,' he told
everyone who would listen. He would settle here and be king,
with Tiarooa and Koa. Fine fish. Fine coconuts and all
refreshments.

But it would be a long time before Omai could make his way
back to these lovely rich islands, even if he really meant what he
said, or could navigate the 600 or more miles from Tahiti, which
all the officers thought highly improbable. For Cook had already
resigned himself to the inevitable and informed his officers
accordingly. They would not attempt the North-West Passage
this coming summer. They would be a year late. The vision
dreamed up in the reassuring security of the Admiralty building
in London of the two expeditions meeting in the clear Arctic
mid-summer water was already dead. Perhaps Pickersgill's party
would find their way through, depriving Cook's expedition of
the prize and the fame, and making this voyage abortive?

The delayed start, the poor state of the ships, adverse winds,
uncharacteristic dilatoriness, above all the needs of the livestock,
had combined to destroy their itinerary.

Sunday 6 April was the day of decision, just before they

raised Palmerston. Omai's favourite rich little isles had served only to keep the cattle alive until they made the Friendly Islands, 'where I was sure of being supplied with everything I wanted'.

'It was therefore absolutely necessary,' wrote Cook in his journal with a heavy heart, 'to pursue such methods as was most likely to preserve the cattle we had on board in the first place, and save the ships' stores and provisions in the second, the better to enable us to prosecute the discoveries in the high northern latitudes the ensuing summer.'

A floating farmyard was one thing, a professional expedition of hardened explorers another. The attempt to combine the two, on behalf of the king and the ethic of romantic idealism, were alone enough to destroy any hope of fulfilling their timetable.

Cook transmitted the new orders to Clerke. 'You have permission to open the instructions issued to you at Cape Town', ran the message.

It was always an especially moving experience for Cook and his men to arrive at a Pacific island which was already known to them and to experience the warmth of the natives' welcome, to recognize chiefs and figures in the crowd; in some cases for past lovers to greet one another on the shore. Several crew members had good reason in later years to judge the Friendly Islands as misnamed. But Cook himself never had reason to regret the name he had given them while holding some reservations, as we shall see. Clerke remembered the natives' 'benevolence and goodness of heart' from his previous visit. 'They show every kind of attention and civility as any people on earth,' was his benign conclusion.

In fact, on their first arrival at Nomuka just three years earlier, there had been violence, much thieving, much un-friendliness, and some gunfire as a consequence. Matters were soon sorted out by Cook's unique blend of firmness and leniency. This time, however, when Cook went ashore from the same anchorage as in 1774 with Clerke and other officers, as well as the ubiquitous Omai and his New Zealand retinue, the natives lived up to their name 'and showed us every mark of civility'.

Tapa, the local chief, greeted them warmly, harangued his people about good behaviour to his friends and urged them to bring their produce for the white men. He also had his palace carried, lock, stock and barrel, on the shoulders of his people a quarter mile 'in order to be near us as well in the night as day'. Another chief made his appearance, one Kapee, who was also given to hectoring his subjects to keep them in good order. The sailors, with their sardonic regard for politicians, nicknamed him Lord North, the current British prime minister.

Cook understood the Tongan hierarchical structure better than on his first visit, but it was always complicated and full of pitfalls. Many chiefs had been superseded since he had last been among these islands, and each chief liked to give a more inflated impression of his status than was justified.

There was also the perennial problem of the identity of the real king of the Friendly Islands. Cook remembered the claimant on his last voyage, a man of 'sullen gravity', and he bore no likeness to the man who called himself king this time, one Feenough. Cook and Clerke met him for the first time on 6 May. Of how many islands was he monarch? they enquired. 'He enumerated them to us by their name,' Clerke recorded dryly. 'I counted till he came to a hundred when I concluded there were isles enough in conscience for any one man, but His Excellency made many additions after I had done. . . .'

Cook found there were difficulties about receiving chiefs in his cabin, the only place of honour, because no matter how elaborate the ceremonial, however lavish the laid-out gifts, the beat of feet on the deck above was undeniable, and intolerable because it was humiliating to be placed beneath their own subjects.

Cook was, as always, prepared to be flexible in order to avoid insulting the chiefs, but when it was made clear that this same insulted monarch expected him and his officers to strip when being received in audience, a message was despatched to the effect that the king of Bretanee, with all his boundless wealth and power, far above even that of the chief, expected only hats to be taken off. Not *naked*.

At several of the Friendly Islands Cook and his men were

treated to the most elaborate entertainments. The girls' dancing performances aroused the usual admiration. One dance by flower-bedecked Tongan girls, Samwell related with relish, 'consisted in moving in couples briskly round the ring, springing up and clapping their hands all together, throwing them by their sides, clapping one hand to the head, the other to their waist, then wriggling their backsides in a lascivious manner, springing up again and repeating the same motions. . . .' The lusty Clerke, too, remarked on the grace and beauty of 'The Ladies' as they performed to the beat of drums.

The sight of female boxing, fierce and sharp, though without rancour, gave them all a nasty jolt, however, and one gallant sailor, on attempting to intervene, was mockingly cheered by the inhabitants.

The dancing could continue for hours on end, always immensely skilful in execution and in a spirit of uninhibited naturalness and friendliness which put to shame the British sailors with their ribald comments.

Cook decided his men should make their own contribution, and he ordered Phillips to bring the Royal Marines ashore to demonstrate their rather different skills in reply. The performance was not as impressive as he had hoped for. Musket volleys were fired at a canoe at a hundred yards' range, but when the natives had recovered from the noise and shock and had run to examine the target, they found only one ball had struck.

Nor had months of shipboard life improved the marines' drill. Anderson noticed that the natives 'easily discerned the awkwardness of some of their manoeuvres which afforded them matter for much mirth'. The band was no more impressive. The natives had little appreciation of the french horns or any of the instruments except the drum. William Bligh thought the performance of Phillips's men disgraceful and humiliating. 'A most ludicrous performance, for the marine officer was as incapable of making his men go through their exercise as Captain Cook's musicians or music was ill adapted.'

This display was made to seem more sorry by a later faultless and spectacular display by a hundred warriors. Something had to be done. 'In order to give them a better opinion of English amusements,' Cook noted, 'I ordered a set of fireworks to be got ready and after it was dark played them off before the chief and a great concourse of people.' This somewhat redeemed the status of the voyagers.

For the two and a half months that Cook idled away among these delectable islands, the crews were employed in the usual tasks of cutting wood, replenishing the water supplies and collecting fodder for the animals, and on shipboard tasks. But again it was a very relaxed routine, and they had plenty of time for the women, who were always available in numbers and for the price of a shirt or an axe for the night. Samwell's description of them, not surprisingly, is the best, combining Welsh romanticism with invigorating ardour. 'In symmetry and proportion,' he wrote, 'they might dispute the palm with any women under the sun . . . as beautiful as Venus herself. As to modesty, these women have no more claim to it than the Tahitians. We have had on board the ships large companies of them dancing stark naked, at the same time using the most lascivious gestures.'

Captain Clerke, his health and vigour improved since New Zealand, recorded his admiration of their perfect form, for 'Chastity is by no means the reigning virtue of these isles,' was his satisfied conclusion. 'The good lasses readily contributed their share to our entertainment and rendered our bill of fare complete.'

But both ship's captain and surgeon's mate recognized that they were getting only representatives of the lower orders and the professional whores on board, their short hair confirming their status. No number of axes nor lengths of red cloth could succeed with the *Agee* girls, the long-haired aristocracy who were kept inviolate for the chiefs, who normally had four or five of them.

Other officers had their women, too, but all of them, whether or not they remained celibate, were torn with guilt at the knowledge that they had left 'the venereals' behind after their last visit. 'Wherever we go,' lamented Lieutenant King, 'we spread an incurable distemper which nothing we can do can ever recompence.' Surgeon Anderson agreed, and was especially agonized that they were 'depriving them at the same time of that intercourse between the sexes which most probably is a principal ingredient of happiness in a country where custom has laid but little restraint upon it.' Clerke, who had had more than his share of the women in the past, now agonized for them. 'This, of all the curses that could befall them, is the worst.'

The self-criticism was misplaced. The introduction of syphilis among the Polynesians by the early explorers was negligible. A certain amount of gonorrhea was transmitted, but again on a small scale, and the healthy native women seem to have cured themselves by abstaining from relations for a short time. There was no venereal disease among the Tongans sixteen years later. The distressing symptoms reported by Cook and others stemmed from endemic yaws.

The women were not the only object of David Samwell's admiration. He loved the islands themselves. Of one of them he wrote, 'Such enchanting prospects does it afford that it may be said to realize the poetical description of the Elysian Fields in ancient writers. It is certainly as beautiful a spot as imagination can paint.'

And on another day when 'all is beautiful, all is lovely', the poet, carried away by the scenery, records, 'Where man lives in the state most agreeable to his nature, undisturbed by those passions, those vultures of the mind, that are found to distract and torment him in artificial society—where nothing but benevolence, love and charity dwell, where even-handed Justice holds her distinguished seat, where happiness for ever reigns—mid scenes like these:

> With joy they search, who joy can feel, to find
> Some honest reason still to love mankind'.

For Jem Burney, brought up in England's most musical family, it was the melodies of the islands that naturally appealed most to him—the girls' lovely lilting choruses, the rhythm of the drums and bamboos. Their music, he noted for his eminent father, 'is mostly (but not always) in the minor key of flat 3d, and they want not for variety. . . .'

For John Gore and the other more sporting and extrovert

officers, the days were occupied in shooting duck and other fowl, and walking and exploring. After the rigours and austerities of the voyage, it was pleasant for a while to be able to relax. But prolonged idleness among ships' crews, as Cook had always understood, and Bligh was to learn to his cost, germinated dangerous seeds. Slackness for the men led to thefts of irreplaceable valuables as well as to petty bickering among themselves. There was drunkenness and outbreaks of violence against the natives. Clerke lost all his cats, and that was no joke, for 'they did not take the rats with them', the captain complained. Others lost their muskets—even Bligh had his stolen, which caused him shame and fury because anything less than perfection in conduct made him miserable.

Among the officers, Bayly and Burney fell out several times. The astronomer was a solemn fellow, not given to vice or high jinks, and was very conscious of his elevation from a humble background. Jem Burney, well born, cultured, effervescently high-spirited, loved to tease him and sometimes overdid it.

There was also friction between King and Bligh. Their relations went from bad to worse through the voyage. King, as an officer, was over-pleased with himself. He was only reasonably able, and did make mistakes which drove the ship's master into barely contained anger. There was a touch of preciousness in King which irritated Bligh, who also mistook his shyness for pomposity. Bligh knew that he would have made a better second lieutenant of the *Resolution* than King; and, as usual, he was right.

The unloved Williamson got on everyone's nerves; and this lieutenant, who had never liked his commander, became more and more critical of Cook. When, to conform with native custom and to please a chief, Cook took off his shirt and let loose his tied hair, Williamson was disapproving. 'I cannot help thinking he rather let himself down,' he commented pompously. It was typical of this self-righteous Irishman.

Too much drink, too many girls, too much time on their hands. The expedition's morale slumped at the Friendly Islands. An incident in which Omai took the leading part, and of which Jem Burney was a witness, was symptomatic. When drunk one day—a frequent condition—he struck one of the marine sentinels on shore. The corporal in charge responded by pushing him away and threatening to give him a good beating. Omai responded angrily. He, Omai, friend of King George, being pushed by a corporal—and in front of these natives. He immediately left the tent with his two young Maoris saying that he was finished with these insulting white men. He soon regained his spirits, of course. But he was to suffer another more serious blow to his pride.

On 10 June at 2 p.m. the *Resolution* and *Discovery* anchored in ten fathoms in 'a very snug place' at Tonga. Cook ordered a boat hoisted out and was rowed ashore with Omai and several of his officers. They could see the portly king with his retinue on the beach awaiting their arrival with every sign of friendliness and goodwill.

What contrasts in receptions Cook had experienced over the years in the Pacific! And how many there had been! At some he had been forced to retreat before a demonstration so fierce that it would have been courting disaster to have gone farther. At so many others, arms holding gifts had been wide open, with cries of welcome to greet him.

Here at Tonga the reception was warm, muted but comfortable. After the formalities of greeting, the king conducted them to a fine house on the foreshore, sheltered from the sun by palm leaves. Omai translated the king's desire that this should be their home for as long as they wished. When they looked out a short while later, the officers saw that a large number of natives had silently assembled on the beach around them and were sitting down awaiting their reappearance. One native approached the king, bending low and presenting him with the knotted root of a kava shrub. The king indicated that custom should be followed and that it should be divided between several people to chew and spit out for the preparation of the traditional drink. Cook, wrongly in fact, considered it alcoholic as well as horrible. He had also seen so often the debilitating effects of much kava drinking—the bloodshot eyes, the hopeless apathy—and preferred to pass it by while following the motions of the ceremony of drinking it. Omai drank for both with relish.

The celebrations and ceremonials at Tonga were conducted at a high pitch. All the animals were brought ashore, securely fenced in and guarded by Phillips' marines, and provided with communal stables. The larger livestock caused great consternation. The rearing goats who butted vigorously whenever a native approached were especially feared and 'often made whole armies fly'. Pigs were the largest mammals the Tongans had seen, and even today cattle are called *puaka labi*, or 'Cook's pigs'.

Fear of the stock naturally diminished with the passing days. And then suddenly, and without reference to anyone, Cook announced that there was to be a massive distribution of the livestock to the king and the chiefs of Tonga on the next day. He instructed Omai to tell the recipients that they should not be killed and eaten right away, that they should be allowed to multiply first, and 'that there were no such animals within many months of sail to them'. With great solemnity, the king was presented with King George's English bull and cow, one chief was offered a ram and two ewes, another a horse and a mare, a third some goats.

What had brought about this sudden decision when Cook's instructions had been clear? King George's livestock were for the Society Islands, for Omai to set up as a farmer. Tonga was not even mentioned in the timetable, let alone as an island on which to deposit a large proportion of the animals, brought to the Pacific, as Cook himself knew to his cost, and wrote, 'at vast trouble and expense'. Omai was dismayed. 'But they were for me,' he was heard to lament.

Cook's own craven explanation, that there would be less tendency to steal the animals if they were given some, was in complete contradiction to his customary attitude towards the natives. Nor did it have the desired effect, for the next morning it was found that a kid and two turkeys had been stolen. Nor did any of the chiefs show much pleasure or interest in their new possessions. The goats were never even claimed by one chief, and as the sheep were so uncared for when they left a month later, Cook reclaimed them.

Cook, proved wrong, reacted strongly to the loss of the

turkeys and kid. The king, his brother, and the chiefs who had just been presented with their gifts, were herded like livestock themselves into the hut lent to Cook, and a guard placed over them. Here they would be held, Omai explained to them, until the turkey and kid, and everything else that had been stolen, were returned.

The island's hierarchy accepted their situation philosophically. 'All will be returned,' the king assured Omai, and settled down to some kava drinking with his cronies. An attempt was made to rescue them, but the marines dispersed the armed natives without difficulty. At dinner time there was still no sign of the livestock, only an adze and an iron wedge having been recovered, so Cook brought them all on board the *Resolution*, amid protests from the assembled natives. This method of holding exalted people as ransom had worked in the past although Cook knew that he was playing a dangerous game. (He had only recently heard of a plot on his life.) It worked again. Soon after Cook had returned ashore with his captives, all but one of the turkeys was brought to him and that was promised for the morning.

Among these Friendly Islands thieving was a perpetual nightmare. It was impossible to keep the natives off the ships entirely; besides, Cook encouraged trading and was obliged to tolerate coupling with the women. In accordance with his health routine, he also encouraged his men to come ashore, and this led to further temptations and opportunities and losses. Tools and metal of all kinds were the first targets. The wily and dexterous natives even contrived a method of extracting the nails holding the vital copper sheathing to the bottom of the sloops, and this was very difficult to counteract.

The men swore, and many were the lurid expressions used against the natives by those who suffered. Jem Burney expressed his observations in characteristic style. 'All the diversions and exercises of these islanders are performed with a natural ease and grace not to be excelled. They are very handy and have great contrivance. Some of their thefts were executed with a degree of genius, or rather finesse that proved them no novices in the art of confederacy.'

Cook began early to punish culprits when he could apprehend them. As time went by, his methods became more savage. A dozen lashes was bad enough, but he took to increasing this number, once to six dozen, and keeping the victim tied up until the ransom of a pig was brought. Miscreants caught in the sea were beaten with oars and stabbed with boat hooks. On land they were peppered with small shot, and at least once with ball, as they ran away. On one occasion a guilty native was ordered into the barber's chair and had his ears cut off. Another had his arms scored with a knife 'that he might be known hereafter as well as to deter the rest'.

The thieving went on unabated, and Cook's officers discussed among themselves the futility and increasing cruelty their commander was practising. None of them had seen him behaving like this before. On the contrary, a large measure of his fame in England was gained by his reputation for wise and liberal treatment of the natives wherever he sailed—by contrast, of course, with the uncivilized 'Dons' who were supposed to treat them like animals.

Anderson, Burney, King, Gilbert, Edgar and others expressed their dismay. 'I cannot account for it', 'savoured of cruelty', 'gave great offence to the chiefs', 'not consonant with the principles of justice or humanity', were among their comments. What had come over their steady and admired commander? It was not as if it was even proving effective. Much more effective was Clerke's method of making them look fools, in the best comic English medieval tradition. He had his victims half shaved—half head, half face, half beard—and slung them overboard to swim ashore and face the mockery of the assembled crowd. He did not get back his beloved cats, but he suffered fewer losses.

Why was Cook wasting all this time—a month at Tonga alone—among these islands anyway, one may reasonably ask? Why had he not sailed to Tahiti and the other Society Islands weeks ago, saving much worry about the stock? Within a few days of arrival they had acquired all the fresh food, timber, water and fodder they needed. Clerke was sensibly salting down pork for the Arctic winter.

At these Friendly Islands they had all heard of an island called 'Fidgee'. The dogs at Tonga had been brought from Fidgee. The natives spoke in awe of the island. They were very fierce people always at war, possessed great weapons, great canoes, ate their captives, were famed warriors. Sometimes, but not often, Tongans went to Fidgee to learn fighting prowess. Clerke even saw one of their canoes and the men who had sailed it from Fidgee, 'the masters of this part of the world'. He noted their curious ears from which the gristle had been cut out so that the loose flesh hung about their shoulders.

Cook learned much about Fidgee, but evinced no curiosity to visit it and its neighbouring islands. He even recorded its distance from Tonga—'three days sail'. Three days, and he spun out two-and-a-half months in this group of islands, which he knew already. Here was another great change in the man. What had happened to the ever-curious explorer, who would in the past have sailed for weeks to locate, chart and sound a group of islands?

He did not so much as point his prow in Fiji's known direction, north-west-by-north. Instead he courted disaster to his sloops when sailing carelessly through a channel, was nearly assassinated, caused more distress than happiness among these child-like islanders, showed a new side of his nature to his concerned officers, lost a large number of his precious livestock, and experienced a lowering in the morale of his sailors.

William Bligh was among those who could not understand his commander's inaction. If he had been in command he would soon have sought out these islands. And by a strange chance of fate, Bligh was to do just that. In these same waters, a group of his men led by Fletcher Christian was to rise up against him and cast him and eighteen of his men—that admirable tough gunner William Peckover and the amiable gardener David Nelson among them—into the ship's launch. He then headed for those islands, sailed through them in the most masterly piece of navigation in history, charted them as well as he could from his tiny overloaded vessel, and thus became, instead of Cook, their famed discoverer.

But all that suffering and glory were still eleven years hence for

William Bligh, and now the *Resolution* stretched east instead of west, heading at last for the Society Islands. It was 17 July, and they soon met their usual crop of misfortunes at sea—contrary winds, then a squall so sudden and heavy that the *Discovery* lost her main topmast and had two of her men badly hurt. Both sloops leaked and leaked. So short of water and fodder were they, even on this short leg of their voyage, that Cook decided that they would have first to land on the south-east corner of the island to top up before proceeding to Matavai Bay.

It took them four weeks to make Tahiti. At dawn on 12 August the familiar mighty silhouette lifted above the horizon. Cook and many of his men shared so many happy memories of this paradise with its benign climate, spectacular scenery, God-given fruit and fish, handsome men and sublimely beautiful women, surely their sojourn here would be a happy one, and from now on they would be blessed by their normal good fortune.

5

'Only in a passion'

COOK, BURNEY, GORE, Anderson, Vancouver, Clerke, old man Watman, astronomer Bayly, and many others knew well the configuration of this massive volcanic island. They had last seen Tahiti on 14 May 1774, when the *Resolution* had slipped out of Matavai Bay, saluting the great chief Tu with three guns, and sailed off on a north-westerly heading. For Cook it was like coming home. He was on the friendliest terms with the natives and was loved and feared by them in return. In the minds of many of the common people, the name Toote was identified with super-natural powers. Although that Frenchman Bougainville had once been here, Cook the stern benevolent patriarch regarded the islanders proprietorially, and in turn was seen as their semi-god-like father.

It was, therefore, with something of a shock that the first news Cook heard—called out eagerly from paddling natives vying with one another to be the first alongside—was that the Spaniards had been here. They had built a fort, landed cattle and other stock, ingratiated themselves with the natives and erected a cross to signify their possession of the island: CHRISTUS VINCIT CAROLUS III IMPERAT 1774 had been engraved upon it.

Strictly interpreted, therefore, Cook was disobeying his instructions in landing on soil now claimed by Spain. He acted

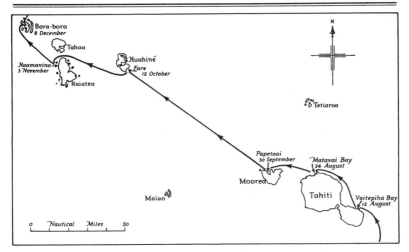

The Society Islands

in angry disregard for the Spaniards' spurious claim and went
ashore at Vaitepiha Bay to learn more. Omai told him that two
great Spanish ships had arrived not long after his own departure.
But the 'fort' was no more than a two-roomed house brought in
sections from the ships' home port of Lima, Peru, with
embrasures for muskets, or perhaps only for ventilation. Tales
had been widely disseminated of Britain's insignificant power
and wealth by contrast with Spain's. Spain had recently
conquered Bretanee, had 'erased the rascally breed from the face
of the earth'. That's what they had been saying. They had also,
more seriously, earned the respect of the native chiefs (and the
scorn of the girls) by refusing to allow women on board, and
appearing ashore themselves only in smart uniform and in full
marching order. All this was in strong contrast to the casual
style and clothes of the British sailors. Two Franciscan friars
and a boy servant had been left behind to convert the islanders to
the Catholic faith, but it seemed that the friars rarely emerged
from their home, and ten months later had embarked in a
Spanish ship and were seen no more.

It had been a very limited exercise in colonization, but Cook
was affronted by the news. After all that they had endured for
the livestock, it seemed that the wretched 'Dons' might have
beaten them to it. Omai, too, was outraged, but for a different
reason. The Spaniards had taken several natives to Lima and

returned two who had survived their experiences. Omai was, therefore, at once no longer the unique world traveller. Perhaps they, too, had brought back with them suits of armour and even more wonderful possessions than his electrical machine and organ?

The other officers could not take the Spanish invasion seriously. One of them met a native who enjoyed mimicking the priests saying grace before meat and counting their beads. Evidently there had been no conversions. Then, in reply to Omai's anxious questioning, the travellers to South America said they thought nothing of Lima—nothing whatever. It possessed no red feathers, and they had brought back nothing of note.

The cattle turned out to be a single tethered bull, though a fine one; and to signify British disregard of bogus Spanish claims, Cook had the cross taken down and 'GEORGIUS TERTIUS REX ANNIS 1767, 69, 73, 74 & 77' carved on the other side. That seemed to settle the point in their favour and to everyone's satisfaction, and trading, forbidden by the Spaniards with the defeated English, began at a brisk tempo.

Amid all this plenty, with yams and breadfruit and coconuts and fish unlimited, the scent of baking hogs and bougainvillaea and hibiscus, bevies of willing girls lovelier even than the Friendly Islanders, and with the relief of being ashore on safe and beautiful land still fresh, Cook assembled officers and men and marines of the *Resolution*. For the first time on this voyage he was going to consult them *en masse*.

The subject was the most sensitive one of all among sailors. It was grog. This was the first time, too, that he had formally divulged to them the ultimate purpose of the expedition. The two were closely related. Because they had lost a year they were going to be short of grog. Did they agree that it was better to cut the ration here, in the warmth and plenty of unlimited coconuts, than in the Arctic, where their lives, and (a further considera-tion, this) their share of the reward, might depend on the sustaining quality of spirits?

The men agreed at once and without dissent, and Clerke received a similar response. It was a rare occurrence for the company of one of H.M. ships to forgo voluntarily their precious, almost sacred, daily ration of spirit, and it was a measure of Tahiti's euphoric powers that these tough and sorely tried men did so. From now until they departed it would be grog on Saturday evenings only, the half-pint 'to drink to their female friends in England, lest among the pretty girls of Tahiti they should be wholly forgotten', as Cook himself expressed it. (A half-and-half mix of grog and coconut juice was highly esteemed, no doubt the better for the long anticipation of it.)

'The pretty girls' were on board before anchors were dropped. With the expectation of a long stay deeper attachments were formed, and for weeks as the sloops cruised among the Society Islands they remained, going ashore only briefly, a welcome feminine softening of shipboard life in place of the obstructive and odorous goats and sheep on deck and below. The comments of the *Discovery*'s master were representative of almost all of them, 'They are angels. I can without vanity affirm it was the happiest three months I ever spent.'

There were plenty of entertainments ashore by the natives, too, for satiated palates. Samwell, of course, was a frequent attender and commented earthily on his observations. By contrast, Williamson, although a keen voyeur at those violent dances called *heivas*, regarded them with pious disapproval as merely gratifying curiosity.

But once again it was Cook and Omai who conducted events and played the leading parts in the drama of the Society Islands that ran through almost to Christmas, Omai a Trinculo to a Prospero whose performance was marred by uncharacteristic slips. Certainly Omai put his all into his performance in his endeavour to make it memorable in the minds of those who observed him back in his homeland. The first of the compatriots he acknowledged—some earlier commoners were ignored— were his brother-in-law and a minor chieftain. To the astonishment of those who watched, they at first treated Omai as if he were beneath consideration. Relations warmed when Omai showed them a drawerful of red feathers in his cabin. When word spread of these untold riches, relations and hangers-on crowded round and he became the centre of all attention.

In no time the upperdeck of the *Resolution* was like a fairground and market place, with trade thriving, the women and children screaming with joy, the men earnestly exchanging a 50-pound hog for 'not more feathers than might be got from a tomtit'. They gave signs that they were long since past nails and beads. Feathers, feathers and more red feathers were what they wanted, with perhaps an axe or two thrown in.

The noise was cacophonous. Everybody was showing off his acquisitions, shouting above the squealing of the pigs, wondering at the alarmed sheep, the neighing, stamping horses, the screaming peacocks, the gabbling geese. Dogs ran everywhere, tripping people up. More and more Tahitians climbed up the sides of the sloop and over the bulwarks to add to the tumult.

Red feathered caps were the greatest rage. A chief wearing one got into the quarter gallery the better to flaunt his finery. Here he settled down 'with great complacency like some Eastern monarch,' one eyewitness recorded, 'adored by his subjects'.

Cook well knew the protocol on Tahiti, and prepared to go ashore to call on more important chiefs and the great chief of this part of the island, a ten-year-old boy. Omai came with him. As Cook had always feared, the returned hero was already showing signs of discarding his thin veneer of sophistication, indiscriminately heaping gifts upon the lowest classes, or anyone who chose to take advantage of his gullibility. He made a foolish and often drunken spectacle of himself, the more so when he attempted to recover a measure of the dignity he had assumed in England. Samwell, the sardonic observer, noted that 'he generally associates with the blackguards of the island among whom he squanders away his red feathers and other things which he has'.

It was symptomatic that he accompanied Cook ashore dressed partly as a savage and partly as a nob of St James's. Cook himself could not make head nor tail of just what he did have on—'Not in English dress, nor in Tahiti, nor in Tonga, nor in the dress of any country upon earth, but in a strange medley of all he was possessed of', which was a very great deal.

The sad and foolish spectacle continued in different forms and guises. There was Omai the great rider, and many a horseman of

Rotten Row could have predicted the outcome of that rôle. The Tahitians were fascinated by the sight of the horses from 'King Tosh' of Bretanee, quadrupeds as big as the Spanish bull but capable of such speed, and of carrying men! Cook and Clerke exercised them frequently on the black volcanic sand after they moved to Matavai Bay, and created a tremendous impression among the crowds. Omai, alas, could still struggle for only a few steps before being thrown.

There was Knight Omai. Fortuitously, a genuine reason for donning his magnificent shining armour arose shortly after their arrival. Renewed hostilities with the satellite island of Moorea were about to break out. Sea warfare was more favoured than land warfare in the Society Islands, and this expected battle was preceded by a naval review. Omai had now acquired a formidable war canoe, which he quite properly named the *Royal George* after the British monarch. As soon as the review was over, Omai resplendent in his armour climbed onto a special stage secured to his canoe, and proceeded out into the bay like a supreme commander inspecting his fleet at Spithead, Toulon or the Tagus. 'Everyone had a full view of him,' Cook observed caustically, 'but it did not draw their attention as might be expected.'

Omai the admiral recovered himself jauntily, and in a mock fight, wearing an additional breast plate, he bettered the 'enemy' and took him by boarding.

Cook, as always, refused to become involved in the islanders' warfare, but it seemed for a while as if he might have to face a battle of his own. Word arrived from the other side of the island that the Spaniards were back in strength, and it seemed to Cook likely that they might try to drive off the British sloops from the 'Spanish' island.

For the first time, the two sloops were placed on a war footing. The decks were cleared of the remaining lumber from the livestock's pens and assumed a more military appearance. The *Discovery*, too, 'put herself in the best posture of defence', and at great trouble and disturbance two four-pounders were brought up from her after hold. Cook ordered Williamson out on an armed reconnaissance trip in the ship's cutter.

This lieutenant, guided by Cook's chart, searched as far as Vaitepiha Bay, where the boy chief boasted reassuringly that he would certainly drive off the Dons if they should appear.

It was all a tiresome false alarm, as the threat of war with Moorea turned out to be. This decided Cook to visit the island, which he had never done before, a curious lapse because its breathtaking silhouette was temptingly visible in all but the worst weather from Point Venus, where his shore encampment and observatory were always set up.

Now in despair at Omai's foolishness and improvidence, he decided to take him along rather than settle him in at Tahiti, which had always seemed the sensible and obvious thing to do. Cook had planned a marriage, selected a steady wife for him and then a job as estate manager to one of the Chiefs, supervising the care of the stock and the cultivation of the seeds and plants they had brought to the island: a distant agricultural emissary of King George III.

But Omai would have nothing of weddings, regarded all the stock as his personal property, a gift from King Tosh, and still preferred to consort with low company, among whom his brother-in-law was prominent, and ignore the great chiefs as if they were beneath his lofty contempt. It was all very disappointing. Another island would have to be found for the foolish young man.

Then there was Omai the pilot. He travelled to Moorea grandly in the *Royal George*. With a hired crew of paddlers, and his Maori aides-de-camp in attendance, he swept out of Matavai Bay in his most vivid finery ahead of the *Resolution* and *Discovery*. He may have lost the greater part of his wealth, possessions and livestock—three cows destined for the pleasure of the Spanish bull, the horse and mare and all the sheep, the English bull, Lord Bessborough's peacock and hen, some geese and ducks—at Tahiti, but his style was as perky as ever.

Seen from the east, Moorea appeared unlikely to have a sheltered anchorage for a pair of sloops. It looked all reef and surf, and near vertical peaks often dark in cloud. But to Cook, working his way along the northern coast, one inlet, then another even deeper, revealed themselves, like slices cut from a cake, the 3000- to 4000-foot peaks towering above the quiet waters. The first is, wrongly, called Cook's Bay; the second, where Omai in his canoe awaited Cook, is called Opunohu.

The sloops slipped through the reef and hove to, and Bligh and Edgar went ahead in boats, sounding the bay for an anchorage. It was as good and secure as they had been informed it was at Tahiti. The ships anchored and were hauled, close to, and secured with hawsers to hibiscus trees on the shoreline.

Even the commander had seen no lovelier setting in all his travels. Clear streams and a river poured into the bay, the slopes were a mass of flowers and flowering shrubs, fruit of every description was for the picking, the waters teemed with fish. Here was a veritable Rousseauesque paradise for the noble savage—and he was here in strength. Among the trees and shrubs on the shore were their thatched dwellings. The Mooreans stood, bare-chested, dusky and wondering, in their hundreds staring out at the great vessels that had arrived so suddenly and silently, while others paddled out cautiously in their canoes; then, finding no discouragement, climbed on board.

This peerless gem of an inlet on one of the loveliest of all Polynesian islands now inappropriately became the scene of the unhappiest and most inexplicable incident in all Cook's voyages. It stemmed, once again, from theft. At Tahiti thieving had been negligible. The wrongness of theft had been learned there after so many European visits. The island may have lost some of its innocence, but for better or worse had acquired the morality of the eighth commandment and the reality of punishment. The authority of the chiefs was firm there, and they had learned how thieving could interrupt the pleasures and profits of trading.

The more familiar semi-innocent daring of Polynesian thievery still applied at Moorea, and when the local chief requested a pair of goats and was refused, two were taken while they were being grazed ashore. In the rising tide of Cook's wrath that followed can be seen, step by step, the events that led to tragedy.

It is the evening of 7 October, warm and still where the two sloops are anchored and moored at the head of Opunohu Bay.

The sounds are of domestic life ashore where smoke rises from fires outside the little thatched houses. Children are running about at play, voices of women calling out can be heard, and the deeper voices of a party of men hauling up a big outrigger canoe. They have been fishing inside the reef and carry ashore baskets richly filled. The canoes look right for this place, their raised prows carved, graceful and handsome and lightly decorated, like the young people. Second to a wife, they are the most prized of all a man's possessions and take much labour and skill to construct. By contrast, the *Resolution*'s two boats loaded with goats and pulling out from the beach appear stubbily clumsy.

The A.B. standing forward in the first boat to come alongside the *Resolution*, painter in hand, calls out, 'They've got another. Seized it and ran while we were getting them into the boat.'

Captain Cook, overhearing the voice, hurries up from his cabin, where he has been writing. Not a second one! He is a fearsome figure when in a rage, craggy features distorted, eyes blazing. Only yesterday the half-blind old chief, Mahine, the recipient of many generous presents, whom Cook had entertained on board, had sent a message requesting a pair of goats. Cook had regretfully refused but had replied by messenger that he had asked Chief Tu at Matavai to send a pair as he had many. Cook had sent full payment in red feathers. Now it seems that old Mahine is not prepared to wait.

Cook interprets this defiance as an insult and is prepared to take the severest steps to recover the goat, which is with kid. He goes ashore at dusk with Omai, his double-barrelled musket loaded, and with two marines. This time there is no curious and friendly reception. The natives slip out of sight or pretend not to see him.

Omai succeeds in recruiting a few natives, however, and with the authority of the formidable figure at his side in support, orders them out into the forest to bring back the goat before darkness sets in. It has not been stolen, protest the natives, just strayed off among the trees. But none of the natives return, a certain sign of guilt.

Instead, the first goat turns up, quite unexpectedly, in the charge of a native. He tells Omai, 'I took it because these men took my breadfruit and coconuts without giving me anything in return. This is my payment.' Cook contains his anger. His sense of justice tells him that he cannot punish this man until his claim is proved false. It would not be the first time that his own men have failed to make proper payment for produce.

There is nothing more he can do that evening, and he returns to his ship, his mind still full of fury and plans. When he looks out the next morning at dawn the bay appears empty of inhabitants, fled for dread of a repeat on the grand scale of the devastation caused in the last Tahitian war. Later, Omai, who is so valuable on these occasions and makes up for all the foolery he has indulged in on Tahiti, discovers from information he collects ashore that the goat has been taken to the house of a chief on the south side of the island, one Haamoa.

Rather than face the heat and exhaustion of an armed march over the mountains that rise up like fairy tale fortresses before them, Cook instructs Henry Roberts, one of Bligh's mates and a steady, bold man, and Midshipman William Shuttleworth, to take a boat with armed sailors and marines to the other side of the island and bring back the animal.

Cook waits restlessly for their return. He had intended to be away from here the previous day. But he will not leave without this stolen animal, not now. His stock has died on board, has been stolen and not recovered, has been left where it has little chance of survival, and goats are the least valuable of all his animals. But this one has suddenly become for Cook a symbol of native defiance of his authority, a refusal to recognize his power and superiority. In this most beautiful setting, his fury has never burned with such heat. Give way, he argues, and there will be no end to it.

The story he hears from Roberts and Shuttleworth that evening determines his plan for the next day. They located this chieftain's village where all day natives pretended to search for and promised to recover the goat, until the boat was forced to put off with the coming of nightfall.

Cook formulates a plan of action overnight. It is on the largest scale he can muster. Lieutenant Williamson is to take three boats with a strong party of marines to meet his own party of 38 with powerful marines escort to the south side, and there force the chief to return the goat.

Led by a guide, the land party marches off into the forest on the lower slopes, and climbs steadily in the high heat and humidity to over 2000 feet, where they are now exposed to the mid-day sun and face steep slopes of raw volcanic rock. Cook himself is by a wide margin the oldest member of the party, 49 in a few days. His physique is as tough as ever, but he feels the strain and there are many pauses for rest.

Messages travel fast in these islands, and news of their progress, their strength and intention, races ahead faster than their own pace, and they see only occasional fleeing figures. Several times they observe significant signs of defiance. Armed men are distantly seen, once a volley of stones whistles about them, and is answered by a ragged volley of musket fire. The heat is appalling and they are in no fit state to fight off an attack when they reach the village.

But at length, with the aid of Omai's party and Omai himself, Cook locates the chief. Omai translates for Cook. 'He knows nothing of a goat. None of his people knows about a goat. . . .'

'Tell him I am determined to recover the goat,' orders Cook. 'Tell him that from the testimony of so many people, I am well assured they have the goat. If not I shall burn houses and canoes.'

When Williamson arrives with his party he boasts that he has already taken punitive methods on his journey, burning 20 houses and many large war canoes—'a damage,' Cook writes in the coolness of the aftermath of this dreadful day of destruction, 'that I suppose will take years to recover'.

When there is still no sign of the goat, Cook carries out his threat, most of the officers reacting with regret, the men with relish, Omai with delight (he had been disappointed that Cook had rejected his advice to shoot every Moorean on sight—better than game on Lord Sandwich's park). All afternoon they burn and sack, devastating the coastline of the lovely island, the natives fleeing before them while behind them the smoke of fires rises into the sky as if a new wave of volcanoes has broken out on Moorea. Only once, and momentarily, does the wrecking cease.

A party of natives, bolder than the rest, emerges from the forest bearing plantain branches as a sign of peace, and lays them at Cook's feet, begging that their canoe might be spared. 'I touched not a single thing belonging to them,' Cook later asserts piously.

On the morning of 10 October there is still no sign of the wretched goat, and Cook's anger simmers as dangerously as ever. 'Send one of your men to chief Mahine,' he tells Omai, 'and tell him I will burn and destroy every house and canoe on the island to recover the goat.' At the same time, he despatches carpenters to smash three or four canoes abandoned on the shore near them. The carpenters dismantle them instead, and bring back the planks, suggesting that they would make a good house for Omai.

All through the morning the men are ashore with axes and cross-cut saws destroying the houses of the natives with whom they had traded peacefully and with so much laughter. The flames and smoke of fires rise high into the sky, much admired by the men's Tahitian mistresses watching from the sloops' decks.

No one else feels much pleasure from their work now. The men do as they are told, but no longer with any satisfaction. Only Cook's anger has not cooled, and some of his officers eye him anxiously. Again they wonder what has come over their beloved commander.

At 4 p.m. a canoe appears at the mouth of the bay, the first they have seen manned and at sea for two days, and one of the few surviving on the island. It is paddled swiftly up the long inlet, and as it comes alongside the *Resolution* it is seen that it contains a single goat.

The Mooreans treat the affair in a very offhand way, as if it is of little importance. Yes, they tell Omai casually, one of the Tahitians took it, took it to Tahiti. That is why is has needed time to recover it. Even the power of the great chief Mahine could not get it back at once. They paddle away without a backward glance. Cook stares at the wake of the canoe scored on the still waters of the bay, then glances at the nearby shoreline where the fires consuming the last of this community's homes and canoes are now dying with the day. 'A rather unfortunate affair,' he records later, 'which could not be more regretted on the part of the natives than it was on mine.'

Many of Cook's officers recorded stronger descriptions of that 40-hour orgy of pillage and plunder and destruction. 'All about such a trifle as a small goat,' exclaimed one. 'I can't well account for Captain Cook's proceedings on this occasion, as they were so very different from his conduct in like cases in his former voyages.' 'The losses these poor people must have suffered!' lamented the *Discovery*'s master.

King, too, was outraged. 'I cannot think it justifiable,' he wrote. 'I doubt whether our ideas of propriety in punishing so many innocent people for the crimes of a few, will ever be reconcilable to any principle one can form of justice.' He particularly deplored the plunder, in which Omai took the most prominent part, filling the *Royal George* to the gunwales.

Williamson wrote that he 'cannot help thinking the man totally destitute of humanity. This once I obeyed my orders with reluctance,' he added with more than a hint of sanctimonious hypocrisy, considering that everyone had witnessed his wholesale anticipation of Cook's instructions.

Even loyal Charles Clerke had to admit that he had never seen his commander behave like this. Why had he not 'secured a chief' instead? 'The losses these poor people must have suffered will be more than they are able to recover for many years to come,' he logged.

On 11 October the two sloops slipped out of unhappy Opunohu Bay, the heavily overloaded *Royal George* in the van, Omai the admiral again in proud command. Nemesis struck at him almost at once and almost fatally. There was a sharp squall, the sound of a musket. It was Omai, in grave distress, his ill-earned cargo having reduced the natural stability of his canoe.

The next day the gods of Polynesian justice struck again. A mysterious sickness that might have been yellow jaundice swept through Cook's ship and the *Royal George*. Omai was very ill, too, and even robust Cook himself.

Omai had survived all the unfamiliar germs and viruses of England, every disease associated with voyaging, all the rigours of the unfamiliar climate of western Europe, the penetrating chill of Antarctic fogs, only to succumb to a mysterious and near-deadly complaint among his own islands.

To add to this burden of anxiety, Watman was not at all well, and Cook regretted again that he had not sent him back to Greenwich Hospital from the Cape. The Scottish carpenter's mate, Alex McIntosh, from Perth, described by King as 'a very hard working quiet man', was sick; and 29-year-old Tom Roberts, the efficient quartermaster, was suffering from dropsy.

Cook, unaccustomed to illness on board his ship, visited the sick in their quarters, where they swung in their hammocks in the heat of below decks. The scene reminded him of below decks in the *Eagle*, under Palliser's command, when she arrived back home with 130 of her crew to be carried off to hospital, after burying 22 at sea in one month. But that was a long time ago, and mass sickness at sea was a foreign experience to him nowadays. Anderson and his two mates, Samwell and his brother Welshman, Robert Davies, were doing what they could for the men, but heat was the first enemy, and Cook was anxious to get them ashore. A short period in a breeze and the shade of trees would do wonders for them.

These suffering men below decks were not the total of Cook's health worries. When he had last spoken to Clerke at Moorea he had seemed in a very poor way; as courageous and as ready to see things cheerfully and optimistically as ever, but weak, pale and coughing badly. Anderson, too, gave Cook concern. Never robust, the *Resolution*'s erudite, stimulating surgeon had lost much of his earlier bounce and eagerness. Cook prayed that it was only the damp, relaxing climate that was slowing him up, and tried to forget that it was on board the *Eagle* that the surgeon himself had succumbed. A weak constitution, heat, poor ventilation, and constant contact with germs were a poor recipe for good health. Cook watched Anderson talking to the sick men, his mates cooling hot foreheads with damp cloths, and made his way up the ladder onto deck again. It was still early in the morning, Sunday 12 October, and the saw-tooth silhouette of Huahiné was clearly visible to the north-west. He remembered drawing it from this bearing more than eight years ago, one more island of so many previously uncharted. He had a health problem with his men then, and had been in a black mood. It was only 'the venereals' from Tahiti, self-inflicted, and temporary; but irritating because in their condition he had not dared to head south as he had planned and make them face the rigours of the Antarctic.

This time the prospect was of the Arctic's effect on the sick in higher latitudes than he had faced in the *Endeavour*. Anderson must get them well, for they would soon be heading north. . . .

The thought of the Arctic was giving Anderson grave concern, too. Not for his patients, who would be well by then from their sickness he had failed to diagnose. But for himself. He had known for a long time now that he carried in him the fatal seeds of tuberculosis. He had known it since August of last year when, ironically, he had recognized the healing qualities of the Tenerife air for tuberculars. Perhaps he could have saved himself then, if he had done the unthinkable and left the expedition, and he had promised himself to return if he should survive. Now he knew that he was unlikely to live to return home. The fatal bacilli had obtained too firm a grip, stimulated by the freezing fogs of Kerguelen and the southern Indian Ocean. Anderson knew his Heberden—'Cold weather and bleak winds,' wrote that excellent doctor, 'will occasion coughs in the soundest lungs, and cannot be too carefully avoided. . . .' He knew, too, that the cold of the Arctic would similarly speed his end.

Before they even reached Tahiti, Clerke had confided his own anxieties to the *Resolution*'s surgeon, and Anderson had reluctantly confirmed Clerke's suspicions. The dry cough, the blood that accompanied the coughing when it was bad, the loss of weight, the occasional pain in his chest, the increasing weakness; all stemming from those dreadful weeks in prison, all spelling out in uncompromising clarity, *phthisis pulmonum*, tuberculosis.

Jem Burney, as the *Discovery*'s first lieutenant, had been told by Clerke to prepare for the possible change in command. Gore would almost certainly be transferred from the *Resolution* as commander in his place if it became necessary through sickness or death. Cook, however, was not told of Anderson's diagnosis,

either of his own or of Clerke's condition. He had enough
worries, Anderson and Clerke had decided. But, according to
Burney, at Tahiti 'Anderson represented to Captain Clerke their
inability to encounter the severities of a frozen climate, and they
mutually agreed to ask leave of Captain Cook to resign their
situations, that they might remain where they were, and trust
themselves to the care of the natives, as the only hope left of
being restored to health.'

They had not done so at Matavai Bay because Clerke said that
he had not sufficient time to get his papers in order. Nothing had
been said to their commander of this plan, which Anderson now
hoped to put into effect at Huahiné or one of the other small
islands they were to put in at. His own consumption was more
advanced than Clerke's, whose sense of duty to Cook and the
voyage was more uncompromising than Anderson's. In reality,
although his loss would be sorely felt, Clerke was a good deal
easier to replace than the surgeon, whose medical wisdom was
unique. Nevertheless, there is a wistful flavour in Clerke's
comment that Bora-Bora enjoyed 'a very salutary air'.

For Anderson it was an unimportant matter whether they
should be left ashore at Huahiné, Raiatea or Bora-Bora. The
only consideration of importance if he hoped to prolong his life
beyond a few months was to avoid sailing north into the deadly
high latitudes of the Arctic. He would discuss the matter again
with Clerke as soon as he had got the worst of the sick ashore at
Huahiné.

There were sensitive officers and warrant officers in the
Resolution who wondered if this dreadful sickness had been sent
to remind Cook of his earlier standards of compassion and his
responsibilities to these simple people. The behaviour at Moorea
had surely been a passing madness, they told each other.

It was not. It still lingered. Shortly before they arrived at
Huahiné, the *Royal George* with the ailing Omai guiding them
towards the island, a Moorean who had remained on board the
Resolution was apprehended with a stolen object. The gentle
Lieutenant King was horrified to hear his captain order him to be
taken to the barber's to be shaved and for his ears to be cut off.
King, retaining his anonymity although he was the leading

character in what followed, wrote, 'After the barber had finished with his head, he began to execute the other part of his orders, and would in a short time have completed it. Luckily for the fellow's ears, an officer [King himself] was looking on and stopped the barber, being convinced that the captain was only in a passion.'

With the loss of the lobe of an ear, the culprit leapt into the sea and swam for his life to the shore.

Omai's final home had for long been a subject of debate amongst Cook and his officers. Cook's own first choice had been Vaitepiha Bay; then, after his refusal to get married and his disreputable behaviour, all Tahiti was ruled out. Now Moorea was out of the question. Omai himself had for some weeks expressed a strong wish to settle in Huahiné, a friendly place where he had family connections, and where, as a much smaller and less populous place than Tahiti, his wealth and splendour would be even more evident. Once, this mercurial character exclaimed 'No! It must be Raiatea!' Burney ironically observed, 'This new revolution, however, did not last above 3 days when he resumed his former plan again.'

Now, at noon on 12 October, the die was cast. The *Resolution* and *Discovery* anchored at the north entrance to Fare harbour at Huahiné, and Cook prepared to dispose of one of his major anxieties with all the care and foresight he could summon. Omai had proved his value time and again throughout their Polynesian cruise, and he and his entourage had given them all much amusement. Cook still felt an affection for the young man, and would miss him, for all the nuisance he had been back in his home islands. But now that they would soon be leaving the last of Polynesia behind them, his value as interpreter and guide to the manners and behaviour of the people would cease, and the space that he and his possessions and the remaining livestock occupied would relieve much pressure.

The *Royal George* lay hove to a short distance away across the harbour. Already the canoes were crowding round her. But there was no sign of Omai. He was still too ill to make his first appearance, and was being tended by his anxious New Zealand boys. It would, indeed, reflected Cook bitterly, be a sorry business if he were obliged to record in his journal that the much travelled Polynesian had died within half a league of his new home.

Huahiné, less than a hundred sea miles west of Tahiti, had been charted during the *Endeavour*'s voyage, and Cook had been here in the *Resolution*, too, in 1773. But because of the difficulties of navigation about its coastline and its nearly unbroken reef, he had failed to discover that it is in fact two islands, Huahiné Iti in the south and Huahiné Nui in the north, now linked by a bridge but in Cook's time separated by a hundred yards or so of sea, where Cook marked a narrow spit of land on his chart. Like its neighbours, the craggy volcanic peaks, where the rainfall is many times that of the low hinterland, dominate the islands' topography.

Fare on the south-east side of the island is today less populous and thriving than it was in 1777, when it was—as today—the best harbour. Even before the *Resolution* dropped anchor in the shadow of a pyramid-shaped hill on the north side of the harbour, the natives were swarming up her sides, full of greetings and eagerness to trade. The tales of destruction at Moorea were recounted wide-eyed by the Tahitian women, who 'multiplied the number of canoes and houses we had destroyed by ten at least, which I was not sorry for,' commented Cook.

The omens for Omai were at first favourable, too. Cook established good relations with the chiefs, the balance of trading was in the islanders' favour, and at one stage of a meeting to arrange Omai's future, a voice was heard crying out that the whole of Huahiné and everything in it was Cook's, therefore he could give what he pleased of it to Omai.

In the end Cook purchased for 15 axes and 'some beads and trifles' 200 yards of the harbour frontage, with an equal depth to the base of the hills. In an atmosphere of the greatest goodwill and co-operation, the islanders and Cook's men created for Omai a miniature replica of the great country estates he had visited in England. With the planks of the unfortunate Mooreans' canoes, the ships' carpenters built a house, stylish and secure but, as a precaution against their pillage, with as few nails as possible. It had a single room some 15 feet square with a loft above for his organ, games, armour and other more precious possessions. It was furnished with a proper English bed and mattress; there were tables and chairs and other European comforts.

Omai regarded his house with the utmost satisfaction. It was, to him, a piece of old Britain, and he so named it. (The area was called Baritani for many years after.) Above the door, as a memorial to the old country and its monarch, was later carved 'Georgius Tertius Rex 2nd Novembrius'. With unusual foresight, he had taken cuttings from some vines left by the Spaniards on Tahiti, and now planted them here. The men dug a complete kitchen garden for him, planting pineapples and melons and sowing great numbers of seeds. Cook himself planted a shaddock tree, which was to flourish for many years.

Privately, Cook had the gravest doubts about Omai's future on his estate. He had seen too much of the foolishness of the young man, and too much of the jealousy of chiefs and minor chieftains, who saw the superiority of possessions in others as the undermining of their own status and power.

With this danger for Omai in mind, Cook 'advised him to give a good part of his moveables, useful as well as ornamental, to two or three of the principal chiefs, by which means he would satisfy them, and secure them in his favour'.

And so, for the present all was well. Omai showed off his horses and pigs and goats and one buck rabbit and monkey, and the key to his front door, which he flourished when welcoming Cook and his officers to dine with him, as they did several times, with afternoons 'spent in mirth and jollity' after passing round the port. There were fireworks, too, one evening, accompanied by the usual screams of fear and wonder from the natives.

'We lived upon peaceful and friendly terms with the natives,' recorded Samwell, 'till Wednesday October 22nd, when an accident happened that destroyed this tranquility.'

The occasion was a candle-lit dance, a special *heiva* featuring 'a young woman as beautiful as Venus' who drew great crowds. The marines' guard, sloppy as always, were distracted from their duties at the entrance to Bayly's observatory, and it was an easy business for a native to get in and help himself to a sextant.

The dancing was still going on when Bayly discovered his loss and at once informed Cook. Omai was summoned and through him Cook ordered the chiefs to halt the *heiva*. As at Moorea, panic then spread throughout the community, many families taking to their canoes to escape the wrath of these white men and the threat of their muskets and cannon. Cook sent armed boats to cut them off. Within minutes 'fear had taken over from all merriment'.

Omai, with his wealth to tempt reward hunters and his nose for conspiracy, had no difficulty in apprehending the culprit, who was dragged on board the *Resolution* and summarily punished with the loss of his hair and his ears. On release he shouted defiance and swore he would kill Omai in revenge. For a start, he made his way straight to Omai's house, trampled his newly-dug garden, tore up all the vines, and was attempting to set fire to his house when he was apprehended. As Clerke said, it was a lucky escape considering the quantity of gunpowder he had stored, which would 'have blown our poor friend Omai's fortunes to the devil'.

The native was again seized and put in irons on board the *Resolution*. Cook determined to take him far from Huahiné before releasing him. Then, very early on the morning of 30 October, Omai hastened from his house and paddled out to the sloop. He was in a state of fear bordering on panic. His tormentor had escaped and was on shore.

Cook confirmed the truth of Omai's assertion. The native had escaped from the quarterdeck, along with the bolt securing him, and the captain's wrath was awful. It appeared to him that both the mate of the watch, William Harvey, and the midshipman, Robert Mackay, had been asleep, as well as the two marines on guard. While he offered a reward of ten axes to any native who brought the culprit back, he ordered the bo'sun to give both the marines a dozen lashes three days in succession and confine them in irons.

'As to you, I want no more of you,' he shouted at Harvey. 'I want you out of my sight and off my ship. You are disrated and will take yourself to the *Discovery*.' As for Mackay, he was turned before the mast—disrated to A.B.

Cook's theory was that the native had waited until his guard and the watch were all asleep, stolen the key to his irons, and slipped overboard. There were other theories. The word on shore was that he had been released. Was it the young Scot, Mackay, perhaps out of pity for the man who he may have judged had already paid the price of his crime? Mackay had been punished for some minor misdemeanour the previous month and was out of countenance with his captain.

Whatever the answer, the native, whom Clerke described as 'the most consummate and most impudent rascal I have met with', was not recaptured and Cook decided that he could delay his departure no longer. Omai would have to take his chance. Some dozen relatives, attracted by his possessions, had joined him; and he had muskets, a shotgun, two pairs of pistols and some swords in his armoury.

Even Omai's detractors—and there were many in the expedition—were touched by the ceremonies of farewell. Here, for the first time, was Omai the penitent, regretting his past profligate ways, his dissolute life in England, his extravagance. So much had he stowed away, and now it was nearly all gone—to unworthy people of the lowest orders. 'Omai too late saw his error,' wrote one of the officers who knew him well, 'and often wished himself in England again, saying his time should be spent in learning what would be useful to him instead of throwing his time away at cards.'

On the afternoon of 2 November, as a breeze got up, Cook gave the order to weigh anchors and sail out of Fare harbour. Omai remained on board as the *Resolution* worked towards the gap in the reef, while the *Royal George*, carrying his New Zealand boys and manned by his paid Tahitian crew, followed astern to collect him. He made the rounds of all the ship's officers, shaking them solemnly by the hand and bowing to each. He was dressed in his most splendid finery, complete with sword and pistols at his waist.

'He sustained himself with manly resolution till he came to me,' Cook wrote in his journal. Then he threw his arms about his friend and commander and burst into tears, trying to express his gratitude for all that had been done for him in a torrent of

Polynesian broken with a few English words. Lieutenant King led him away, and together they climbed down the gangway into the waiting boat. Omai continued to cry all the way to the *Royal George*, King reported later, and was obviously deeply affected.

Tiarooa and Koa were distressed at the parting, too. Both had said they wanted to remain with the expedition and return to England, but Cook had thought it unsuitable and an additional responsibility in the cold and dangerous voyage that lay ahead. Besides, Sandwich, at the end of Omai's long and demanding stay in England, had suggested to Cook that it would be inappropriate to bring back any more natives.

Tiarooa succeeded in hiding his feelings during these last minutes. But little Koa fell into a paroxysm of grief, calling out again and again across the water, and at length leaping into the sea in an effort to catch up the *Resolution*, swimming as fast as he could. Watched and encouraged by a number of the ship's company who had formed a great love for the boy, he continued to cry out until the natives in the canoe fished him out of the water.

Now, as the light fell over the Huahiné lagoon, the *Royal George*, with Omai now on board and like an extravagantly carved figurehead standing at the prow, his arms held high, became smaller until the reef cut off the canoe from sight. The sun was setting over the peaks and the *Resolution* and *Discovery* picked up the stiff easterly wind and headed west for Raiatea.

In the short time—some 20 hours—that it took for the sloops to sail to this island, it is worth attempting to puzzle out why Cook was set on visiting yet another of the Society Islands at all, for it perplexed many of his officers at the time. The expedition had completed their task of 'landing Omai at such of the Society Islands as he may choose and to leave him there'. They had salted down countless pounds of pork in casks, they had disposed of all their bad ship's biscuit and had plenty remaining, as well as their original stock of salt pork and beef. Their 'anti-scorbutics' were in ample supply, and their fresh fruit and vegetables would last them for several weeks. They were fully stocked with fresh water and wood fuel. In every respect they were as well equipped as they could expect in order to face the northern coasts of New Albion, the Bering Strait and the Arctic.

Before them, stretching north for thousands of miles, lay the vast and little known waters of the north Pacific, crossed only by a handful of circumnavigators and the Spanish galleons to and from Manila. The hazards were unknown, and already time was only just on their side. They had lost one season, and now there was the risk of losing another. The original instructions were to leave the Society Islands not later than February nine months ago. Already they were into November. They were not to get away until many more weeks had passed.

These last weeks among the Society Islands brought the expedition more troubles and anxieties, and very little benefit. There were quarrels and harsh punishments over thefts. Natives and British sailors were flogged with impunity. There were several attempts at desertion, and in one case Cook held chiefs captive on board until the men were brought back. Very little that reflected credit on Cook and his men took place.

After Raiatea, Cook steered for Bora-Bora, where the most warlike natives of all lived, on the most spectacularly architected of all the Society Islands, the whole dominated by what might have been a slice of Table Mountain from the Cape. Here, it was rumoured, lay a lost anchor which had belonged to Bougainville, and Cook reckoned it was worth trying to retrieve it for its iron. They had been so lustful, and so improvident in their trading, that they had few axes and knives left for the natives of New Albion, and iron for the blacksmiths was sorely needed.

The anchor was located and traded for, but it was only a fragment and made few axes. They stood north at last from this island on 8 December after tearful farewells to their girls.

No sailor knew the Society Islands better than James Cook, no one understood better the way of life and the character of the islanders, their idiosyncracies and vices, their childish cunning, their warm hearts, their ephemeral view of things. Understanding their weaknesses and simple natures, Cook also held them in warm affection.

But by any reckoning—and certainly by the reckoning of his officers—this third visit had been a singular failure. At every island, he departed less loved than when he had arrived. No one was better for these weeks, in spirit or health. Old Watman was weaker than ever, there was more gonorrhea and jaundice about on land and on board. And the health of those two brave consumptives, Clerke and Anderson, had deteriorated so badly that it is difficult to believe they would have lasted for long even if Clerke had got his papers 'in order' before they left, which he failed to do.

One sees a clear and haunting picture of William Anderson at this time, the one man on the voyage who knew by his training and experience every stage of deterioration by consumption, and knew now that he was suffering it in its most advanced form.

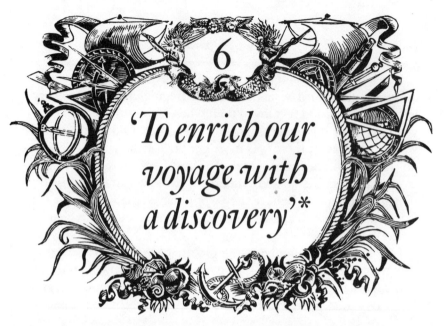

6

'To enrich our voyage with a discovery'*

GEORGE GILBERT, WHO later nearly drowned falling overboard when drunk, spoke for many of his fellow seamen on their departure. 'We left these islands with the greatest regret imaginable, as supposing all the pleasures of the voyage to be now at an end, and having nothing to expect in future but excess of cold, hunger and every kind of hardship and distress.' Gilbert might record their dejection, but the *Resolution* especially had a volatile company and the young gentlemen usually raised spirits high again after a little time with their tricks and pranks and robust jokes. They all missed Omai and his Maori entourage and often speculated on their fate. The last they had heard, by a prearranged code of coloured beads despatched by swift canoe from Huahiné, was that everything was well. But no one predicted a tranquil domestic life for him.

A mere three weeks passed before they made their first discovery, proof once again of Cook's extraordinary talent for finding islands in a waste of ocean. Christmas Island is one of the loneliest in the world, but the *Resolution*'s lookout spotted the low, flat coral speck on the mid-Pacific Ocean just after dawn on Christmas Eve. On closer inspection it appeared an unpromising atoll in the shape of a reversed C and was pounded by a ferocious

Cited W. Ellis, Narrative of a voyage through Hawaii (London, 1828)

surf. There appeared to be virtually no vegetation. Cook had thoughts of turtle and fish.

Boats were despatched from the two sloops with lieutenants in command, and again the following morning. All failed to find a landing place. Cook decided on one last attempt, calling on Bligh, who so often brought success after the failure of others. Bligh's way with a small boat impressed the most seasoned and sceptical mariner, even those who had often felt the lash of his tongue at some slackness. So, after breakfast on this Christmas morning, the *Pesolution*'s boat was seen standing north-east along the flat coastline and precariously close to the breaking surf, with the master's sturdy figure standing in the stern, hand on the tiller. It soon disappeared from sight and was not seen until shortly before noon. 'Yes, sir,' reported Bligh on board again, 'there is a way through the reef and into the lagoon a league and a half north.'

'And the soundings, Mr Bligh?' asked Cook, whose understanding with his master was absolute.

'They are the same as where we lie now, sir.'

The *Resolution* and *Discovery* weighed and worked north to their new anchorage off Bligh's inlet and a small sandy island at its entrance, now called Cook Islet. After this strenuous work in great heat, the men settled down to their Christmas dinner— 'fresh pork, fish and double allowance of liquor, which enabled them to spend this evening with mirth and jollity,' recorded one of Bligh's mates.

The revels continued for some days, combined with the light tasks of fishing and turtling. The turtles were as abundant as Cook had hoped, and were caught by turning them over while asleep on land or, more excitingly, by pursuing them in the water, a task for skilful swimmers only working in pairs, each seizing a fin and often being carried far and into deep water before overcoming them. An eclipse of the sun was expected on 30 December and Bayly took his telescopes ashore to observe it. As they were almost on the equator ar 1 the sand acted as a reflector, the heat at noon was almost unbearable and Cook was forced to give up his observations.

Clerke and Anderson were both going through a bad patch

and suffered greatly in their cabins. But most of the ships' companies were inured to the tropical heat. Their skin was brown and hardened from eight months in the Pacific and they thrived on their swimming and games. For all but the consumptives and several seamen who contrived to get lost in their wandering ashore and almost succumbed to the heat, it was a happy and unexpected break, neatly coinciding with Christmas and the turn of the year.

When they stood out to sea again on 2 January 1778 everyone was convinced now it really was the end of the easy life and the tropical warmth. Four days later, with the temperature in the 80s, the Fearnought jackets and trousers were issued, and Clerke put his men on to a ration of two quarts of fresh water a day. Clerke, his health improved, dined with Cook one afternoon when they were caught in a temporary calm. Mostly the winds were fresh and favourable from the south-east so that they made good progress north, being excited and puzzled towards the middle of the month by indications—turtles in the sea, the nature of the birds in the sky—of land not far distant. According to their sketchy charts, New Albion was still far distant.

At dawn on 18 January Cook could just make out the shape of the first of the Hawaiian islands he was to note in his log and describe in his journal. It had 'the appearance of being high land'. Then, a short time later, the lookout at the masthead, Midshipman James Ward, called down and pointed more to the east. The first island was Oahu, and the second, almost equidistant, Kauai. Bligh, who was to do more than anyone else to chart the whole chain accurately and for the first time, was one of those on deck studying the undulating profile of these distant islands through his glass. They were clearly on the brink of making the greatest discovery of this voyage so far, and Bligh, with an explorer's instinct and enthusiasm as great as Cook's, again blessed his good fortune in having been selected as master of the *Resolution*, even if his fellow officers were such fools.

The day was calm with only occasional light breezes, and their passage was frustratingly slow. The profile remained unchanging so that they could have drawn it from memory. At sunset the nearest island, which now bore due north, was still 30 miles distant. In the annals of exploration, there was no greater excitement than to observe by the light of a new dawn a discovery last seen at nightfall. Would its shape be more clearly defined? Would other new shapes have lifted above the horizon? At what distance would they be from the land? And was it inhabited, and if so be what nature of people?

On this dawn the answer was yes to the first two questions, and the last was shortly to be resolved.

Oahu bore almost due east, its mountains sharply defined in the clear air, but no nearer than before. Kauai was directly ahead, mountainous, too, and already giving evidence of rich fruitfulness. A third much smaller island bore north-west. Cook wrote, 'We had now a fine breeze at EBN and I stood for the east end of the second island.'

Gore 'saw a high hummock of land' at 5.30 p.m., rising straight from the sea at the east end of the island, then gentler slopes along the south side with trees higher up, and along the shore and hinterland villages, plantations of some root crop, sugar and plantains. Then a great surf. The natives were massing in groups on favourable headlands and staring out wonderingly at the strange sight of these great vessels running before the wind half a league off the shore.

Canoes put out, keeping their distance. All the sloops' companies were on deck, calling and waving encouragingly to them, smiling and cheering when the first paddled close along-side. Cook himself threw down a red cloth into the canoe, and then a bag of nails at the end of a rope. The natives grinned and began calling back, reassured now and tossing over the side the stones they had been carrying and holding up fish instead.

To the astonishment of the sailors, the words they heard were in familiar Polynesian—hogs, sweet potatoes, plantains, bread-fruit, fish—words the sailors had listened to every day at Tahiti. All the sailors had learned a little of the language, some of the midshipmen and officers were quite fluent, Jem Burney almost bilingual. Burney was full of questions—'What is the name of your island?' 'Is the fish good?' 'Where are your women?' 'Do you have heivas?' 'Do you have morais?' Some sailors held up one of the surviving turtles from Christmas Island, and the canoeists looked astonished, then claimed that they had them too.

These islanders were dressed in no more than a loin cloth. Their skin was dark; King likened them to the New Zealanders, Edgar described their skin as of a dark copper colour. 'They were not tall, but of strong, muscular make, and there was great variety in the shape of their visages.'

How could these people be so widely and distantly spread across the face of this ocean, itself occupying a third of the earth's surface? As Cook now observed, almost wherever he had sailed they were to be found. 'We find them from New Zealand to the south, from these islands to the north, and from Easter Island to the Hebrides; an extent of 60° of latitude or twelve hundred leagues east and west.'

Although he had met in the Friendly Islands some native survivors of a desperate canoe voyage from Tahiti, his mind could not encompass the idea that great Polynesian outrigger or double canoes might sail these vast distances in migrations, navigating by the stars and the winds, the flight of birds and the piled-high cloud above the volcanic islands of this ocean.

The natives were bolder the next day. 'I never saw Indians so much astonished at entering a ship before,' Cook noted, confirming his belief that these were the first ever that they had seen. 'Their eyes were continually flying from object to object, the wildness of their looks and actions fully expressed their surprise and astonishment.'

King took some down to the gunroom and noted the same amazed effect. 'In their behaviour they were very fearful of giving offence, asking if they should sit down, or spit on the decks, and in all their conduct seemed to regard us as superior beings.'

In the *Discovery*, Clerke took them down to his cabin, too. Everything was fingered, with expressions of amazement. Iron especially attracted them, and a native seized one of the open window supports, causing the frame to slam shut. Believing that they were all going to be trapped, they struggled to the windows that were still open, diving into the sea and leaving the windows behind them smashed.

Cook awaited the first thefts fatalistically. They occurred almost at once, some blatantly, some by deep guile. With all the elaborate precautions, he knew he could only limit them. Their passion for iron was equal to the Tahitians' for red feathers. This was because they understood its value. Washed up ship's timbers with iron set into them had been found; only a few, but sufficient for them to learn what could be done with the metal. One of the butcher's cleavers went that first day.

The second problem was, as always, the women. On sighting these Hawaiian islands Cook asked Anderson and the *Discovery*'s surgeon, John Law, to inspect the men for gonorrhea. Any who were still suffering from it were forbidden to go ashore, no shore parties were to remain overnight, no women were to be allowed on board, and all intercourse with women forbidden. It was as impossible to prevent as the thieving, and Cook knew it. Several women got into the *Discovery*, and ashore it was even more difficult to escape the attentions of the women than at Tonga. 'They seem to have no more sense of modesty than the Tahitian women,' Samwell recorded. 'And in general they were as fine girls as any we had seen in the south sea islands.'

Williamson, with his talent for raising trouble, and in charge of the first shore party, created as much excitement among the men as the women, and the violence of their reception—part joyous, part covetous of the iron—caused him to lose his head. The native he shot 'was a tall handsome man about 40 years of age and seemed to be a chief,' the lieutenant noted in his journal, 'the ball entering under his right pap, he instantly dropped down dead in the water.' Edgar said that when they saw the body floating, his friends snatched him up and made off with him, crying mournfully.

Able Seaman William Griffin, present on this occasion, described Williamson's attack as 'a cowardly, dastardly action'. Williamson did not tell Cook. The lieutenant's popularity fell even lower when the word got about; and when Phillips heard he was outraged. The two lieutenants were at constant loggerheads, and had already fought one abortive pistol duel at Tahiti in connection with the inefficiency of the marines.

Later in the day, the sloops anchored off the village of Waimea. Cook's reception was different to Williamson's. 'The very instant I leaped ashore,' he wrote, 'they all fell flat on their faces, and remained in that humble posture till I made signs to them to arise.' He was being received as a king with the highest degree of submission. Later, while the men watered, he and Anderson took a walk inland, and Webber completed a drawing of the village showing their houses, the natives going about their business, the sailors rolling their casks.

Down on the beach, trade was brisk, 'and the cheapest market I ever yet saw,' observed Clerke. 'A moderate size nail will supply my ship's company very plentifully with excellent pork for the day.' Everyone agreed, too, that they were the most honest traders they had ever met.

Kauai on that January day in 1778 marked the high point of the entire voyage. Besides the deep satisfaction of discovering this paradise—this 'garden island'—the weather was perfect, the natives friendly (Williamson's outrage already forgotten), it was pleasant just to look at the smiling women even if they were forbidden fruit, there was turtle and fresh roast pork and good fish to eat, and to cap it all, grog was served out again.

There was not another day among these islands to compare with Wednesday 21 January. The weather soon broke. Vexatious winds and currents first drove the ships off Kauai, then separated them, and for some days prevented the *Resolution*'s successful passage to Niihau, which Cook was anxious to chart and land upon. He had also not completed watering at Waimea and wanted more for the last leg to New Albion. Once again it took Bligh to resolve their frustrations. He took a boat, ranged the coast westward from the south-east point of Niihau, and found a landing place. But no water. Gore found some later and then was forced by the rising seas to remain ashore for the night.

This was just what Cook had been so anxious to avoid. He knew the lieutenant would be unable to prevent his men from consorting with the women. But whether or not half-caste children were conceived that night, John Gore, already the first

American to land on a Hawaiian island, made a small footnote to history as the first American to sleep on the future American 50th state.

Cook made a signal finally to the *Discovery* at noon on 2 February to weigh and stand north from these exasperating islands, which he now named Sandwich after his patron. After the first satisfaction of their discovery and charting, and the pleasure of their friendly reception, it had been a mainly frustrating visit. Cook and Bligh agreed that these were devilish awkward waters, whatever the splendour of the landscape.

Cook was not in the least satisfied with the results of his lengthy stay. 'After spending more time about these islands than was necessary to have answered all our purposes, we were obliged to leave them before we had completed our water,' he wrote in his journal. Then there was the Williamson affair, which he now learned about, and that made him explode with wrath. The *Resolution*'s quartermaster Thomas Roberts at last succumbed to the dropsy. Over in the *Discovery*, Clerke was unwell again, and Burney and Bayly had had yet another tiff.

Three islands had been added to the map of the Pacific. Five more weeks had been lost. The anxiety lest he lose another season was already gnawing at Cook. He would be relieved and thankful to sight the coast of New Albion. But there were many leagues yet to sail.

The stark silhouette of Kauai in the south-east faded in the falling light of the evening. But he would be back among these islands.

As usual after leaving a newly discovered island, Cook descended to his cabin and in his carefully formed hand and with not too much regard for consistent spelling, wrote his conclusions. Many generations had passed since these people of Kauai and Niihau had experienced any contact with others of the Polynesian race, and it was fascinating to note in which ways they had advanced more swiftly and which more slowly, and the degree to which natural conditions had influenced their lives.

Certainly there was little difference between the language spoken here and at Tahiti, and many of the tribal customs were similar. In everyday dress they were less covered than the

Tahitians, which Cook thought accounted for their darker hue. But their chiefs' formal attire was most magnificent, a cloak sewn with multi-coloured numerous feathers and a helmet-like headdress. Tattooing was practised, but it was crude stuff compared with the Maoris', while their carving was much superior in design and execution. In fact they only saw one chief, the rest being on the other side of the island at the time of their visit, which must have caused them much chagrin.

In tools they had advanced little beyond those of the Tahitians', stone axes and adzes. Their iron, probably derived from the wreckage of Spanish ships, might have been brought here be a combination of the north equatorial current and the north-east trades.

Their food was typically Polynesian—mainly fish, roast hog, plantains, yams, breadfruit, eaten off leaves or wooden bowls.

Cook noted that their houses were more elaborate than those in the Society Islands, with solid wood frame and coarse dry grass thatching for walls and roof. The entrance was a small cavity, for temporary illumination you punched a hole in the wall and pulled it together when no longer required.

They saw few trees, but knew that there must be forests inland from the size of the canoes. In boat-building they showed more skill than any other islanders they had observed. But then they must have been great sailors to have reached this far north. Cook measured their boats at 15 to 18 inches in beam and 24 feet in length, of one piece shallowly hollowed out, pointed at stem and stern, and built up with lashed one-inch boards. Stem and stern were slightly raised, and 'those that go single have outriggers, which are shaped and fitted with more judgement than any I have before seen', Cook noted. Some had a single triangular sail with a mast and boom. Paddled with muscles and skill, and with sail hoisted, they were very fast.

All the officers agreed that in most respects these Sandwich Islanders were superior to any other Polynesians they had met. King wrote later, 'The eager curiosity with which they attended the armourers' forge, and the many expedients they had invented, even before we left the islands, for working the iron they had procured from us into such forms as were best adapted to their purposes, were strong proofs of docility and ingenuity.'

Day by day with the advance of Spring, so the weather became more autumnal. Clerke, who had learned from Anderson the desperate risk to his life he was running in the increasing cold, refused to be down-hearted. There was no more he could do now that they had left behind the warmth of Polynesia, and there is a robust and cheerful note in his entry: 'We have been so long inhabitants of the torrid zone that we are all shaking with cold here with the temperature at 60. I depend on the assistance of a few good north-westers to give us a hearty rattling and bring us to our natural feelings a little, or Lord knows how we shall make ourselves acquainted with the frozen secrets of the Arctic.'

Towards the end of February the first evidence of not-too-distant land appeared in the sea. It was a foggy day with a light wind from the south-east and the temperature not quite touching 50°. They saw kelp in the water, and some wood. Cook had read Walters' account of Anson's circumnavigation. Walters had told how relieved the Spanish mariners always were on their long haul from Manila when they first sighted weed in this area, the whole ship's company assembling to chant a *Te Deum*.

On the night of 5 March, John Gore observed stars on the water, 'a great number of little sparks which exhibited a fairy light and swam about very briskly'. Later, he wrote of objects in the water that 'shone like bits of bright silver'. This land of New Albion was far distant from his native Virginia but there is a prescient quality in this vision—recorded by no one else—of another part of the world which would one day be under the stars and stripes. He and his fellow Americans in the expedition were to be the first by a wide margin of time to sail these future North American waters.

The coast of New Albion was sighted at noon the following day. There was nothing remarkable about it—wooded hills and valleys, a more prominent mountain of around 4000 feet a little distance inland, 'a remarkable flat-headed high hill,' as Clerke recorded it. They were, according to Bligh's calculation, in 44° 55′ north. He did not name the mountain St Mary's Peak, but now Cook for the first time began to use saints' names, out of respect to Spain, the nearest colonizing nation southwards.

The weather's reception did not prove hostile until the following day. Then, and for long after, it was hail, sleet, fog, haze and howling westerlies. There was nothing saintly about his first-named landmark, Cape Foulweather. It appeared ominously clear that the whole of the western coast of North America might be a mariner's lee shore nightmare. They were driven south, back to 42° 45′, and named a cape after St Perpetua and another after St Gregory. Cape Blanco was more prosaic.

The Spaniards had once reached at least this far north, but how much farther they were uncertain. Then the two sloops, battered and leaking, bore north again, farther out to sea for safety. A fierce lee shore infuriated Cook and Bligh as it prevented charting the coast. Cook observed how the wind backing south might give them some heading but always signified a storm, short but fierce from the north-west. Clerke was getting his hoped-for conditions, but now described their frustrations and dangers as 'a lamentable business'. He was coughing worse than ever.

Miserable weeks passed. On 22 March they were off a point which Cook named Cape Flattery. He thought he was at 48° 15′ north but was nearly two degrees out, a reflection on what the weather was doing to their navigation. He was, however, correct in his comment, 'It is in the very latitude we were now in where geographers have placed the pretended Strait of Juan de Fuca, but we saw nothing like it, nor is there the least probability that ever any such thing existed.'

But here at least is one of Cook's fairy tales that could have a basis of historical fact, blurred by the years and boastful elaboration. The small opening near the cape that had 'flattered us with hopes of finding a harbour' was passed by in daylight. The 15-mile-wide opening, now called Juan de Fuca Strait, was passed in the darkness. And it was not for another 14 years that Cook's young midshipman would find it, sail through it and discover what Cook never learned, that Vancouver was an island. It is not beyond the bounds of navigational possibility that the Spaniard had already done just this and pretended to himself—or really believed—that he had found the Atlantic at the other end and returned from it.

No one in the world knew the east coast of present-day Canada better than Cook. Newfoundland, Nova Scotia, the St Lawrence estuary, the river and its tricky traverse—all this and much more he had surveyed in his late apprentice years as a master navigator and hydrographer. He had even been in attendance at the birth of British Canada, a violent one at Quebec, and his contribution to victory had been substantial. Now, on 29 March 1778, with his sloops desperately low in water, in need of wood and extensive repairs and fresh food, Cook sighted an inlet and with a blessed stroke of good fortune was gently blown into it by a north-westerly breeze. Almost at once the breeze died and the *Resolution* anchored in 85 fathoms. It was six o'clock in the evening, there was a fine freshness in the air, scented with pine, the dark water appeared rich in fish, the sky was full of birds.

Cook named it St George's Sound, later renamed by the Admiralty Nootka Sound, and they were in the more easterly of the two arms, now called Zuciarte Channel. All about them for as far as they could see in the evening light were forest-clad mountains, one piling upon another, the highest snow-capped, and rising from maze-like channels, inlets, headlands, coves and islands that would have engaged Bligh's hydrographic skills for weeks.

Nothing is much changed today. It is still, as Cook recommended it in his journal to other mariners, one great forest of cedars, spruce and hemlock for those in need of wood, and a good place to water can be chosen from countless opportunities. Only the inhabitants are different. Only one member of the ships' companies had seen man in this form before, in appearance, speech, dress or habits. And, except that they crowded about them in dozens of canoes even before they had dropped anchor, the characters and the setting could not have been in stronger contrast with the Polynesian islands.

It was John Ledyard, with his missionary experience of Red Indians, who claimed, 'I had no sooner beheld these Americans, than I set them down for the same kind of people that inhabit the opposite side of the continent.'

Their noise was the strongest first impression on that March evening. They first came off from a point Jem Burney marked on his chart as 'Indian Town' (Yuguot village today) at the western entrance to the sound. They were in massive 40-feet-long dugout canoes, at least seven feet in beam, with raised head and stern, which many of Cook's sailors likened to a Norwegian yawl. No carvings or ornaments of any kind, just a hollow cut out in the prow on which to lay their harpoons and spears, and paddled with the usual dexterity of people who live with the water. Their paddles were comparatively small and light, shaped like a large leaf, and with a secondary use as a drumstick against the side of the canoe, which they beat in sturdy, precise rhythm.

When they were close alongside, the men stood up in their great seagoing canoes, shouting at the tops of their voices, which slowly came together in a wild chorus. The *Discovery* had an able seaman who had once sold potatoes about the streets of London, and the voices of these natives were compared with his. There was certainly nothing else to which to liken them. Nor their looks. 'It will require the assistance of one's imagination to have an adequate idea of the wild, savage appearance and actions of these first visitors,' wrote King, 'as it is difficult to describe the effect of gestures and motions. Their dark, coppery-coloured bodies were so covered over with filth as to make it a doubt what was really the proper colour. Their faces were daubed with red and black paint and grease, in no regular manner but as their fancies led them. Their hair was clotted with dirt, and to make themselves either fine, or frightful, many put on their hair the down of young birds, or plaited it in seaweed or thin strips of bark dyed red.'

Their clothing was equally individual, shaped according to inclination or the configuration of the animal from which the skin was taken, with little regard for covering private parts, and with no regard at all for cleanliness.

Their manner of greeting the intruders was like no other they had experienced, too. A figure stood up in a canoe, worked himself rapidly into a frenzy, waving his arms and pointing at the sky and the shore, uttering half howl, half song, holding a rattle in each hand, which at intervals he laid down, taking handfuls of red ochre and birds' feathers and casting them onto the water. More deep, guttural shrieks followed, then the native would simply sit down again in a posture of repose as if nothing had happened.

In spite of this violent demonstration none of Cook's men regarded them as hostile, and this was confirmed minutes later when trade commenced: priceless furs—beaver, bear, sea otter, wolf—for a nail or two; and (memories of London's Billingsgate market) a pound of sprats for two English copper halfpence, which were much preferred to the silver money.

This first evening had an air of unreality about it, even to these hardened mariners who had already seen some strange sights and heard many strange sounds. A chief arrived, causing an interruption in the trading, recognizable as a figure of authority by the raised plank in his canoe to offer greater height when he stood up—gaudy in his paint and furs, red and white, his head ornamented with many feathers tied to strings falling about his shoulders and back.

Cook lowered him a piece of green baize cloth, which he examined and indicated by signs was of no interest. All he wanted was iron, iron tools. Then, as the light faded, a voice from one of the canoes repeated the same word several times 'as a parish clerk gives out the first line of a psalm', the delighted Burney described it, other voices joined in, and taking up their paddles again and beating the sides in strict rhythm, burst into a chorus of syncopated song, which all agreed was pleasing to the ear.

Jem Burney loved their rhythmic singing, the most pleasing and melodious of the voyage. 'Their song was composed of a variety of strange placed notes, all in unison and well in tune,' he wrote. It had a swagger to it, like a vigorous passage in an opera, with the canoes circling the ships, the foremost paddler in each making a flourish at every third or fourth stroke. 'The halloo is a single note in which they all join, swelling it out in the middle and letting the sound die away. In a calm with the hills around us, it had an effect infinitely superior to what might be imagined from anything so simple.' This was one of so many occasions he looked forward one day to describing to Fanny, and especially what followed on that dream-like evening.

A young native man with a remarkably soft, effeminate voice began to sing a solo, holding equally in admiring silence the fur-bedecked and daubed natives in the canoes, and the crews of the two ships at the rails, like a standing opera audience in the upper gallery. Then he suddenly stopped in mid-note, frozen into a grotesque stance, the whole effect so sudden and unexpected that the sailors began to laugh. This the native took as a signal for an encore, and gave it, and another, and again. What a performer!

It was, the officers considered, time for their own contribution, and fife and drums were ordered to play a tune, which was listened to in silence and with evident respect—the first rewarding experience for the fife player, who had so far never enjoyed an appreciative audience.

The natives replied with more songs, and then as a last item, the *Resolution* and *Discovery* produced their French horn players. The Indians loved it. They might stink of seal oil and ochre, converse in deep-throated grunts, seemingly throw hysterical fits, and appear almost as primitive as the Fuegians, but here, amidst the lapping of water and the sigh of the wind in the yews in the last light of day, was a music-loving people. It was just one more incident—and such a moving one—to impress on these sailors, who were not yet at the half-way point of their great voyage, how varied and unexpected were human conduct, manners, taste and appearance in a world they were opening up from the sub-Antarctic to the Arctic.

This dream world changed to one of severe practicality with the dawn. Down-to-earth Bligh was off early in one of the *Resolution*'s boats, ranging the sound for a suitable cove for the extensive repair work they must rapidly put in hand. The big island in the centre of the sound dividing the two main arms, and along which he searched, is rightly now called Bligh Island; and other present-day names—Discovery Point at the entrance, Cook Channel, Resolution Cove at the end of Clerke

Peninsula—commemorate the expedition's sojourn here; though with some names, like Williamson Passage and King Passage, flanking Gore Island, their eternal juxtaposition did not reflect their relations in real life.

King and Edgar were both out in the boats, too, and good sheltered anchorages were discovered up this sound that could have accommodated the whole British navy. But Cook chose 'a pretty snug cove' close to where they were anchored, and got the sloops moored head and stern the following day.

Entries in the logs and journals now begin to read like a daily work report on a ship in Deptford dock, except that this work was carried out with the probing care and conscientiousness of men whose lives were to depend on the soundness of their vessels, and not shipwrights, joiners and hammermen who were after corruption and cash.

They had given up cursing the men of Deptford now. It was with expressions of resignation that they found, in cutting into the masthead and examining further into it, both cheeks to be rotten, and unrepairable without getting the mast out. Out came the foremast, then, to be hauled ashore, and the carpenters set to work on repairing it. Eleven days later, exhausted and half asleep at their work, the carpenters were at work on a new mizzen mast. It was more than half completed when they found the tree had been sprung in felling, and they had to start all over again, selecting, clearing, felling, dragging to the shore. After that it was a new fore topmast.

The caulkers worked equally hard and for equally long hours. Tropical rain pouring through the decks was an inconvenience; in a few weeks time, secure decking could mean the difference between life and death.

Against this background of industry ashore and on board, and daily trading and fishing, Bligh and Edgar were the most enthusiastic, nosing about the creeks and inlets that seemed to wind on for ever. The two consumptives—Anderson very weak now—were also the two best informed ornithologists, and there was much to report from here: from minute humming-birds to great albatrosses, geese to bald eagles, gulls, shags, mallards, the red-breasted merganser.

Cook employed his young gentlemen in rowing him about the straits, sounding and landing to study the rocks and flora and fauna and the natives' dwellings—any occupation to soothe his impatience and vexation. He unbent a shade, but not much, on these day-long expeditions, and in spite of the hard work, the young men enjoyed them, especially the better quality of rations and drink that went with them. They were also expected to test the local greenery; but not as they witnessed the natives sampling their plants, pulling them straight out of the ground and into their mouths without a shake.

The young gentlemen, when not employed with Cook or elsewhere, did their best to maintain their lusty reputation. At first, few women were seen about the ships, and those who came awoke no passions among the seamen. The midshipmen, undeterred, succeeded in making clear their wants and the rewards, and one day three girls were brought on board the *Discovery*, and a price agreed. They appeared very modest and timid, not at all Polynesian, but they had been carefully prepared to attract, their hair and faces well daubed with ochre, their bodies, as always, well larded with seal oil against the cold.

Fortunately we have Samwell's account of what followed. 'Our gentlemen were not to be discouraged,' he wrote, securing buckets of warm water and much soap. 'This they called the Ceremony of Purification and were themselves the officiators at it, and it must be mentioned to their praise that they performed it with much piety and devotion, taking as much pleasure cleansing a naked young woman from all impurities in a tub of warm water as a young confessor would to absolve a beautiful virgin who was about to sacrifice that name to himself.' As to the poor girls, they were puzzled that all that had been added apparently to improve their desirability was now removed with such thoroughness.

However, these Nootka natives were quick to pick up lessons, and in future (and in ever-increasing numbers) girls were provided for both ships. A pewter plate was the most desired payment, and soon there was scarcely one left in the gunrooms so that meals were eaten off tables and chests. Old Watman once again proved his worth at this time. With the wisdom of experience, he had anticipated that his shipmates would probably trade away their plates before the voyage ended, and he had carefully preserved and put away a number of half coconut shells. His appearance with them at dinner was greeted with cheers.

Like an actor in a long-running drama, Williamson played his part here as at other anchorages. He found it as difficult to come to amiable terms with the natives as with his own shipmates. There was petty pilfering at Nootka Sound, pocket-picking, the cutting off of an attractive button and the like, but this lieutenant seemed especially to attract thieves and to resent losses. When two of the local tribes put on their war dress and assumed an aggressive stance, and for a while Cook's men misunderstood the situation and thought they might be the object of an attack, it was Williamson who was first to call for arms for the shore party. He got them, but there was anxiety among the officers that he might panic again and fire into the natives.

Later, when the crisis had passed over, he determined to demonstrate the deadly power of a musket. 'With this I can pierce your war dress,' he told them, patting the butt. 'Eight times over, I can pierce your war dress.' And he held out his hand for the loan of one. This he secured to a tree, three times folded, took aim and fired at 20 yards. 'See now how deadly are our muskets.' Williamson took out his knife and prised the ball from deep in the tree bark, to the amazement of the natives gathered round.

Judging by the short length of New Albion coast they had so far traversed, they had many dangers and difficulties still ahead before they even began their exploration north of latitude 65°, some 1600 miles distant. They were into the third week in April already, leaving them a mere six weeks to be into the Arctic. It was now probable rather than possible that again they had lost their season, and this was reflected in Cook's brusqueness and short temper. Every day there were Cook *heivas*, as his men called them, after those violent Polynesian dances. Never had the strain and anxiety of commanding this voyage been so evident. Small incidents caused flare-ups. He complained about the greed of the natives. When one stole a small piece of iron

from the *Resolution* and dived overboard, climbing into a canoe,
Cook took out his double-barrel musket and fired, wounding
three or four of them in the back.

Nevertheless, when sails had been bent and they weighed and
cast off moorings on Sunday 26 April, they enjoyed one of their
happiest and most splendid departures. A chief on board the
Resolution was given a gift by Cook, who received in return a
beaver skin cloak so magnificent that he gave him one of the very
special gifts he still possessed, a broad sword with a brass hilt.

The boats had to tow the sloops out of the cove, and that
added to the pageantry of the scene. It was misty and still in
Nootka Sound and all the canoes within miles had assembled to
escort them out towards the sea, the large ocean-going kind as
well as the river canoes which were much smaller. Suddenly, by
some pre-arranged signal, all these water-borne natives burst
into song, a special parting song, it seemed, at the same time
holding aloft and flourishing the largest and most valued objects
they had acquired from their guests—hatchets, saws, a sword or
two. The centrepiece to the entertainment was a dancer on a
stage of loose boards, held to the gunwales of the canoe by his
friends, who in rhythm with the singing danced in different
guises, wearing the grotesque mask of a man, then of an animal,
next of a bird.

The entertainment continued as the sails filled, the boats were
hoisted in, and the two sloops stood out to sea and headed north.
The barometer was falling ominously. Cook knew that a storm
was imminent but dared not lose another day.

7

'As compact as a wall'

NOW THEY WERE embarked on the last leg of their voyage to the Arctic. Their provisions were adequate, they were well stocked with wood for the ships' stoves, they had become acclimatized to the colder weather and had prepared themselves for a much greater temperature fall. They believed their ships were in good order. If they did not delay, if they were free of mishaps, they might yet make their season. A rapid Atlantic voyage back home after finding the Passage, and their share of that prize, were in everyone's thoughts as the last canoe fell astern outside Nootka Sound.

Almost at once the wind changed from the north-east to south-east, further confirmation of an imminent storm. A squall of rain and a gale hit them a double blow. It was a horrible night, teeming with rain, the gale tearing at the rigging, and they could not see a yard in the inky blackness. Cook's concern was to get clear of the coast, and at the screaming dawn they appeared to have succeeded. But before the day was out the wind had increased to hurricane strength. To add further to their dangers, the *Resoluion* sprang a leak. After all the time and care they had put into refitting the sloop for this northern voyage, the sea was pouring in under the starboard buttock. Cook went down, and he could see and hear it coming in. There were casks floating about in the fish room. While the ship rolled and pitched as never before, the men manned the pump. On all the voyage, they had never before felt such concern for their safety in a storm.

Later, the hurricane abated somewhat, then the gale turned to a strong wind from the south. When the *Resolution* heeled over less acutely, they were relieved to see that they no longer took in water, indicating that at least the leak was above the waterline. Cook closed the land again when conditions permitted. His judgment was to be sorely exercised all the way up this coast, for he must treat it with caution in case he should be thrown onto a lee shore, but he also needed sight of it as a guide to the course to steer. So the coast of New Albion was at once an essential guide and a dangerous companion. There had been Russian discoveries in the waters he was approaching, and he had maps supposedly based on them, but the most optimistic navigator could place no reliance on the chart of, say, Gerhard Müller, 1761, with its wide brush strokes indicating no more than the rough shape of the land. No one could be sure even of the broadest configuration of the coastline: the land was *terra incognita*, the sea equally unknown, certainly hostile.

It was not until 1 May that the lookout sighted land again. Bligh calculated they were in 55° 20′ N, 500 miles nearer the Arctic than Nootka Sound. Cook needed a harbour to repair his leak. With a favourable wind, he pressed on north. Never had been more evident the unpredictability of voyaging in unknown extreme latitudes than on this drive to the north. Suddenly all was serene in the 60s, and he could even hoist carpenters over the side to carry out emergency patching on the leak. Clerke, in tolerable health, unlike Anderson, who was weakening, said that he had never in his life in any climate seen for such a length of time 'the air so perfectly serene, the sea so perfectly smooth, and the weather altogether so perfectly pleasant'. Now Cook could match the earlier Cape Foulweather with a Cape Fairweather. Gore was altogether delighted with this side of America. 'The land high and very hilly,' he recorded. 'Much snow on the hills, some low land on the coast and much wood and many appearances of inlets.' A great mountain (Edgecumbe) with a round head 'beautifully capped with snow' could enjoy only one name, 'Beautiful Mountain.'

Their experience throughout their Arctic voyaging was of occasional days like this of crystal clarity, without a breath of breeze, with blinding sun and unlimited visibility, air tasting like mountain spring water. Then a puff of wind, a gathering of clouds, mist turning to fog, breeze turning to wind turning to gale, an unhealthy clamminess in the lungs, and sudden new fears in the heart. These brilliant, joyous days might be rare but were God-given rewards for the suffering of long dreadful periods, and made life just tolerable.

By the middle of May, midsummer a mere month away, they had reached the ultimate north-east of the Pacific Ocean; and the omens were suddenly favourable, especially in the eyes of John Gore. At midday on 12 May they had sighted the entrance to a great inlet, which Cook named Sandwich Sound, as if his patron had not already been sufficiently honoured. On Gore's own chart, but no other, there appears the name Cape Hold-with-Hope at the entrance to what the American believed might well be a passage that would take them through into the Arctic. And, a week later, while still in that great stretch of open water that was renamed Prince William Sound, he judged that their way ahead was through a channel to the north-west. 'A great bay of bays and islands, harbours and inlets,' wrote Gore with relish. 'Perhaps it passes into some great waters as yet unknown to Europeans.' Cheerful optimism could turn the practical hunter into a dreamy sentimentalist.

The need to repair the leak permanently gave Bligh the opportunity to hoist out a boat and occupy himself with one of his favourite pursuits, the destruction of stupid myths. Gore, not yet disillusioned, occupied himself shooting but hurriedly returned to the *Resolution* when pursued by a force of 20 natives in canoes.

They seemed to be friendly enough, however, and trading began, the usual beads and knives for fish and furs. Then, without provocation or notice, it turned to plunder, in a particularly businesslike and implacable form. A party of natives, armed with spears and dressed in loose sealskins shaped like a shirt, climbed into the *Resolution*'s cutter, threatened the few seamen on board, cut loose the painter and began to tow the boat away.

Bligh's considerable voice boomed, calling out the watch, which tumbled onto deck, armed with cutlasses. The show of strength was quite sufficient to halt the thieving. Without sign of guilt or even concern, the natives returned to their own canoes and their own business. 'Do not panic, white men, we know our place,' their gestures seemed to indicate. 'Lay down your arms, which are too powerful for us.'

Later they paddled across the cove to the *Discovery* and climbed on board as if to trade. There were only a few sailors on deck, who were now cornered and threatened with knives, and the party's leader, after glancing down several hatchways and seeing no signs of life — the men were at dinner — considered the sloop theirs and began plundering her, cutting free everything that was not loose. They were hurling a boat's rudder into the sea when the cries of alarm brought up the crew, flashing cutlasses and driving the natives off the deck, from which they dived into the water like seals, whose skins they wore, but again re-emerging without sign of fear or shame.

They were back as families, and in strength, the following day, dressed in skins of hares and squirrels, raccoons and beavers and seals, some with a huge bearskin like an overcoat as well, the bearded men in mittens of bear paws and with high crowned conical hats; the women with their black thick hair piled high on their forehead and chins stained black to emulate their men, and all with bored lips for inserting bone strips hung with decorations. Noses were bored, too, and ears for smaller ornaments and beads. All other features were heavily and vividly painted.

It was as if some demon had cast a malignant spell over the local animals and driven them from their lairs. In their arms they carried more skins piled high; they were for trading, but added a new grotesque element, as if these beasts were dragging with them their victims — in triumph or in grief, who could tell? The young gentlemen were, as usual, first off the mark in the trading, James Trevenen acquiring a sea beaver skin, which he later sold in China for 600 dollars.

But any imbalance of trade was later rectified. The *Resolution* had been heeled over to port so that the carpenters could better work on the sloop's damaged bottom, which brought the scuttles close to the water, close enough for one canoe-load to smash in every one and make off with the broken glass before anyone noticed.

More repairs, more delay, another outburst of anger from Cook. It was 15 May. They were not yet at the 61st parallel, and Bligh, always quick with the bad news but always right, had established not only that there was no hidden passage inland but that the coastline to the west trended south, indefinitely.

The sloops weighed from this sound at 6 a.m. on 17 May, sailing after long delays inside an island which they marked Montagu, Sandwich's family name, and the southern tip of which the disappointed Gore named Cape Lost Hope. As they headed south-west along the fractured southern coast of what is now the Kenai Peninsula, Bligh's pessimistic observation was proved to be all too accurate, until the afternoon of 21 May when the coastline terminated abruptly with a massive headland.

There was no sign of land ahead, and to the north there stretched a great spread of water, irresistably tempting. Bligh had no use for it at all. Gore, buoyantly optimistic again, disagreed. He was confident that here was an opening that would take them through. Cook, compromising, decided they should explore further to the south before entering it; and meanwhile, the day being her birthday, and he being always ready to honour a royal occasion, named the cape that signalled the entrance Cape Elizabeth, after the king's third daughter.

This was not the end of the American continent. That they soon established, but the entrance to this gulf was wide enough and so redolent of cheer that Gore named an island at this southern entrance Hope's Return. Beyond to the south the coast seemed to trend ever more to their disadvantage. Surely, argued the American again, this was worth a diversion?

Never in all his years of voyaging had Cook faced such a dilemma. Never had he appeared so uncertain of himself. He was back at the 59th parallel. His instructions were specific: '. . . taking care not to lose any time in exploring rivers or inlets, or upon any other account, until you get into the latitude of 65°, where we could wish you to arrive in the month of June'. The last days of May were running out, May 1778, not 1777 as in the instructions. His instinct told him that this inlet would lead him nowhere. Bligh was emphatic, as always. 'Here we have a great river, sir. No more.'

But the first lieutenant remained confident that this sea, being so great, would take them through into the Arctic, by-passing the strait of the Russian, Bering. King was an optimist, too. Clerke was anxious, which was unusual for him, because of his weakening health, and was reflecting Cook's own anxiety, so long had they sailed together. 'A fine spacious opening,' he agreed. But if it proved abortive, 'It might,' he knew, 'have a most unhappy effect upon this season's operations.' David Samwell thought it appeared promising. Anderson had no opinion. He was confined to his cabin, wasting away, a pathetic huddled figure who could no longer even write.

Gore still strongly and persistently pressed for exploring north. It could bring them into the Arctic in June, which no other course could satisfy. Cook yielded. Bligh cursed to himself. A ship full of fools! Gore was triumphant, bursting with delight. Of a headland he wrote, 'I distinguish it by the name of Good Prospect.' When they passed east of some dreary islands, Cook called them Barren Isles; Gore insisted on Entry Isles. The names corresponded to their moods.

They passed now close to Chugach Islands. Banks was honoured with a cape, and so was St Bede, and the sloops stood briefly into a fine bay, still called Port Chatham. They were heading due north, but winds were contrary, currents and tides tiresome, progress agonizingly slow. Far to the west they could make out a snow-clad mountain, a massive volcanic cone in the distance. Gore called it Mount Welcome, Cook returned to his saints: Mount Augustine, whose day it was—and one of whose tenets is of absolute predestination. Bligh drew it. They should not be here, but he could not keep his pen still, recording this gaunt land of white-capped peaks, piled one above the other as if they continued into eternity.

The fog came down, lifted, the wind remained from the

north, blew up into a gale on the 26th. Off Doubtful (Kalgin) Island they picked up a southerly breeze at last. They could see clear across to the other side, and the inlet appeared no narrower, except for a headland Gore named after himself, so perky was he feeling (now, prosaically, West Foreland).

Day after day passed, and they were still only creeping forward. On 28 May, to prevent the *Resolution* from drifting south on the current and wind, Cook ordered a kedge anchor to be dropped on an eight-inch hawser. It parted, and Bligh went in a boat to try to recover these irreplaceable items. His crew hooked the hawser, but lost it again and never recovered it. His rage was as great as Cook's. Gross incompetence on top of all their troubles! The next morning, Gore wrote, 'To the northward is a gulf, river or strait—the latter I hope.' Even his conviction was weakening.

But just as Cook felt all hope lost, the sky cleared and there was nothing but open water ahead to the north-north east. Gore interpreted the gestures of natives to mean, 'Our ships could go that way.' It was easy to be convinced that they were already half way through this land mass, and to recall the rise and fall in the hearts of Magellan's men before breaking through from his Strait at the opposite end of this continent.

Clerke was among those tossed between hope and despair during these anxious days. Now he wrote, 'This western land appears low and seems to form a curve easterly, so as nearly to shut in with our north-eastern extreme; if that is the case, the Lord knows which way our passage extends itself; some way it must, for the strong tides bespeak the source of it at some distance from us.'

John Gore named a headland, opposite the one carrying his own, Nancy's Foreland, 'a fair foreland for a favourite female acquaintance'. He wondered if Banks had been in touch with her and their child, perhaps reassuring her that she must not feel anxiety: Banks's Pacific voyage had been much longer.

Every day tests were applied for evidence that might lead to proof that they were in a river, or encourage them to proceed farther. The water was carefully weighed, and proved as saline as the sea. Currents were checked. Sludge and tree trunks in the water told a different, pessimistic story. Natives came off in kayaks, but only a few and they could hardly articulate to trade let alone provide them with the information they so desperately needed.

On 30 May, saline tests close to the shore showed the water much fresher, the tide ripped through at almost five knots. Clerke made his own independent test and found the water close to the surface pure and fresh, 'a discovery I was sorry to make, for I think it a very cogent argument against this being a strait betwixt two seas'. Cook was now claiming that he only agreed to this exploration to satisfy his first lieutenant, and that it was a waste of time. His officers were already convinced. King was calling it a river, Bayly with a surprising turn of romantic rather than scientific nomenclature called it Seduction River. Gore's claims were now even more muted.

Yet Cook was determined to punch his point home to satisfy others in the future who, he claimed, might feel he had not searched with sufficient diligence. It had been a struggle almost all the way. Now he would take the sloops no farther and would send the boats instead. On the last day of May he anchored some six miles off the west shore and due east of an island (Fire Island). It was 9 a.m., they were in 16 fathoms, the ebb tide was already made and ran just three knots here. It was a horrible morning, misty with drizzling rain. Out of the mist there appeared two large canoes, 20 natives in each and with a fur jacket of white hare skins hoisted on a pole, whether as an ensign or as an invitation to trade no one could tell. Cook was in no mood to develop relations. He threw them some beads, and ordered out two boats on more serious business.

In brief clearances of visibility, two large inlets could be seen, one trending north-east, the other east-south-east. Bligh stomped across the deck to the gangway and climbed down, settling himself into the stern self-confidently, the complete master. He took two boats, and rowed off for the northern inlet. He went ashore on the island, found fruit trees and currents nicely set, proceeded past present day Anchorage, and up what he already knew to be a dead end. He continued for nine miles, resting his men from time to time, sounding all the way and noting the likely trend of the river.

This was a spectacular land. No one could deny that. But unattractive. To Bligh, who combined a keen geographical curiosity with a need for tidy trimness, this landscape was unsatisfactory. The foothills rising to mountains, rising to higher mountains, were in turn part concealed and part revealed by clouds in long grey strips. One minute they might cut off the pure white peaks, the next the lower dirty summer snow slopes; then both. Dirty and deceptive. There were glaciers, which he had never seen before. Like the mountain snow, they were white higher up, but lower down like giant soiled stair-carpet awaiting laying, and dropping untidy chunks of ice of all shapes and sizes into the water, unwashed flotillas drifting without discipline upon the tide.

The streams, tumbling vertically, and the rivers making more stately progress towards the water, were slate-grey-muddy. In spite of the pure green trees and shrubs and grass on the lowest slopes, this was an unclean, untidy landscape. The sooner they were away from it the better, but meanwhile he must complete his duties. He noted the direction and configuration of the mountains to the north, sounded for the last time—17 fathoms—rested and fed his men; and in sub-Arctic midnight dusk made south again. He was back on board, sharp and efficient, at 2 a.m. on the first day of June.

King went with two boats up the south-east arm. He failed to get far against the tide, and returned. With appropriate fatalism, Cook named it River Turnagain. (In fact neither are rivers, but arms with many rivers pouring into them.)

They had been, as Clerke put it, 'Accursed unfortunate'. Or misguided? One would like to give Cook the benefit of the doubt as a gambler. But James Cook was no gambler. He was a man who had always possessed a precise, firm line of thought based on logic, experience and instinct. And now they had lost more than sixteen days when they could least afford to. He had not gambled. He had yielded, 'very much against my own opinion and judgment' because some of his officers believed 'we should certainly find a passage to the north'.

They had not, and it was a disastrous expedition, despite his striving to justify it. There remained only the naming and the taking possession of this land. The north entrance to King's Turnagain, opposite Bligh's (Fire) Island, Cook named Princess Charlotte; the south King George's Foreland (Point Possession). King went ashore with Bayly and others, with a staff and union flag. He took solemn possession in the name of King George III, raised the flag, and buried a bottle containing the names of the ships, the date and the commander's name. Then they all drank a bumper of porter to the king's health, and traded for dogs rather drunkenly with some natives, who, by virtue of the recent ceremony, were now subjects of the king. The dogs reacted by biting their new owners so savagely that Dr Law of the *Discovery* had to shoot his. It frightened the natives, but otherwise did not matter as they were only for the pot.

The north-easterly winds, which had made so difficult their passage up Cook Inlet and would have been so favourable if they had continued their passage west and resisted the temptation to explore, now veered to the south, making their return to the sea as difficult. Then the *Resolution* struck and stuck fast on a bank in the centre of the inlet, just above Nancy's Foreland. Cook raged and swore at the leadsman. Gore marked it as 'The Snare' to warn future navigators. The *Discovery* nearly grounded too. Cook ordered her to anchor and await the flood tide, which refloated his ship. Some natives came to the *Discovery* with fresh salmon and a gallon of cranberries, which made excellent puddings and tarts to offset the rigours of the passage, running with the tide against the wind, and anchoring at the flood.

It took them a week to recover their earlier position in the open sea, missing Shelikof Strait. The fog came down like a suffocating blanket on their hopes for three more consecutive days. No conditions could be more trying for Clerke's lungs, and he prayed 'that our darkness be enlightened'. Another week passed, mostly out of sight of land, before they observed and named the Trinity Islands at the south of Kodiak. Again, a shaft of hope pierced the gloom. Was this the turning point? One of the maps had indicated that they would have to sail as far south as 53°N before they could make for Bering's Strait.

They were soon to discover it was not. Under these damnable

conditions they could not be sure of anything, but in fact, between brief clearances of rain and fog, they could only recognize that they were being forced south-west just as they had feared, and just as they had been more or less consistently forced since 'turning the corner' of the Gulf of Alaska; and they were now following the warning finger which points down into the Pacific, the Alaska Peninsula, which in turn fractures into the Aleutian Islands.

When the fog thickened so that they could not see prow from stern, they fired guns, sounded rattles and drums and shouted. Then there would be a slight lifting, sometimes offering a glimpse of some hellish shore, sometimes not. Once or twice a tiny kayak was sighted, and it would sheer away as the natives recognized in these fearsome great vessels the reality of their legendary nightmares.

Once a great volcano was sighted briefly, pouring smoke up into an already over-full sky.

Midsummer came on 18 June, and Cook managed to get a sighting at noon which set them at 55° 18′ N. In the afternoon there occurred an odd incident which made them all, for one reason or another, faintly uneasy. The *Discovery* suddenly fired three guns. Cook, nerves on edge, was greatly alarmed, and searched for evidence of an attack or a natural catastrophe to his consort. It was neither. Clerke was making a signal that he wished to speak, and brought to.

Cook at once sent a boat for him across the two miles that separated the sloops. Clerke came up the ladder from the boat falteringly, not at all like the Clerke of old, who always bounded; and in his cabin, Cook noticed how he was losing weight and wondered what this awful weather was doing to his lungs.

Clerke was carrying a sack from which he took a wooden box. 'Some indians in canoes had been following us for some time, sir,' he recounted, 'and at length came under our stern, indicating they wished to send this up to us. So I had a rope flung down. They were bowing and taking off their caps as if taught in Europe, though that is not likely.'

Cook examined the box. Clerke explained that it had been tied with string, and indicated the slit in the side. 'We thought it might be a bird call,' he said. 'The indians kept repeating "Killy midgy cally ka!" or something like it. Then we untied the string and it fell apart into two pieces.'

Clerke demonstrated, and withdrew from the box a piece of paper. There was writing on it, in the Russian script. They could understand nothing except '1778' and '1776'. 'My belief, sir, is that it may be a message from shipwrecked mariners — perhaps Russians from St Peter and St Paul.'

Cook thought for a moment, and then put this theory aside. 'Rather, I think it to be a note of information left by some Russian trader lately in these parts. No doubt the indians suppose us to be Russians and it would make us stop to read this.'

Whatever the truth, and however indirect it might be, this first contact with the civilized world since leaving the Cape should not have been ignored, the men considered. It *could* have been a message of distress, they believed, and with the historic loyalty towards all others in their dangerous trade, were outraged that Cook took no further steps.

It was no discredit to Cook that he missed the ten-mile-wide Unimak passage through the Aleutians, just above 54°N, though he was being uncharacteristically cautious. He saw what might be a passage, then saw what he thought was land beyond, and refused to risk becoming trapped. This, the new cautious Cook, became the new wildly rash Cook on 26 June, running before a moderate wind to the west with fog so thick that Bligh could not see a hundred yards. The previous day, with a little visibility, they had passed close to three lethal islands; and no one in the world knew what lay ahead of them.

At 4.30 p.m., with all on watch recognizing the risks they were running, a sharp-eared seaman suddenly cried, 'Breakers!' Cook ordered the lead, found 28 fathoms, then 25 next time. 'Heave to!' he cried, and urgently hailed the *Discovery*, 'HEAVE TO!' BREAKERS!' With her bows to the north, the *Resolution* was anchored; and the *Discovery* anchored close beside her. Everyone could now hear the thunder of the breakers to the south.

Just how close to catastrophe they had come was revealed later when the fog cleared enough to show them they were no more than a few hundred yards from the rocks, and three-quarters of a mile from a rocky island, guarded by foaming reefs and rocks. There were more ferocious rocks on two other sides. They had anchored in the only clear water about them. The Cook luck of old had saved them by perhaps 60 seconds. But it had never been tested so severely.

The ever loyal Clerke remarked dryly, 'Very nice pilotage, considering our perfect ignorance of our situation and the total darkness which prevented our attaining any kind of knowledge of it.' Others expressed themselves more forcefully, including Bligh, inevitably. Gilbert was struck with horror. Edgar told of his surprise and terror. Midshipman Riou drew a chart which, better than any exclamation of dismay and relief at providence's favour, shows how nearly the voyage ended for both ships on that day.

However, after losing the easy passage through the Aleutians because of caution, improper pilotage brought them through here at around 54°N, after two days to recover themselves, and at the cost of the *Discovery*, caught in the ebb tide, being thrown about and round and round in a race—'confoundedly tumbled about for an hour or two', as Clerke laconically expressed himself. They put in to a bay for wood and water and fish, finding none of the first and little of the last. Cook named the island Providence.

But this time not even Bligh doubted that the worst lay behind them, that the clear water that stretched ahead was open sea that must take them to the Arctic.

Here, of all places, on this God-forsaken island with its God-forsaken climate and vegetation, Cook's men found the nicest natives they had ever encountered in the Pacific, right here at the ocean's ultimate north. They were polite, with much bowing and doffing of caps; honest; obliging. They had clearly been trading for some time with the Russians, who had introduced the habits of taking snuff and smoking tobacco, a cynically calculated policy to ensure continued trading and the hunting for skins. A leaf of tobacco could work wonders, Samwell and the lustier young gentlemen quickly discovered.

The Welsh doctor, who was always prepared to give the girls the benefit of the doubt when it came to assessing their attractiveness, found them very comely; and on being invited into one of their huts was offered the fairest of them all by her husband and father, there and then. Samwell always felt it necessary to preface a trip ashore in this style, and then afterwards became the most industrious observer of the people, their customs and habitations. He may not have been fastidious, but he was a great student of human behaviour.

Midshipman Riou marked this bay as Sammaganooda (Samgunuda). Later, the Russians obligingly named it English Bay after Cook's visit.

When they stood north from this bleak but hospitable island, there were few in the expedition who believed there was now any chance of recovering the season in the Arctic. They were already into July, and it seemed impossible that there were not as many dangers as leagues ahead of them before their search for the Passage could begin. But Cook knew, too, and his officers agreed, that they must persist, that it would accomplish nothing to return without even an attempt, having come so far and suffered so much. There was certainly no qualification in Clerke's support. As to his fellow consumptive, these long and arduous weeks of cold and damp had now reduced him to a state of total invalidism.

Anderson had not been seen on deck for a long time. Cook visited him at least once a day in his cabin, and David Samwell did what little he could to ease his sufferings. On 2 August, high up in the Bering Sea and not far from the strait, the Scots doctor was seen to be dying. He lasted through the night, but on Monday 3 August he gave up the stuggle and expired. Bligh had just sighted the coast of an island, as dour and uninviting as any they had seen, but Cook thought that it was the least they could do to name it after his friend and companion on so many expeditions, and to whom they owed much for their good health. It might be said, and was, that he had given his life for them. Everybody had liked Anderson, from the lowliest seaman being examined for 'the venereals' to Clerke ('a sensible young

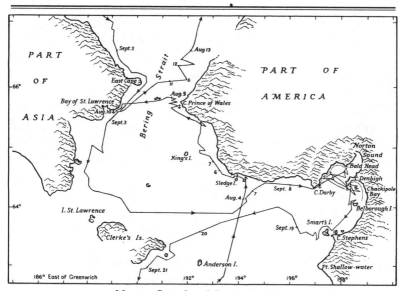

Norton Sound and Bering Strait.
(Redrawn and simplified from the chart in the published Journal)

man and an agreeable companion'), King and John Gore. He had been one of the few of his shipmates for whom Bligh felt nothing but regard and affection. He was going to be dreadfully missed.

Cook wanted to bury him ashore and provide him with an appropriate grave, but that would take perhaps two days and he wanted to lose no more. So his poor shrunken frame was wrapped in sacking and he was committed to the deep with all the honours.

Now they closed and hugged the coast of Alaska again until they reached the uttermost western point of the American continent, and named it Cape Prince of Wales. Ashore they could see the westernmost American settlement, too, and some claimed they saw moving figures. But no one was sure, and soon a storm arose in this 50-mile-wide strait, and just as Cook triumphantly recognized that the Arctic was now open to him to the north, he was driven clear across, and forced to seek shelter in Siberia in St Lawrence Bay.

For the first and only time in his voyaging he was on Asian

soil when he landed from his pinnace, with two cutters as support. There were frightened natives ashore, many of them, the women fleeing to the hills with their children and meagre possessions. And now we see once again, as if reincarnated, the explorer's marvellous talent for 'cultivating a friendship with the natives'. Alone, and disregarding the aggressive stance and spears and bows and arrows of some 50 of the men, Cook walked towards them, a massive figure but his every gesture and movement expressing gentleness and peace. They could see that he carried no arms, and his signs were of a peaceable nature. They backed away from him, indicating that none of his men should follow him, but eventually he managed to get in amongst them, taking from his pockets beads and trinkets and tobacco, for which they gave him two fox skins and two walrus teeth.

Several of the *Resolution*'s officers followed him, while the marines continued on guard at the shore. Suspicion among the natives was never entirely allayed although several of them were prepared to put down their bows and perform a dance to the beating of drums. Soon the whole shore party was mingling with the natives, laughing and trading—a perfect picture (which Webber drew) of peaceful and compassionate understanding between races so distantly separated from one another and with such different ways of living.

Like the Aleuts, their last hosts, these Mongoloid Chukchi appealed strongly to Cook's men in the short time they enjoyed with them, quite lacking in the guile and treachery, the dishonesty and hysteria, of the Polynesians. Their qualities again seemed to confirm that the farther north they probed, the nicer were the people.

Cook remained only long enough to record economically and accurately details of this remote and barren place and these fine tall people dressed all in leather—cap, frock, breeches, boots and gloves.

St Lawrence Bay provided them with one of their shortest and happiest visits, and the following day was one of the most promising and joyous of their entire cruise, combining as it did one of those rare spells of sparkling clear visibility, a touch of real summer in the air and a favourable breeze, with sightings and conclusions that seemed to favour the completion of their ultimate task.

From the centre of the Bering Strait they saw Cape Prince of Wales with its characteristic peaked hill behind, on their starboard quarter; and 25 miles distant on their larboard quarter East Cape (Cape Dezhneva), the uttermost east of Asia and unimpressive considering that honour, although the coast falling away on each side paraded high cliffs; close by were the Diomedes Islands, Little and Great, equidistant between the two continents, like two permanent guardships—say a first rate and a frigate.

All this they saw in the clear, sharp air. But farther still, and even more exciting, as if half the world had been laid out for them on a massive relief map, they could see the first shaping of both continents, the Alaskan Arctic coastline trending away, fractured and mountainous north-east and south-east; and Asia filling out south-west and north-west to the giant land mass that continued, through steppes and plains and forests, the Polish wastes, the rich German grand-duchies, the mellow vineyards and farmland of France to Cape Finisterre; which they had sailed past just two years and one month ago on the other side of the globe.

It was as if they had threaded together the whole world, that the secret of the earth's geography had been revealed to them in this one magic moment of suspension between the continents.

Their hopes had never been so buoyant. King spoke for all of them: 'We are in high spirits in seeing the land to the northward of these extremities trend away so far to the north-east, and the other north-west, which bespeaks an open sea to the northward free of land, and we hope of ice.' Then, later: 'All our sanguine hopes begin to revive, and we already begin to compute the distance of our situation from known parts of Baffin's Bay.' The temperature was in the upper 30s; so long as they were not forced too many leagues farther north, surely they could feel that they were close to success. Cook hugged the American shore, which must lead them at length to Baffin's Bay, Davis Strait and the Atlantic Ocean as it had earlier brought them to the Bering Strait.

The freak fair weather left them, as they knew it must unless this Arctic Ocean was all miracles. Gales and rain struck. They caught only glimpses of the coast, but what they saw was encouraging, if desolate: low land, snow free. No snow as they approached the 70th degree of latitude! It was more than they could have hoped for. If it was as mellow as this in mid-August, what could it be like in June, the required mid-summer month?

On 15 August the sun came out again and they could observe their latitude as 68°18N. The next day, farther east and farther north, quantities of land birds, pretty little red phalaropes, descended upon them. Webber drew one. They were lost and weary from flying in the night fog and were in such distress that many died. This had never happened to them before. Was it an ill omen? With everyone in such a high state of nervous expectation, smaller incidents than this catastrophe in miniature were read as pointers to their fate.

On the morning of 17 August both sun and moon shone out at intervals, scarcely a phenomenon, but curious and noteworthy: Cook himself was one of those who did note it. 'We got some flying observations for the longtitude, which reduced to noon when the latitude was 70° 33' gave 197° 41' E.' They were off present-day Point Collie.

The first glimmer of eventual defeat flashed warningly in the sky just before noon. There was a sudden brightness on the northern horizon, a glimmer they remembered from their deep Antarctic probes. It was called 'the blink', a warning light of ice ahead. Cook at first shrugged it aside. 'It is improbable that we shall meet with ice so soon. . . .'

His illusion did not last for long, scarcely more than an hour. At 1 p.m., north of a headland they were inevitably to call Icy Cape, the ice came into sight through the chill mist. At 2.30 p.m. the two sloops tacked close to it, and a sense of shock and dismay, an agony of disappointment, swept over them as they saw the 12-foot-high wall of ice stretching from horizon to horizon for as far as the eye could reach, as impenetrable and as bright in the grey gloom as a band of steel. Cook himself described it 'as compact as a wall'.

Not a man believed there was a way round. At 70° 44' on 18

August they were as far north as they could sail; and, suddenly, in as great danger as they had ever found themselves. Bearing out for some eight miles north-west from Icy Cape on this coastline are Blossom Shoals. The wind from the west was increasing in strength, and at the same time that this shoal water was recognized as a deadly outlying hazard to the lee shore, the wind was driving the wall fast down upon them, a threatening trap between ice and rock.

'Our situation,' wrote Cook, within such a short time of uncompromising optimism, 'was now more and more critical.'

8

Russian interlude

ONLY SUPERLATIVE SEAMANSHIP could have extricated the two sloops from the trap into which Cook had allowed them to be drawn. He made a short board north and then ordered the *Discovery* to match the *Resolution*'s short, awkward tack.

Some 175 lives depended on the timing of this manoeuvre, the combined superb skills of Cook and Bligh, the speed of the men aloft, the instant responses of the helmsman, with Clerke following, his ship handier than the *Resolution*.

The rocks in such close proximity could have smashed the ships to pieces in no time. Beyond them was the most un-promising shore any of them had ever set eyes upon—bogs, pools and rivulets, islands of mud sprouting tussock grass; no more than that to the north-east, south-west and into the far distance, an everlasting half-land.

The manoeuvre brought them into a marginally more favourable position, and the wind took mercy on them as if offering a small reward for their skill, and they were able to lay up for the short period of darkness.

Cook was still not free from all danger from the ice pack on the following day, 19 August. But now, or so it seemed to Gore and Bligh and King, their commander was no longer primarily interested in getting away from it, but rather had succumbed to its fascination. He told Bligh to take the *Resolution* close alongside the ice. He noted it was not formed into a wall at all, that there were gaps that could tempt the unwary into stretches of open water beyond, where you could be trapped within seconds. He sent boats to land men on the floes and sound the depth below the waterline. He noted that the pack had drifted five leagues—15 miles—in ten hours. The restlessness of the ice provided its own warning note, a booming sound which Clerke likened to a heavy waterfall, as ice floe drifted against ice floe with the lift of the sea.

There was another sound, which blended in grotesque harmony with this roaring, to signal danger to mariners. It came from the throats of countless walruses. No one had ever seen them in such numbers, male, female and young packed so close as often to be seen half on top of one another; a dark mass of bodies, individually indistinguishable from a distance, stirring into reluctant movement as a boat approached, the warning spreading amongst them in a slow-moving wave until all were alert but not yet determined on leaving. In a fog or at night their hoarse braying several times warned the sloops of imminent danger.

The reward for many walruses for this service was death by musket fire when the fog cleared. Rowing fast in the ships' boats, Cook's men fired musket volleys into them as they tumbled panic-stricken into the sea. Walrus hunting was not a nice business, with young clinging onto dead mothers, and many escaping though mortally wounded. Even when secured and brought back to the sloops, only a little nourishment and a great deal of misery were derived from them.

Cook, with his abiding interest in the health of his men and the economy of supplies, saw the animals as a God-given source of fresh nourishment that would provide one consolation for reaching their destination too late in the season. But after hoisting on board the 1000- to 2000-pound carcasses, skinning and draining them of their oil, hanging them to drip for 24 hours, towing them astern for another 12 hours, boiling for four hours, and then cutting them into steaks and frying them, many found the meat quite indigestible, or that they merely vomited it up.

Petitions were presented for a return to salt rations for those who could not eat the rich greasy walrus. Cook fumed. 'You damn'd mutinous scoundrels who will not face novelty!' Opinion became violent even among those who could eat the steaks. Cook refused all rations except ships' biscuit to those who would not comply. In this harsh climate, with the physical rigours of their life, men began falling with weakness. Gilbert found the flesh 'disgustful'. Able Seaman James Trevenen, complaining that the walrus fat was like train oil, came some way to explaining Cook's ruthlessness by speaking of his captain's taste as 'the coarsest that ever mortal was endued with'. But so was his treatment of his men.

Here, up in the fogs and ice and unpredictable winds of the Arctic, the *Resolution* came nearer to mutiny than ever before. Cook had to yield. There was no other course. He did so with the worst grace, and lost the maximum face.

It was now that Cook informed Gore, King and Bligh that he was going to make for Siberia in an attempt to reach Europe by the Arctic western route. They were aghast at the prospect. They had no evidence that the latitude of Russia in its far north was less than America's, and with the ice pack rapidly advancing with the onset of winter they must inevitably sail into another trap between ice and frozen shore. Cook was implacable. 'Those are my instructions!' he repeated; no matter that it was now almost September and not June, and that the Admiralty orders had already been flouted several times.

On 29 August they sighted the Russian coast, nearly 200 miles north-west of East Cape. Drizzle fell through the haze, and the land was so featureless, so lacking in trees or vegetation of any kind, that there seemed to be no means of describing it. 'A mossy substance gave it a brownish cast,' was the best the verbally resourceful Cook managed. To the north, the ice packs were still moving south. He could just make them out, like relentlessly advancing hordes of a pitiless enemy. The ships were also becoming critically short of wood and water.

Suddenly Cook seemed to have accepted that the idea of attempting to force this passage above the Asian continent was suicidally insane. He ordered Bligh to gather together the ship's

company, and with the fog now cutting off sight of the land and
the ice floes that flanked them addressed the men:

'You will know that the service we are sent on is to find a
passage west if such exists if we fail to make Baffin's Bay. Now
you see the season is too advanced for either course, and we will
head south from the ice and Arctic seas.' A cheer arose from the
men, and he held up a hand to continue. 'We shall sail as fast as
we can—' another cheer, '—and I advise economy in all things
for we shall be back for the season next year in another effort to
perform effectually our service. We are low in wood and water,
and I propose to replenish in these things in America before we
proceed to St Peter and St Paul in Kamchatka.'

The men returned happily to their tasks, and King wrote of
'the general joy this news gave'. Next summer was a long time
ahead. As if to confirm the wisdom of Cook's decision, a great
fog fell over them, and snow fell for hours without a break.
When the fog lifted and the snow ceased they saw that winter
had come to Siberia. For as far as they could see, from the
distant inland mountains right down to the sea, a mantle of
white had fallen over the land. Even the buckets on deck were
frozen hard and snow covered. They sighted an island, a white
lump on a steel grey sea, and Jem Burney accepted it as his
(Kolyuchin Island).

For five days as they groped south-east along the Siberian
Arctic coast they saw not a glimpse of the sun. When it came at
last, it was a repeat of the miracle of 11 August when they had
been given that brilliant geographical vision in the dead centre of
the Bering Strait. And it occurred in the same place as before,
leaving them with the impression that this gateway to the Arctic
was always bathed in deceitful sunshine. They anchored off St
Lawrence Bay, where they had made friendships and traded on
the way north. They could see the natives on the shore but they
affected to take no notice of the ships, which Cook, accustomed
to being received at least with curiosity, found remarkable.
Later, when he was charting what he thought was a small rock
within the bay, someone pointed out that it was a dead whale;
moreover, it was being towed in towards the shore by a group of

natives who were now huddled behind the carcass in an effort to conceal themselves.

On the following day, 4 September, out at sea in the fine weather that had prevailed since leaving the Arctic, they noted an island, which Cook marked on his chart as St Lawrence Island, previously noted by Bering as long before as 1728. On the following day a short stretch of land was again sighted. Cook presumed it to be another part of Anderson's Island; and on the 6th the massive, mountainous coast of America lifted to the north-east.

They all felt a new comfort at the sight of the valleys and rivers, and above all the forests, for they had been economizing on their fuel at a season and latitude when this was uncomfortable. Featureless Asia had been a land bare of all promise. America seemed at least to live, and by now, having ranged it for so many hundreds of leagues, a familiar and friendly place. Clerke especially felt relief at the sight of this living coastline. Both spirits and health rose with the temperature into the high 40s. 'We are now blessed with a prospect we have been strangers to since we left the river,' he wrote that evening.

They made the coast just east of present-day Nome and worked their way east into the deep bite of the sound Cook named after the undeserving Sir Fletcher Norton, 'Sir Bull-face Double Fee', who had laid on that dinner for Cook and his officers. It proved an awkward place for, while amply provided with what Cook wanted most, there was no good anchorage for procuring it easily. They filled their immediate needs by sending boats for driftwood, which in many cases burnt better than new-cut timber, and managed a few casks of water.

On the afternoon of 9 September, Cook committed another of those navigational indiscretions which were raising increasing fears in his officers and men. They were deep in Norton Bay, which is in the deepest heart of the sound, searching for a suitable beach off a suitable anchorage. A bare bluff he called Bald Head bore north-by-west. To the north-east, from a deep valley cut into the mountains, he felt sure a river must emerge. A few huts of a native village were visible on the shore west of the head. To and fro Cook plied across this bay, sounding all the time and in very shallow water, down to 3½ fathoms. Then the wind got up from the south-west, and in this tight corner williwaws could strike unpredictably. One experienced seaman commented that 'I doubt strongly whether any other man in the world would have ventured so far as he had already done, and indeed whether it was not highly imprudent.'

It was the same story as off Icy Cape, off Bonavista, and other crisis moments in this voyage: a sudden rashness or failure of judgment, critical minutes when disaster seemed inevitable and then was averted by brilliant and desperate seamanship. As before, it was as much the skill and speed of his crew as his orders that saved them. But this time the danger continued all night, with the sloops plying back, until daybreak when they managed to get into deeper water.

Norton Sound was carefully charted, and searched for good landing places, but the best were only indifferent, and the coast from which they had had such high expectations proved a disappointment. It was while the two ships were in this sound, picking up driftwood here, felling some spruce there, picking berries to cheer their diet and top branches for making beer, at the same time contriving to find themselves in several more difficult situations, that Cook reached one more of his sudden and far-reaching decisions.

It is difficult to account for them: for staying so long at the Cape; for deciding to divert first to Adventure Bay and then to New Zealand, which had led to their losing the first Arctic summer; for the many smaller decisions that had delayed them so long that they had lost their second summer; for deciding to search for a Siberian passage in the teeth of the advancing ice pack.

Now, on 16 September, still deep in Norton Sound, Cook suddenly announced that they would not, after all, winter in Asia according to his instructions. They would winter far south, in the warmth of the tropics, among the Sandwich Islands they had recently discovered, where everything they needed for replenishment, refreshment and recovery from the rigours of the Arctic lay awaiting them. Then they would make for Kamchatka to arrive in May, giving them ample time to attack the Arctic again in June.

The reason Cook gave for this radical change of plan was that he preferred that his men should not be idle at St Peter and St Paul—'inactive for six or seven months' as he put it, as if this was a prospect that he was considering for the first time, as if the Cook who had never wasted a day of exploring and charting on previous voyages, was, for more than half a year, going to have his sloops swinging at their moorings after replenishment at this remote Asian port.

No, they would proceed down the American coast to find a satisfactory watering place—now their chief need—and, in the event of failure, return to their friendly Aleuts at Samgunuda, where there was plenty of water; and where, seen through Clerke's still-lustful eyes, they would go ashore with their tobacco to revisit their 'good Friends'.

From Stuart Island, at the southern entrance to Norton Sound, Cook gave up further search for water, although every sighting along the coast revealed tumbling rivers, and bore west out to sea. On 20 September, in dirty weather, they were in shoal water again, and only got clear, in Cook's words, 'just in time'. What was this island upon which he had nearly shipwrecked them again? Too far west to be Anderson's Island. Not St Lawrence. It must be a new discovery. He named it after friend Clerke.

This was a doubtful honour. Cook had now charted four sightings of an island in the centre of the Bering Sea, and given it *three names*, believing there to be that number. He had sighted first Anderson's Island on 3 August, the good doctor's date of death; then St Lawrence Island on 4 September; the next day Anderson's Island again ('or some other land near it'); and now a new island entirely, Clerke's Island.

Giving due allowance for the unfavourable weather, this was an astonishing lapse by the great navigator, which left the *Resolution*'s master amazed and furious, as slack cartography and hydrography always did. 'A gross mistake!' he exclaimed. 'A blunder!' To Jem Burney he later wrote, 'This unaccountable error arose only from sheer ignorance . . . a disgrace to us navigators.' A navigator who had given the world the shape of New Zealand with breath-taking accuracy, in often foul conditions, and in a few weeks!

Five days later, in a gale that reduced them to two courses and a close-reefed main topsail, the *Resolution* began to leak again. As the sea poured in and filled the sloop's spirit room, a fateful weariness seized the company. Was there no end to their misfortunes?

They reached the Aleutians on 2 October in hazy weather that prevented a sight of more than one of the curving string of islands that seem to have been laid down to protect the unwary from Arctic hazards. It was Unalaska, jagged of silhouette, sawtooth in its coastline. Cook had made a perfect landfall across 800 foggy miles of an uncharted sea he had only once before sailed across. It was reassuring for them all to witness this happy consequence of his real navigational genius.

The following afternoon the sloops anchored in Samgunuda harbour, and Cook at once set his men to work, the carpenters on the *Resolution*'s leak, the seamen and young gentlemen fishing and collecting berries, which were at their peak and were as rich and varied as on the mainland in Norton Sound. The fish also provided great variety and a relief from salt rations for so long: fresh salmon and salmon trout, and huge halibut—one of 254 pounds—which was relished by everyone. These waters were a fisherman's paradise. A single boat, with hook and line, could bring back enough rich halibut for all hands of both ships in a few hours.

There was rich food on shore, too, for their tables, and from an unsuspected source. On 8 October two large pies, in the shape of big loaves and each containing a highly seasoned salmon, arrived for them by messenger from another part of the island, together with a letter written in Russian. Cook returned the compliment with some bottles of wine and rum and porter. John Ledyard, a ready volunteer for any adventure, told his American friend that he would like to carry them. Gore agreed. The marines corporal returned two days later with an account of his harsh journey, including a passage across a lake lying in the bottom of a kayak. He had been taken to a Russian trading settlement, and moreover had brought three of the Russians back with him.

The drink that Cook had sent with Ledyard was the only liquor the Russians had drunk for many months, and now the night on board the *Resolution* became a very jolly occasion, with laughter, goodwill and sign language becoming ever more excitable. Cook tried to extract some geographical details of the islands from them. He had no success, although one of them claimed to have sailed with Bering; but by that stage of the evening no one took him very seriously. Cook was obliged to await the arrival of the commander of the Russian settlement for any serious cartographic discussion. His name was Erasim Gregorioff Sin Ismyloff, all furs and beard, a magnificent colonial governor escorted by many local chieftains, and nodding acceptance of the numerous tributes of fish laid out for him by the Samgunuda natives.

His entourage set up tents by the shore, in sight of the two anchored ships, to which Cook was invited. Cook found him a sensible and intelligent man, and was mortified that he could not speak a word of Russian, nor Aleut which the governor spoke fluently. With the aid of a bottle of good brandy, Cook managed to extract some information and received confirmation that the Russian-based charts he had been carrying were indeed woefully inaccurate. It seemed that the Russian had once sailed with a Lieutenant Sind, that he had been as far north as St Lawrence Bay with him, but he knew nothing of the American coastline to the north. The Russians had been island-hopping along the Aleutians over the past years, subduing and disarming the natives, but had been halted by the warlike natives of the Alaskan peninsula—and the Russian pulled up his furs and revealed his scars as evidence.

Governor Ismyloff had, it seemed, led an adventurous life, having voyaged to the Kuriles, to Japan, China and even, once, to France. Yes, he nodded, he had heard of their earlier visit, but had surmised that their ships were Japanese, hostile and too powerful for them, and they had not therefore made their presence known.

The next day the governor dined with Clerke, and, it would seem, dined very well, departing amid a volley of his own pistol shots fired joyously into the air. Delighted at the English hospitality, Governor Ismyloff returned later with charts over which he and Cook and Bligh pored for many hours, exchanging information by sign language and drawings. It appeared that the Russians had settlements on all the larger Aleutians, their sole occupation after mastering the people being the trading in furs, above all the fur of the sea otter, which was so highly valued. Four years was a usual time to remain in the settlements, and the austerity and dangers of the life were compensated for by the high profit. But there was communication between the islands. Governor Ismyloff had a 50-ton sloop, and Cook thought it worthwhile to write a report to the Admiralty on their voyage so far in the hope that it might reach London before they returned. (It did so.)

The young gentlemen saw much of the Russians, too, making the overland 15-mile journey to their settlement with plenty of liquor for a party, and receiving in exchange leather boots and furs, and always a send-off salute of pistol shots.

In spite of the harsh climate, social life on board for Cook's men was almost Polynesian. Many had selected for themselves a woman, although as Samwell pointed out they all looked the same. They also smelt the same and were equally vermin-infested. A good public wash, as at Nootka Sound, disposed of the vermin and grease, but in spite of all their endeavours the infernal smell of sulphur remained; the sulphur, from a nearby volcano, used as a fire-lighter. Other discouragements to passion were the white stone ornaments drilled into their lower lips, the string of beads secured to the gristle of the nose and hanging down to their chin, and the tattooing everywhere. Yes, less desirable than 'the lovely ladies of the South Seas', and by no means free of gonorrhea either, but their kindliness and modesty had a certain attraction, too.

Except for the carpenters, who always had the hardest life at anchor, the three weeks on this desolate, chill island were mostly relaxing and interesting, perhaps the best feature being not the women, for once, but the food. On the long voyage south, back on hard tack and salt pork, the scent of roast halibut and salmon seemed to linger in their nostrils.

Winter was setting in, and Cook now wanted to be away. The two sloops weighed and put to sea on the morning of 26 October. It proved to be a bad day to choose. The next morning Cook's luck was out again, on this of all days, his 50th birthday. They sailed straight into the teeth of a gale, some said the worst they had experienced, and certainly the longest. For a week they were battered, stood to, progressed a league or two under storm sail, then shortened sail again. On 30 October they were just one league from Samgunuda, sighted briefly through hail and snow squalls.

One especially heavy gust tore out the *Discovery*'s fore and main tacks. John McIntosh, from Perth, Scotland, was hurled down the main hatchway and killed instantly. He was Clerke's personal servant, and was greatly missed by him. The bosun Aitken and two others were badly hurt, too.

Nor was that the end of it. On the night of 2–3 November the *Discovery* suffered the loss of her fore staysail, her foresail was split. With all headsails disabled and in howling wind, the crew furled the topsails, and later had no alternative but to lay to under the mainsail, with starboard tacks on board. It was blind dark, Clerke had lost contact with the *Resolution*, and he now ordered guns to be fired at intervals and false fires to be lit as signals. The *Resolution* returned the cannon fire but the howling gale drowned all sound.

For twelve hours they were out of touch. At dawn, the wind eased, the *Resolution* was in sight ten miles away, and by mid-day the battered *Discovery* resumed station in a very heavy sea. The Arctic had given them a final thrashing send-off; and now they headed south for the Sandwich Islands, and for the commander's greatest discovery of the voyage.

9

'Infinitely
their
superiors'*

ONCE THEY WERE out of the storm, the run south back to the
tropics from the Aleutians was mainly peaceful, the only
uneventful leg of their voyage. Spirits rose with the temperature,
everyone's health improved, even old Watman's, though Clerke
did not experience the benefit he had hoped for with the end of the
cold and damp, and Bayly was confined to his bunk with an
abscess. For the first time for many weeks the ships could be
properly aired and smoked, the ships' boats, which had taken a
battering in the storm, were repaired by the carpenters; the
sailmakers worked on the sails, and all hands worked on
oddments of rope, spinning and splicing and picking oakum.
The forge was kept busy making adzes and knives and hatchets,
every additional one turned out representing the imminent
satisfaction of their appetites.

Cook, however, was determined that his officers should
control the trading strictly, that it should be for provisions only,
that women should not be allowed on board and that all
connection with them should be prohibited under the threat of
severe punishment. This was black news for the men, who
remembered the enthusiasm of the Sandwich Islands women
and had been looking forward to Tahitian-like weeks of

* 'It is very clear that they regard us as a set of beings infinitely their superiors.'
Lieutenant James King.

hedonism. With Williamson's outrage the last time they were at the Sandwich Islands in Cook's mind, he ordered that no firearms were to be taken ashore.

What no one except his officers knew was that Cook had formulated a new trading policy altogether. In the past there had always been the difficulty of receiving an initial embarrassment of riches, so that the produce of many natives had to be refused, and they lost heart and failed to return later. By standing off and sailing slowly along the coast, Cook hoped to achieve a steadier return from different communities, and for a while to avoid the temptation of going ashore at all.

On 26 November, in clear weather and with the temperature in the 80s, land was sighted ahead, instantly recognizable as a new island to them. Cook had drifted too far to the east to strike Oahu or Kauai. As at Kauai and Niihau, they could see the white slash and hear the thunder of a great surf, then steep cliffs, and the country beyond rising to a great height. The island, which they later learned was Maui, was dominated by what they took to be a massive saddle-shaped mountain, summit and base divided by a layer of cloud. They were in fact looking at the extinct volcano of Haleakala, 10,000 feet high, its northern lip long since collapsed.

The canoes came out to them as they hove to off this hostile looking coast, and the men climbed on board with the usual agility of Polynesians. One of them shinning up the side of the *Discovery* clutched a wet and dismayed black cat that had fallen overboard and been rescued. Clerke loved his cats. At Tonga the natives had stolen them. It seemed a good omen.

At first it was only small quantities of fish and fruit and roots that the natives brought out, but as soon as Cook made known his wishes, he was answered with extravagant gestures indicating plenty. The next morning more canoes came out, well supplied with breadfruit, plantains, pigs and fruit of many kinds. This time the women came too, bare-breasted and provocative; and then, when refused entry, grimacing and mocking the sailors who so ardently desired them. The native men, too, were in a high state of excitement, gazing and exclaiming at the nails and tools laid out for them. Later the king of Maui was paddled out and solemnly received by Cook. Then, on 30 November, a chief named Terreeoboo (Kalani'opu'u) arrived alongside the *Resolution*, escorted by several canoes, and was hoisted on board with great pomp and great difficuly. He was of indeterminate age, disabled by the effects of drinking kava, eyes red, skin encrusted with scabs, and shaking all over as if from the palsy. On his head was a cap of yellow and black feathers, and he wore a magnificent cloak also of birds' feathers. His smile was good-natured, and there was no doubt of the warmth of his welcome.

For the present, Chief Terreeoboo, as they regarded him, was content to look about him with wondering and watery eyes, and ordering one of his courtiers to present Cook with three pigs. After two hours he was carried off the ship with equal difficulty, leaving behind eight nembers of his entourage for the night, their double-canoe being towed behind the sloop.

It was on that same evening that Cook set eyes on Hawaii for the first time. On the first day of December, the ships stood south for it, and soon he recognized that he was raising the greatest of all the islands he had discovered: what the natives appeared to call, and Cook wrote, 'Owhyhee'. By the next morning they were close in to the spectacular shore of massive cliffs, spines of land thrusting out into headlands, white streaks of great waterfalls tumbling into the white surf, more rivers emerging from deep valleys. Inland there were ravines with thundering torrents, a landscape of mixed barrenness and fruitfulness, a pocked landscape rising slowly and then higher and higher to the summits that were snow-capped. Snow in the tropics! Another new discovery, another new paradox. Here, it seemed, was another rich land, and far greater in extent than even Tahiti. Through a telescope, thousands of natives could be seen pouring from their dwellings and their places of work, and streaming towards the cliff tops to stare out and hold aloft white strips of cloth as if greeting a new messiah.

More white streamers flew from the canoes that were racing out through the surf towards them. Cook ordered his ensign to be broken out in reply. The sequence of events was predictable. Precautionary stones were tossed out of the canoes, and then everything was for sale, noisily and enthusiastically—bread-fruit, sugar cane, plantains, potatoes and other roots, all for sale; squealing pigs and giggling girls, too. Later some of the girls got on board against orders but before a price could be agreed they were struck with seasickness and returned thankfully to their canoes.

Ironically, Cook, who was unaware of this novel reaction, relaxed the recently and severely laid down rule. Yes, he suddenly announced, they could come on board, but not to a diseased seaman—that would result in a dozen lashes. At the same time he imposed on his men a severe new restriction. He had earlier ordered experiments to be conducted with the sugar cane in the hope of making it into a palatable drink. He liked the result; 'like new malt beer'. He considered it pleasant and wholesome, and above all its consumption would save their supplies of grog for their next Arctic assault.

At Tahiti he had taken his men into his confidence and consulted them. Now, for no reason that any of his officers could make out, he stopped their grog on alternate days without consultation and issued this beer in its place. With as much amazement as fury, he noted, 'when the cask came to be broached, not one of my mutinous crew would even so much as taste it'.

Foolish, unreasonable or over-cautious or even superstitious they might be, but the seamen judged the concoction to be dangerous to drink and refused to do so. A young gentleman claimed the seamen did taste it and disliked it. One of them, better educated than most, wrote a letter of appeal to Cook. The captain ordered all hands aft and berated them:

'So you will not drink this beer because it may be prejudicial to your health,' he shouted at them. 'It is something extraordinary that you should think it unwholesome when I and my officers have been drinking it and benefitting greatly from it. I notice that you think nothing of stealing the sugar cane and eating it raw without any scruple.'

His eyes ran over this body of men—shirtless, tattooed, bare-footed, bronzed, hardened, long hair tied back—with whom he had sailed for two and a half years, some for much longer.

His expression held only contempt for them. 'I can help you no more. Every innovation of mine—portable soup, sour kraut, all of them—have been designed by me to keep my people generally speaking free from the dreadful distemper, scurvy. I cannot help it if you choose not to drink this healthful decoction. You will be the sufferers. Had you drunk it, you would have been served grog every other day. Now the grog cask will be struck down in the hold and you can content yourselves with water. This is a very mutinous proceeding,' he concluded. 'In future you cannot expect the least indulgence from me.'

The men were dismissed and Cook stamped back to his cabin.

The sugar cane affair brought the *Resolution* nearer to mutiny than any other event on the voyage, even the walrus meat business; much nearer, for past upsets had only momentarily brought the temperature high. Cook knew better than most of his officers that small deprivations in their tight little community, two years from home and depending so strongly on the ritual of regularity, could become almost absurdly enlarged in the minds of simple men and lead to irrational violence. He had known this for twenty years. He had also known that withdrawals of privileges, small pleasures though they might be, if related to their provisions are the most dangerous of all. This time he chose to ignore these facts. So did Bligh, who knew so much and so little of the sailor's mind and responses. On these mid-December days in 1778, the *Resolution*, driven far out from the Hawaiian coast by heavy weather, was seriously close to mutiny.

How it was averted, who brought about a change of heart in Cook, will never be known for sure. But the finger points first to John Gore, and then to James King, sensible and steady officers both, who had compassion and the gift and experience for steering the great navigator between dangerous reefs. The sugar beer disappeared, but not before the cooper was given a dozen lashes for an indiscretion. It had been a sorry and nasty business. By 20 December, the grog and the girls were back, and life began to assume the pleasant pattern of gratified appetites they had dreamed about on that month-long voyage south from the sub-Arctic.

The pattern of trading until Christmas was set to satisfy all parties. Take, for example, 21 December. The *Resolution* and *Discovery* are hove to four miles north-east of Cape Kumukahi, the eastern tip of Hawaii. A great number of canoes have come out from the shore stacked high with fruit, vegetables and pigs, dead and alive. Both sloops have lowered boats which lie rolling in the swell some way off, with shipped oars, each carrying a quantity of crudely contrived knives and axes, adzes and chisels, forged from some of the last bits of iron and cask bands found in the ships.

The canoes jostle among themselves to be first close alongside the boats, the natives holding aloft pigs and breadfruit, plantains and bundles of sugar cane. There is much covetous gesturing and good-natured shouting. The sailors show off their few words of Polynesian. Some of the girls stand up briefly to make sinuous movements of their hips and clap their hands before the roll of the canoe forces them abruptly to sit, laughing at the sailors' laughter.

The trading is fast-paced, spurred on by the competition, but no one loses his head, neither the officer conducting it in the boats nor the pressing natives on both sides. When their stock is exhausted, they paddle off, calling out to the next the going rate, and more canoes struggle for the place alongside. Several enthusiastic natives leap into the sea and swim with their goods—a dead pig held high here, a bunch of big breadfruit there—emerging alongside the boat's gunwale, treading water effortlessly.

The noise mounts as the struggle for the remaining goods in the boats intensifies. There are quick flashes of temper among the natives, a struggle, a theft of a prized axe, a pursuit under-water, a shout of rage.

Before long the sloops themselves are invaded. Such is the press of numbers that they cannot be stopped. Private trading for the sailors' personal possessions adds to the din and pandemonium. Several seamen have cannily stripped buttons from their jackets and sewn them onto pieces of red cloth. This is currency of very high denomination, worth the pick of the girls, who can no longer be kept off. There are more girls in canoes slowly circling the ships, sometimes almost colliding in the heaving swell. They are trying to attract the attention of the men in the rigging, at the rails and windows. An exchange of glances, a wave by the sailor, and the chosen girl dives in, swimming speedily towards her partner, 'where we receive her in our arms like another Venus just rising from the waves', as David Samwell happily records. It is very hot.

There are sharks in the water, big killer sharks ten feet long. The natives appear unafraid of them. Edgar sees one making for a man, jaws open and on his side ready to grasp his thigh. The man strikes it hard on the head with his fists. It is as casual-seeming as it is effective. But later, when a boat's crew have hooked it successfully, and it is dragged on board the *Discovery* to be hung up, the same native bursts into tears and expresses terror.

The tumultuous waterborne fair continues until shortly before sunset. Then the boats are hoisted in, there are lingering farewells, brown figures dive into the sea and swim to a canoe. The decks of the ships and the sea about them are both left empty of the eager, gregarious and attractive brown figures. The crews are set to clearing up the wreckage like any stallholders at the end of market day. Very little has been stolen, and that of small account. The merits of the girls are discussed; and everyone seems to agree that there are no Polynesians to equal these of the Sandwich Islands. And they will be back the next day.

Two days before Christmas, the inevitable occurred. A native was left behind. The last canoe was too far distant when he came up from below. He did not appear to be put out in any way, and settled down between decks with the seamen, eating with them and sharing their life, a reminder of those far-off days with Omai, Tiarooa and Koa. Only Christmas Day proved too much for him. The *Resolution* had now been driven far to the east and out of sight of land. The double grog ration took its usual effect, and the traditional boisterous horseplay became rougher on the lower deck as the day wore on. Later, the 'poor Indian' was found cowering in a corner, evidently convinced that these insane white men were hellbent on mutual genocide. Terror of a dead shark defied while alive; terror of a bit of horseplay. Two more Polynesian mysteries for these sailors to log.

Days of satisfactory trading and seduction, ample provisions, fair skies and the prospect of several months among these delectable islands, suggested to many of them that their misfortunes were now all past. The terrors and discomforts of the Arctic, the weeks of groping through the fog and sleet of the North American coast and the Aleutians, those series of navigational crises that had them all on edge: all this now seemed a long way away. But a number of the old hands like Able Seaman Watman, Gunner Peckover, Lieutenants Gore and Burney, sensitive to the tone and character of a long voyage, had recognized almost from the departure from Plymouth the difference between this and other expeditions. The cause was difficult to identify. It had an uneasy fateful element, and it stemmed from the commander himself.

A sharp reminder that this voyage carried some kind of curse upon it, that weather and reefs and the uneven judgment and temper of Cook had all combined to their disadvantage and danger, occurred when the ships tried to double the low, rocky Cape Kumukahi to make the south-east coast of Hawaii. It was an unsuitable moment to choose to weather a headland as dangerous looking as this cape, especially considering the difficulties they had experienced in these Sandwich Islands waters on their last visit. The wind, in Cook's own words 'was continually varying from one quarter to another, blowing sometimes in hard squalls and at others calm, with thunder, lightning and rain.' In the evening with the cape fifteen miles distant and the wind blowing from the south-east, the *Resolution* stood to the south, close-hauled.

Bligh recognized the potential danger of their situation well enough, and he was on watch at 1 a.m. when the wind died and a strong north-easterly swell drove them fast towards the land. Cook was roused from his bunk as thunder crashed about them, like a portent of shipwreck; the rain lashed the decks; the flashes of lightning revealed the oily swell nudging them towards their destruction.

Two hours later the wind got up in squalls from the

south-east-by-east, and Cook attempted to tack into it, making no headway. From time to time through the rain they thought they could see a light between themselves and the shore, suggesting that the *Discovery* was in even greater danger than themselves. Then, as the first touch of daylight relieved the denseness of the moonless, rain-washed dark, they saw more lights and recognized that they came from the fires of native villages close to the cape. A short time later they discerned the white raging surf and heard its thunder above the wind. They were little more than a mile from disaster.

The wind was now from due east and rising, and it was all Cook could do to maintain their station. In much 'suspense and anxiety', as King described their state, they set all sail. But the main topsail suddenly split in two, and the main top-gallant sail was carried away, too. Rigging parted, and the men swarmed aloft to repair the damage and get spare sails to the yards. Their own speed up the ratlines probably saved them, yet again. Slowly the *Resolution* clawed herself off the shore. The reef and cape became perceptibly more distant. By 8 a.m. they were out of danger, pitching and heaving in the heaviest seas Cook had ever experienced in the tropics. The *Discovery*, far from being in greater danger than themselves, had discreetly held to the north, and could now be seen, a great distance away.

Cook retired angrily and wearily to his cabin and loosened upon the Admiralty a diatribe against navy cordage, canvas and blocks. On the *Resolution*'s first voyage she carried merchant service rigging and he had had none of this sort of trouble. Navy dockyard equipment, not for the first time, had almost made an end of them. Cook's observation was never made public. On reading it later, a shocked and mortified Palliser, primarily responsible for the scandal, saw to it that the passage was deleted from the published Journal.

Cook returned on deck in the afternoon and ordered Bligh to make another attempt at weathering the cape. It was even worse-timed than the first. Bligh was forced to give up, but this time before there was any danger to them. Learning of this, Cook made the astonishing observation, 'It was of no consequence to get around the island since we had seen its extent to the south-east which was the thing I aimed at.' Where now, his officers might ask, was the James Cook who would take bearings and soundings along every league of the Newfoundland coast, even going ashore to take triangulation bearings for a complete and accurate chart? And here, off Hawaii, he even had time to spare, and every bay and headland was new to the eyes of Western man.

A few days later, the *Resolution* did double the cape after all, and in doing so in the dark and in misty weather lost the *Discovery*. A week passed, ten days, and still there was no sign of their consort. Nor did they have a rendezvous. 35,000 miles they had sailed together, through sub-Antarctic, tropical and Arctic seas, always with a rendezvous, and never separated for more than a few hours; until now, in these waters off Hawaii.

The *Resolution* plied off the south-east coast of the island, seeing in the New Year in cloudy, rainy weather. The aspect of the shore had changed, too, from fruitful to barren—almost lunar. It was like no shore Cook had seen, except perhaps Ascension in the Atlantic, where he had last been in May 1775—'barren hills and valleys, on the most of which is not a shrub or plant to be found'. Later, he suspected the cause of the barrenness of this Hawaiian coast but was puzzled that he could see no volcanoes. Was the brownness of the soil caused by tilling the land, or was it really just a desert?

It was a difficult coast to approach, too, with no visible landing place, let alone sheltered harbour. Bligh suggested he should take a boat and sound it and look for fresh water, of which they were now in need. He got ashore somehow, as Cook knew he would, and came back with a report of rain water only, lying among the rocks, brackish from sea spray.

There was little or no trading during those first days of 1779, and what there was from the occasional daring canoe-paddler was for salt only, a reflection on the poverty of the land. Sometimes, in breaks in the cloud, a vast desert was revealed, rising higher and higher, and then more steeply towards the towering snow-capped summit of Mauna Loa, almost 14,000 feet above them.

The men's mercurial spirits fell, and touched their lowest

point as they ran down this coast. For ten weeks they had cruised off these islands, and never once been ashore. They were without women, without fresh fruit, now severely short of water, and back on hard tack and salt beef. All they had in abundance was salt itself, with nothing to preserve in their empty casks.

The *Resolution* was in a sorry state, with tatty rigging, doubtful yards, leaking decks, another leak in her hull, and generally in sore need of a refit. No one could understand why they did not complete their circumnavigation of this island in search of an anchorage; and failing that, try one of the other islands.

To add to their misery and feeling of resentment was the burden of concern about the *Discovery*. Had she after all foundered on the rocks which had so nearly claimed them? They had many friends, shipmates almost, on board this smaller sloop.

In fact, the *Discovery* was safe, but hardly sound. Her rigging was in a worse state than the *Resolution*'s after her last battering. They had even been unable to swab down the decks as all the water ran through into cabins and mess decks. But, as was often the case, her morale was better than the *Resolution*'s. Weak as he was, Clerke was better able to keep up the spirits of his men, and Cook *heivas* were unknown in this ship.

Clerke had cruised for five days in the same waters after losing the *Resolution*, having no knowledge of Cook's intention to double Cape Kumukahi. Then he had steered south in search of his commander, weathered the cape far out to sea in safety, and then made for the coast again on a westerly heading. There was no sign of the *Resolution* along the barren south-east coast, and risking that he had not slipped past on an opposite course in the night, he weathered Kalae (South Cape), and just before midday on 6 January, after 13 days of separation, Clerke was told that the lookout had sighted the mast-tops of the *Resolution* to leeward.

As soon as they were close enough, Clerke ordered a boat lowered and made for Cook's ship, hove to in choppy seas and trading with the canoes surrounding her. Neither commander thought the other looked well. Cook appeared all right physically, but his old shipmate had never seen him so taut and irritable. His nerves appeared on edge, and he seemed satisfied with nothing.

As for Clerke, the deterioration in his appearance after the passage of weeks since their last meeting was most marked: grey, parchment-like skin, sunken cheeks, more evidently weak than Cook had seen him. He would never last another passage to the Arctic. He would never last for more than a few months, surely, even under the best conditions. Yet it was remarkable how his good spirits prevailed, and an undimmed eagerness was in the eyes that had always reflected mischief and sprightliness.

The two captains agreed that a safe anchorage must soon be found. Not only was it essential for the men and the ships. But the winter was already passing, and the work that must be carried out to make their ships again fit for the Arctic ice would certainly be lengthy. Neither Cook nor Clerke held out great hope for success. It was only essential that their original instructions to be in the Arctic at June midsummer—even if two years late—be adhered to. The thought of missing three seasons was not to be entertained.

The happy rejoining of the ships did not spell the end to their anxieties and frustrations. This island was fast confirming their conviction, established earlier when they were struggling with the intractable currents and winds off Kauai and Niihau, that these Sandwich Islands were as deceitful as any they had sailed among. The winds backed and veered, and for all their skilful efforts, the currents took the sloops out to sea and back to the coast as if they were two pieces of driftwood. There could be a flat calm at noon, a gale at dusk. Clear skies one hour, a rapid build-up of cloud, torrential rain blotting out everything, .the next hour.

The land looked as unpromising when they glimpsed it distantly between rain squalls as on the rare moments when they could put a glass on it in clear weather from less than a league. A heavily indented coastline, few white banners now, and without promise of shelter and always with a raging surf; a bleak hinterland rising to distant forests; a steeper slope of gaunt brown desert rising to the same towering volcanic peaks that were like hubs governing the whole configuration of the island—a shape they could now trace as a stubby arrow-head pointing east towards America.

Score marks, black or deep brown, or even touched with green, cut broad swathes from the mountain summits across this landscape, lava trails of centuries of disturbance, the oldest sprouting recovering vegetation. Nothing much grew along here, as evidenced by canoes that came out with nothing to barter except their women. How did they live? was a reasonable and unanswered question. But the women looked well enough fed, and on 10 January the men recovered their spirits for a while when girls from three canoes that had been paddled ten miles out to sea, white streamers aloft, clambered on board and at once broke into a dance routine. 'They strike their hands at the pit of their stomach smartly and jump up all together,' wrote one delighted onlooker, 'at the same time repeating the words of a song in responses.' Very Maori-like and quite unlike the Tahitian dances. It was a brief welcome break in their troubles.

12 and 13 January were the two low-point days of this frustrating passage. The wind varied from a fresh gale from the west, to a calm, to breezes from the south-east and south-west. For the whole of the 12th they were too far offshore for any canoes to venture out. On the 13th a few intrepid paddlers came out, but they had little or nothing for trade. Everyone on board was heartily sick of the sight of the barren south headland of the island, and the sterile coast north of it. The next day was little better. Cook at one time thought he had sighted the northern point of the island, but any progress they made in the morning was lost later.

One more of the abrupt changes in their fortunes occurred on the 15th. The weather cleared so that they distantly glimpsed for the first time the southern shores of Maui, and a fresh breeze took them briskly up Hawaii's west coast, which was perceptibly changing its aspect from brown to green. Groves of coconut trees, tilled green land, grass-thatched huts, told of fertility as sudden as the steadiness of the wind and the clarity of the air. This wayward island had once more changed its aspect, and in time with this change came the canoeists, white streamers aloft, plying their paddles in swift rhythm—a dozen, then many more, all loaded with the fruit and the pretty girls of this shore.

Suddenly, as Cook remarked, they had 'an abundance of everything'. On that evening, nearly every seaman had a girl in his hammock or wrapped in his arms in some corner of the deck. They could have had three or four. They were replete with fresh fruit and pork, and many of the girls were tipsy with their share of the grog ration. A few of the Hawaiian men remained on board that night, too, wondering at the great size of these ships, which they measured with outstretched arms, trading trifle for trifle from time to time. Their canoes, some of them large double sailing canoes with accommodation for 40, were towed behind the *Discovery* and *Resolution* as they progressed slowly up the coast.

Early on the morning of 16 January, Cook said to his master, 'Mr Bligh, be so good as to take a boat, well armed, and take soundings.' They could both make out what Cook called 'the appearance of a bay'.

'It seems promising, sir, and the indians friendly enough,' said Bligh.

Cook spoke harshly. 'Whatever the nature of the indians, if it is a safe anchorage, I shall resolve to anchor in it. This has been a poor island for shelter and our need to refit is very great.'

Bligh, accompanied by Edgar in a boat from the *Discovery*, set his men to row on a north-easterly heading for a deep cup cut into the cliffs, meeting on the way a great armada of canoes of many sizes, all bustling towards the ships at twice their own speed and waving their paddles and streamers and singing out as they passed.

As Bligh closed the shore he became more than ever confident that this would be a safe anchorage for them. It appeared protected from all points, except the south-west, and from his recent observations gales from this quarter were unlikely. The dominant feature of this bay was a cliff like a knife-cut through black volcanic rock in a slight curve, falling from some 400 feet at the eastern extremity to a point a mile to the west where it shelved into gently rising land from the western promontory of the bay. This cliff, this black insurmountable barrier to the hinterland, appeared to fall directly to the sea, but as the day wore on and the tide ebbed, Bligh observed that there was a narrow beach at its base—black rocks and pebbles. As they were to learn later, the name of this bay, Kealakekua (Karaka-kooa, Cook called it) means 'path of the gods', deriving from this great slide in the hill to the sea.

The village beneath the cliff on the east side gave its name to this bay, the next to the south was called Waipunaula, and there were several more on this side. Across the bay on the western promontory was Kaawaloa, which Bligh could see as a scattering of thatched huts and one or two larger buildings among a grove of coconut palms.

The eastern end of the cliff became a steep slope of scrub which in turn rapidly flattened with the curve of the bay, to form the deeply indented, flat but rocky eastern side of the bay. At the north-eastern corner, close to the shadow of the cliff at its highest point, was a remarkable-looking structure some 18 feet high and rectangular, which he guessed was some kind of *morai*.

Bligh measured the bay at just under a third of a league (⅞ mile) across the inner basin and rather greater from what was to be called Cook Point to the west and Palemano Point almost due south. There was a reef off Palemano Point but no other navigational hazards.

Bligh brought his boat in close to the big stone religious structure and waded ashore ahead of his marines escort. The natives came out to greet him, without signs of fear or shyness, and offering gifts and girls for their pleasure. Bligh treated them coolly but with friendly words and gestures. He had no time for trading or for nonsense with the women, and he ordered his party to keep together and follow him.

A little way north, in a pretty setting among palm trees, he found a large pond. He tasted its water and found it brackish, which was to be expected so near to the sea. But not far from it was a rock pool, covered at high tide but filled with fresh water from a stream at low tide. It would supply them with all their needs, and the distance to the beach was short enough for rolling casks.

Bligh contented himself with a rough sketch, returned to his boat, and took soundings off shore before ordering the boats back to the ships. His exploration had taken all day, and the light was failing when he came alongside the *Resolution*, which was still surrounded by canoes.

'It is a good, safe anchorage, sir, 14 fathoms with a sandy bottom where I sounded,' he reported to Cook in his cabin. 'There is pure water on the east side here.' He pointed to his rough sketch. 'And there is plentiful wood not too far inland. There is a great forest from which these indians have taken the timber for their canoes. The indians are friendly enough.'

Cook nodded. He was clearly relieved at the report. 'We will stand into this bay tomorrow. And the indians are indeed friendly. Too friendly and too numerous. I have a chief named Ka-haw-rooakea on board as a guest. But there are too many girls. I have asked Mr King to rid us of a number of them.'

While Bligh had been exploring and reporting on the bay and its facilities, the ships hove to were experiencing the biggest invasion they had ever suffered in the Pacific. At first it was in hundreds, the vanguard that Bligh had met while rowing ashore. Later the numbers swelled into thousands, 10,000 was one estimate, from a thousand canoes of all sizes, besides others who swam out the great distance like porpoises, and clambered on board from the water.

Samwell counted no fewer than 150 large sailing canoes each with some 35 on board.

The *Discovery* took on a list from the weight of bodies, and parties of men were deputed continuously to drive a number overboard in order that the ships could be worked. Men and women, boys and girls, with their pigs and plantains, their breadfruit and root crops, swarmed over the decks, below decks and up into the rigging. The girls threw themselves into the arms of the sailors, exciting them by any means to lie with them, in full daylight, anywhere amidst this press of bodies. Their appetites, one sailor observed, were unquenchable.

The same pandemonium and noise prevailed as on the other side of this enthusiastically hospitable island, and as this first

day drew towards its end, a feeling close to hysteria prevailed
about the ships. It was not only that the press of numbers was so
great, that as soon as fifty shrieking bare-breasted brown girls had
been driven back into the sea on one side, more than this number would appear over the waist rails on the other side. Then
wholesale thieving began on an unprecedented scale. The
Discovery had all her backstay tackles cut out of the chains for
their iron hooks and thimbles. The *Resolution* suffered the loss of
all the lids of the ship's coppers, and some enterprising under-
water swimmers began prising out the nails securing the copper
sheathing. The firing of muskets loaded with small shot, and
even a four-pounder cannon or two, did not deter the thieves,
who clearly thought themselves innocent of any wickedness,
though the range of the cannon balls greatly impressed some
chiefs.

But neither the thieving, nor the unprecedented numbers,
accounted for the hysterical element which grew rather than
diminished as this day of noise and pandemonium wore on. It
was rather as if the ships had by chance arrived at some
culmination in the lives of this community, a climax that would
affect their destiny. Polynesian excitement was one thing, and
they were familiar with that. In this bay the whole population
gave the impression of being on the brink of mass madness.

Two more chiefs who came on board the *Resolution*, tall,
handsome and authoritative, called Parea and Kanina, did
something to diminish the hysteria in the air by assisting the
crew in clearing the decks until only a manageable number of
women were left for the seamen. Kanina simply picked them up
if they were dilatory, and threw them like rocks into the sea.

Cook presented gifts to these chiefs and talked to them
haltingly, with much sign language, until the next visitor arrived.
He was a holy priest, a man evidently much feared and
respected by all, who came on board with great ceremony and
deference. He was very old, very ugly, his skin peeling, his body
shaking from kava-drinking. His name was Koa, and he was the
High Priest of Hawaii. With him were members of the hierarchy
of the island's priesthood, Priest Hiapo, Priest Kaireekeea, and
others.

It was soon evident from the behaviour of High Priest Koa that, however much he was feared and respected by the natives of this bay, in his own turn Cook was the first object of their veneration. First, with elaborate gestures of respect, Koa presented Cook with two coconuts and a small pig; then, on rising, called for a red cloth from one of his aides, and wrapped it about Cook's shoulders as if preparing him for some divine ceremony. Next a large dead hog was produced and laid before Cook, along with a great quantity of fruit and roots. The word 'Orono' was repeated many times, the new title by which Cook would be known in this place.

Later, after High Priest Koa had dined with Cook, had withdrawn and been carried down the gangway to his canoe, Parea and Kanina indicated that Cook was invited ashore for a further and greater and even more holy ceremony. So far Cook's predominant feeling was one of relief that they had at last found a safe anchorage with all their needs available. The ceremony with Koa he accepted stoically as one more of his duties as commander, to be endured in order to strengthen their relationship with the natives. Throughout his voyages over a period of more than ten years he had participated in native ceremonies, in the Society Islands, New Zealand, the Friendly Islands and elsewhere, many of them involving the payment of tribute. This was only one more of the same kind. Or was it? In the afternoon Cook went ashore with King and Bayly escorted by Parea and Kanina and their staff, prepared to face the tedium of the formalities that lay ahead, and determined at the same time to select the best site for Bayly's observatory and for a carpenters' work area.

The canoes directed Cook's boat to Kealakekua village on the eastern arm of the bay. As soon as they were ashore Cook, King and Bayly were conscious of the silence by contrast with the bedlam surrounding the ships. They were conscious, too, that the atmosphere was quite different from any previous ceremony, as if they were at the same time venerated yet restricted: half god, half captive. Kanina took Cook firmly by the hand when they landed on the volcanic rock shore and led him away as if he were his prisoner. A native walked ahead of them incanting a dirge which was repeated again and again. The word Orono was predominant, and when the natives who had come out to greet them heard it they prostrated themselves.

The party proceeded along the length of a wall of lava rocks, through the village, towards the *morai*, here called a *heiau*. It was as huge and impressive as Bligh had described it, a rectangular black block set among the waving coconut trees and about 20 by 40 yards in size, surrounded by a fence.in a state of disrepair on which were set 20 human skulls. Crudely carved grotesque wooden images grinning down at them from poles added to the threatening aspect of this holy place, which also featured an elaborate but dangerous looking scaffold with 12 more images set in a semi-circle, and a high altar upon which lay some sacrificial offerings, among them a lot of fruit and a huge half decayed hog.

Four natives had now appeared, ceremonially dressed and bearing wands tipped with dogs' hair, and chanting the word Orono. Other officials conducted Cook towards the altar. Here Koa was given a small pig which he dedicated to Cook by smashing its head on the ground and then holding it over a fire until it was dead, when he began chanting a song with one foot resting on the body. Next, Koa, with much more chanting, then raised the stinking hog, held it high and let it fall to the ground with a heavy thud and a scattering of dust.

Another firm hand guided Cook, with King and Bayly following, towards the scaffolding, which they ascended by ladder, hesitantly and doubtfully because of its ancient and precarious construction. Ten more assistants to the priest appeared, bearing a hog—a fresher one this time—and a large piece of read cloth. They all prostrated themselves when they came near to the platform and repeated the Orono incantations.

The ceremony had already lasted a long time, but was by no means at an end. Cloth and hog were raised onto the platform where Cook's party stood uneasily, expecting the scaffolding to collapse beneath them at any minute. A bearded priest, who introduced himself as Kaireekeea, passed cloth and hog to Koa, who in turn wrapped the cloth about Cook and presented him with the hog. A very long exchange of litanies was conducted between the two priests before Koa suddenly seized the hog and threw it onto the ground below as if attempting to dash it to pieces.

King described the next stage, reserving special praise for the patience and endurance of his commander. 'The captain descended,' he wrote, 'and Koa led him to different images, said something to each but in a very ludicrous and slighting tone, except to the centre image, which was the only one covered in cloth and was only three feet high. Before this image he prostrated himself, and afterwards kissed, and desired the captain to do the same, who was quite passive and suffered Koa to do with him as he chose.'

These high rituals developed by slow stages into a feast, brought on by more natives. But before that there was a very long exchange of responses between the priests, with the shrivelled, shaking figure of Koa in firm command; and then a ceremony of rubbing Cook's face and hands, arms and shoulders, with a cloth soaked in saliva-sodden coconut chewed by Koa. Then came the familiar kava-chewing and spitting. And finally the hog was cut up into pieces, which in turn were passed by Koa to Cook with signs to eat. Recalling the putrid hog the priest had so recently been handling, Cook's endurance at last broke, and even after Koa had, in a gesture of kindness, chewed the pork first for him, the captain found it impossible to swallow.

The long and tedious ceremony and feast were at last over, and Cook indicated that they would like to set up an encampment at the *heiau*. Chiefs Parea and Kanina understood at once, and when Cook selected a walled field of sweet potatoes, with many assurances of compensation for the owner, the priests stuck their wands on the wall to consecrate and 'taboo' it.

They now returned to their boat and as they passed through the village, Cook in his red cloak, men, women and children all dropped onto their knees and lay with their heads to the ground until they had passed. 'Orono! Orono!'

Koa was there to bid them farewell, small, aged, bent and shaking, his sore eyes staring out at them from his dreadfully peeling face. Cook indicated that a party would come ashore the next day, distributed some small iron gifts to the send-off party of priests and chiefs, and embarked in his boat. Out in the bay, the *Discovery* a quarter mile away, the *Resolution* a little farther off, were still surrounded by hundreds of canoes, and the sound of thousands of raised voices, of shrieks and laughter which they had heard as if coming from a distant surf, was now much louder. It made a strange contrast to the silence that had prevailed in the village.

King said to Cook, 'With all the encumbrances, sir, I should still have been better pleased to be received by the Friendly Islanders than here.'

Cook agreed. He, too, had been made to feel uneasy by the overcharged reception from the natives on board the ships, and equally by the reverence and abasement with which they had been received on shore.

What he did not know, and never did learn, was that he had been acknowledged as the incarnation of the god Orono. His arrival was the greatest event in Hawaii's history. *Orono makua* was the Hawaiian god of the season of abundance and relaxation, who was said to process clockwise about the island to be greeted by white banners and elaborate ceremonies of obeisance. Cook had arrived, at the appointed time, and by reason of his decision to sail slowly offshore for better trading, had indeed progressed slowly and clockwise about the island, his standard at his masthead a divine acknowledgement of the white banners ashore. And properly, and according to tradition, he had come to rest at Kealakekua, 'the path of the gods', in his miracle giant canoe opposite the *heiau* in the middle of the god's season, in time for the great ceremonies of worship annually accorded to him for the abundance of riches he caused the soil to grant them.

Cook may have been late for the Arctic summer but the timing of his arrival off Hawaii could not be faulted. His subsequent actions did have a near-divine verisimilitude, and the climax had now been reached with the ceremonies he had just undergone. Everything that he experienced over the following two weeks conformed with the legend of the god Orono. It is little wonder that his reception—'this remarkable homage' as King described it—here at Hawaii was so different from that at any other

Polynesian island, and that the natives had been thrown into a state of near-hysteria. Not even the oldest citizen with the longest memory could recall hearing from his oldest ancestor of the appearance in incarnated form of the great god Orono.

Some days later Cook learned that the king of Hawaii, no less, had arrived at Kealakekua and was to visit him. James King was at this time stationed ashore in command of the encampment to ensure its security. He had had no troubles at all from the natives. The men would sometimes sit on the wall watching the incomprehensible activities of Bayly and his assistants and the impressive activities of the carpenters with their wonderful tools that could work timber with such seeming ease and accuracy.

From his point of observation ashore, King watched the long-heralded arrival of Hawaii's monarch in a great procession of canoes that came round the headland and into the bay. He saw the king's 60-foot long canoe stop at the *Resolution*, and a figure in a multi-coloured cape being helped up the gangway. The king and his staff remained on board for some time, and then re-embarked in their canoes and made for Kaawaloa on the western arm of the bay, the seat of the king of Hawaii.

On the following day, King was informed that this monarch would be visiting him with Cook, and that Bayly's observatory was to be the scene of more ceremonies. There were many preliminaries to this event, which clearly attracted the attention of all the people. The king came off in a great canoe, attended by a second with many chiefs and a third stacked high with the island's finest produce, from yams to hogs.

The escorting chiefs, dressed in elaborate cloaks and hats, began to sing as they approached the *Resolution*, chanting with great solemnity, and then standing up. As they came near, the reception party on board observed that the second canoe held also High Priest Koa, hunched and shaking as always, elaborately attired and surrounded by hideous busts made of basketwork. These were covered with multi-coloured feathers, the eyes represented by pearl oyster shells, the distorted mouths filled with the teeth of dogs.

The king himself remained seated when his canoe came alongside the gangway. He was dressed in a magnificent cloak and with an equally magnificent feather cap on his head. The chanting died, a voice called out. It was suddenly clear that the king had come out only to escort Cook to the shore, where the ceremonies were to take place, and would not again be coming on board.

Cook was pulled ashore in his pinnace. King had already turned out the marines' guard, who made their usual dishevelled and sloppy showing. The formal meeting was to take place in Bayly's largest tent, and the lieutenant observed carefully the king and his entourage as they approached from the shore. Flanking the king were his sons, and following behind a number of chiefs; the king's nephew Chief Kamehameha, a ferocious-looking individual with his long hair plastered all over with paste and powder; a particularly vigorous and important looking Chief Kalimu; another muscular individual, Chief Ku'a, and several more. A parade as formidable as it was bizarre.

As to the priesthood led by Koa, they formed up beside the Royal Marines to present a combined ecclesiastical and military reception for the island's monarch and his first shore reception for the ship's captain.

King watched Cook waiting patiently for the ceremonies to begin, a weary expression on his face, towering above all these islanders in spite of his middle-aged stoop. Then the king stepped forward, standing erect and without assistance but shaking all over as badly as High Priest Koa.

It was not until this moment, when in turn the king tore off his cloak and put it around Cook's shoulders, and then lifted his hat and placed it on Cook's head, that he exposed his face for the first time. Like the high priest's, it was peeling and covered in sores, the eyes were red and watery, but the expression through the ravages of kava was happy and benign.

To the lieutenant's astonishment, the King of Hawaii was none other than the Terreeoboo they had met off Maui: it was King Terreeoboo receiving the great god Orono himself.

IO

'We have lost our father'

THE BEST OF all the Polynesian islands—that was everyone's verdict. Neither at Tonga nor the Cook Islands nor Tahiti, and certainly not in New Zealand, could they feel such confidence in the goodwill of the natives that they could wander about freely on their own or in parties. Never had they met Polynesians who seemed to possess all the qualities of their race—cheerfulness, good manners, generosity—and none of the demerits of dishonesty, violence, and cruelty.

As soon as Cook had completed his ceremonials as the god Orono, even the initial hysteria of their reception, which had made some of the men uneasy, had died down. Hawaii might not be the most beautiful Polynesian island, the stark volcanic landscape contrasting unfavourably with Kauai, but Kealakekua Bay was still the most pleasant place to be.

David Samwell and two of his friends went for a long walk into the country, noting the excellent state of the plantations of taroo, sweet potatoes, ginger and sugar cane, black volcanic dry rock walls neatly dividing the fields. Four miles inland they came to the beginning of the forest, rich in breadfruit, mighty koas, thorn trees, and with a marvellous population of birds with beautiful plumage and sweet songs.

Another enterprising party, inspired by John Ledyard, who would have walked to the moon if there had been a rough track to it, set out to climb Mauna Loa from which they hoped to see the full extent of the island. The ever-adventurous George Vancouver was joint leader with the corporal, and the sturdy Scots gunner from the *Resolution*, Robert Anderson, was among the others. Koa provided this party with an escort and guides, who had in fact never been up the mountain, clearly considered the expedition insane, and nearly died of the cold at night. Ledyard and Vancouver never reached the summit, but David Nelson collected a great number of rare plants for Kew gardens, and they were able to sketch a long stretch of the coast from the highest point they reached above the line of the forest.

Another party of young gentlemen went canoeing, upset in the surf and were rescued by eager natives, including children. The courage and skill of the islanders in the water was a constant source of wonder, and it was an extraordinary sight to witness quite young children swimming out with their surf boards, plunging through rollers that, seconds later, broke crushingly on the rocky shore. Surfing looked exciting but no one had the swimming confidence to emulate the natives.

There were many other spectator sports for their amusement on shore, from a diabolically complicated form of draughts, to wrestling and boxing. There was dancing and singing in the evenings, and no end of interesting and attractive sights and experiences. The to-ing and fro-ing with the ships was an entertainment in itself. King Terreeoboo his wife and family were frequent guests on board the *Resoluion*, the young boys especially enjoying themselves. The king and Cook had sealed their friendship by exchanging names as well as almost daily gifts, including from Cook a complete chest of tools. Every visit was a spectacle. On another day a very fat and very grand lady was paddled out to the *Resolution*. She wore about her waist a great quantity of red and white striped cloth, round her neck a thick bunch of plaited human hair with a bone ornament suspended from it. On both her fat arms were rattling bracelets of boars' tusks, and in one hand she held a fly swat, in the other a live cock. When god Orono was pointed out to her, she presented Cook with both, and condescended to receive from him some small gifts in return.

There was little that the visitors could offer in the way of entertainment in return. After their disastrous showing on that earlier occasion, the Royal Marines did not go through their evolutions again, and there were very few fireworks left. However, Cook ordered these to be let off one evening. They were received without evident response, but several of the men claimed hopefully that the natives were silent in astonishment.

For the carpenters there was, as always, very little leisure. They had set up their workshop alongside the observatory and made several expeditions into the forest to fell trees. Again High Priest Koa was an invaluable help, providing them with labour and escort and provisions. The sailmakers were busy, too, and there was much caulking to be done on board. But for most of them, it was a pleasurably relaxing time.

Clerke, on a day when he was feeling strong enough, came ashore. As a great priest to the god Orono, he was received with almost equal reverence. Characteristically, he expressed impatience with all the prostrating, and instructed Koa ('the bishop', he called him) to get them to their feet. When it came to accepting honours and obeisance from the hierarchy, however, he knew that there was no alternative to suffering them as patiently as he could. Chief Parea met him at Kaawaloa, with a servant carrying the inevitable pig, a hen and a coconut. Clerke was bedecked by Parea with red and white cloth strips, and carried to the chief's house. Here hogs were roasted. It was difficult for the fastidious Charles Clerke to retain any appetite after watching the customary Hawaiian method of preparing them for the table: first part-suffocation with a hand over the snout, the singeing over a fire and extraction of the guts while not yet quite dead, and the filling of the belly with hot stones before covering over for baking. Twenty minutes from suffocation to the plantain leaf plate, while the spitting and preparing and drinking of kava went on as an appetizer.

Twenty more live hogs were presented to Clerke before the end of this particular ceremonial, so that, fresh or salted, he began to feel that he could never eat pork again.

Just as George Vancouver and John Ledyard demonstrated their adventurous inclinations, so the other young gentlemen and the officers followed their own enthusiasms—John Gore fishing, Bayly making observations, Nelson botanizing, Bligh making a detailed survey of the bay that was later printed in the official journal; although to his fury, without proper credit to him. Samwell observing, too—the prettiest girls, of course, but also canoe-building methods, the many uses to which the natives put plantain leaves, comparing a dancing girl's evolutions to those of the hornpipe in England; Burney listening to the singing and making a record of it in his journal.

Apart from gonorrhea, the health of the men was good here, but several who had still not quite recovered from the rigours of the Arctic were taken ashore and sent to convalesce in a well-aired tent beside Bayly's observatory. Among them was old William Watman. He did not seem to be at all well and Samwell was concerned for him.

Then, of course, there were the girls; numerous and all so beguiling. During the early days there were so many that even the most licentious seamen had to agree that they were interfering with the work on board. Every morning more swarmed into the sloops than could be driven off. However hard the officers strove to eject them without too much harshness, offence was often given. Cook consulted Kanina and Parea about the problem, and the two chiefs again agreed to thin the ranks. The mere presence of these two powerful men should have been sufficient to cower the girls and send those not wanted about their business. But such was their enthusiasm that the chiefs had baskets of stones brought on board, and the seamen were shocked to see their lovely creatures being pelted with them and driven into the sea to swim ashore, bruised and disconsolate.

For all those at the tabooed encampment, the difficulties in getting a girl for the night were insuperable. Their duties kept them within the confines, but the girls knew that it was more than their life was worth to break the taboo and leap over the wall. Even Queen Terreeoboo would not dare to do that. Several lusty marines approached Koa about the problem, offering him bribes to break the taboo, but to no avail. This body of men suffered enforced celibacy at night for the length of their duties ashore.

As the last days of January ran out, the gifts for god Orono continued to be brought in from the country in the quantities demanded by King Terreeoboo and 'the bishop'. One officer compared the officials who appealed for produce for the white men's great canoes to a bellman striding through an English town. In the centre of a coconut grove the yams and sweet potatoes, breadfruit and sugar cane and dead hogs, grew higher every day until Cook and Clerke wondered how they could accommodate it all, and the salting down of pork went on apace.

Before the month was out a subtle change came over the generous, gregarious people of Kealakekua Bay. King was one of the first to sense it, so did Jem Burney, and Bayly at his observatory. There was no diminution of friendliness, more an interrogative note entered into the natives' attitude to them. At first one or two were observed rubbing their bellies and glancing meaningfully at seamen passing by in the villages and even patting theirs to suggest satiated appetites. Cook reported that, at their last meal together, King Terreeoboo enquired about the likely date of their departure. It was the first time that such an enquiry had been made by a Polynesian community, who normally regretted any suggestion that they might be leaving. Moreover, the king expressed pleasure when Cook said they would be leaving soon. Yet there was no lessening of the pomp and abasement when Cook came ashore: everywhere prone bodies, and a hush of respect for the divine presence.

Were they over-staying their welcome? Was the great Orono, god of abundance, exacting too great a tribute? There was a growing conviction amongst Cook and his officers that it was time they were away—off to chart the other Sandwich Islands more comprehensively, and then head north again, back to Asia and the Arctic for their final assault on the North-West Passage.

Until this time, towards the end of January, they had been remarkably free from thievery. Cook and Clerke had taken special precautions to reduce the risks to a minimum, but since the first hectic days little of value had been taken. Every night the ships' boats moored to anchor buoys were filled with water to their gunwales as double protection, against the powerful morning sun as well as the temptation of theft.

Nevertheless, thieving began on an accelerating scale—a length of rope here, more metal objects, personal possessions. King found himself trading with a native who had the carving knife from the *Resolution*'s gunroom tied to his wrist. Ashore, a thief contrived to get into the tent where King and Lieutenant Phillips were sleeping, ignoring the taboo and making off with cutlery and pewter plates. Clerke was reduced to flogging a thief on board the *Discovery*, an inconceivable action a week earlier.

Then there occurred two events which were often talked about in the months ahead, and many sailors—not all of them superstitious either—related them to the catastrophe closing about them with relentless inevitability.

There is evidence that seems to justify what at first sight appears to be an act not just of tactlessness but impiety in Cook's first order of the morning of 1 February. He wanted firewood—like water, his appetite for firewood was insatiable. On closing any shore his eyes studied the terrain first for signs of water, and then for evidence of timber. At some pains, and with native help, they had brought down much timber from the forest over the past weeks. But the long, decrepit fence about the *heiau*, with its carved figures, was immediately to hand and would make excellent kindling.

Cook asked King to talk to the High Priest and say that he would like to buy it *in toto*. 'I must confess,' recalled King, 'I had at first some doubts about the decency of the proposal, and was apprehensive.' But Koa appeared to treat the matter as of no importance and shrugged his shoulders at the idea of any payment. However, King presented him with some iron tools, and ordered a party of seamen to rip up the fence and cart it to the shore. Several natives who, it seemed, had already taken some of the rotting palings for themselves, vigorously assisted them.

When the task had been completed and the boats were about to put off, King noticed that all the carved images had been taken, too, the seamen recognizing their value as mementoes when they returned home. Koa did not appear to be much troubled by this profane pillage either, when King drew his attention to the images in the boats, and asked for the return only of the small one which he and Cook had kissed at the ceremony and two others that had been standing in the centre of the *heiau*.

It is a curious incident for which Cook has been both heavily blamed and strenuously defended over the years. Its effect on the natives, on the priests and on Koa in particular, remains a matter for speculation. There can be any number of reasons for Koa's seeming indifference: pride or generosity or a wish to ingratiate himself with such an important chief as King, for whom he had a special regard. It is equally possible that King misunderstood his gestures, expression, or words, or all three. It would not be the first or last time that there had been such a misunderstanding.

Whatever the reason, the incident cannot be considered in isolation from events two weeks hence. Some related it to another, more solemn event that occurred later that day.

Able Seaman Watman had assured Samwell that he was recovered, was discharged from the convalescents' tent, and resumed his duties on board the *Resolution*. He was welcomed back by Cook after his absence, and appeared to be better than for a long time. But he was suddenly struck by a haemorrhage of the brain, lingered on for two days, and expired on the first day of February. His loss was felt severely by all ranks. Watman was a thoroughly good, generous, obliging and unselfish man, and he had that rare quality in the navy of remaining equally popular with the lower deck, the warrant officers and commissioned officers. The young gentlemen loved him, and for Cook he had always been a talisman of good fortune with a special place in his heart.

The news of his death soon reached the chiefs ashore, and knowing of his relationship with god Orono—a great priest perhaps?—they begged that he might be buried by the *heiau*. It was a curious and moving ceremony, combining the solemnities of the complex and inscrutable Hawaiian religion with plain Church of England. Cook conducted the ceremony on behalf of his church first, and with the reading completed, Priest Koa took over. As the grave was filled he threw in a dead pig, coconuts, plantains and other provisions to keep him fed on his long last journey.

At the head of the grave, Watman's shipmates erected a post, with a board attached to it (wooden pegs, not nails) carved:

'Georgius tertius Rex 1779
Hic jacet Gulielmus Watman'

Far into the night they could hear across the water the lamentations of Koa and his priests about the grave where hogs were sacrificed for the able seaman from Reigate, Surrey, around a fire at the foot of his grave.

The familiar preparations for departure were carried out during the following days. The last of the massive supplies was ferried out to the sloops. The carpenters, weary from their work, returned from the forest with the last of the timber, which was stowed on board the cutters and smaller boats. The tents were struck, the delicate business of carrying out Bayly's instruments was completed. On the evening of 2 February, the natives of Kalama put on a boxing contest, and two of the *Resolution*'s last rockets were ignited as a signal of farewell.

For James King, however, it was an unusual last evening. With the departure of the last of the shore equipment, he indicated to Koa that the field could now be un-tabooed. This was done by the priests with the same speed and seeming perfunctoriness as the original tabooing. Expectantly awaiting this command was a large number of natives, who rushed in the moment it was safe to do so, searching every inch of the ground for any lost trifle.

Koa turned to King and told him that, as the son of Orono, he would like it very much if he should stay behind. If you do we will make a great man of you. Then, anticipating King's objection, he added, we will hide you in the hills until the ships are gone.

King, taken aback but touched by this extraordinary offer, refused with as much regret as he could muster, and proceeded to his boat after last farewells and much lamenting on the part of the little shaking old man and his priests. King later learned that both King Terreeoboo and High Priest Koa had broached the matter to Cook. King wrote, 'The captain, to avoid giving a positive refusal to an offer so kindly intended, told them that he could not part with me at that time but that he should return to the island next year, and would then endeavour to settle the matter to their satisfaction.'

Koa seemed pleased by this promise, and in order to extend his time with god Orono and his 'son', asked to be taken to Maui on board the *Resolution*. 'And I wish henceforth to be known as "Bretannee",' announced the high priest with solemnity.

It was 4 February, a fine, warm early morning. The natives of Kealakekua Bay were up early for the word had got about that the great ships were leaving. The shores on both sides, divided by that great black slab of cliff, were thick with dark bodies, some waving white cloths. Many canoes had already been launched and were about the sloops as they unmoored and sailed majestically out of the bay on an east by south course with many canoes following, and with many of the most determined and faithful women still on board.

For Cook's men there was a strong measure of regret at parting after the contentment occasioned by this visit. For the Hawaiians, it had been a strange two and a half weeks, busy, emotional, traumatic even, like no other period in their lives or their history: an unpredicted divine descent upon the steady round of the seasons; an event of great satisfaction paid for at a great price.

These Hawaiian waters, which had always proved so treacherous and vexatious to them in the past, appeared at first predictable and serene—almost too calm, so that they made scarcely perceptible progress and many canoes with many girls and chiefs and priests, and even the king, came out to visit them. So often their departures had been accompanied by hostile seas and adverse winds that they felt that this fine weather matched their pleasant experiences at Kealakekua Bay.

By the early morning of 6 February they were at the northern extremity of a deep bay just south of the northern tip of Hawaii, Upolu Point. They had all but completed their clockwise circumnavigation of the island, in accordance with the legendary annual practice of Orono.

Bligh wished to chart this bay. There was the appearance of a good harbour, and many waterfalls suggested good watering, too. To locate another anchorage on the wild coastline of this island would be a hydrographical bonus. Koa—or Bretannee as he continued to call himself—said he would like to accompany him and assist with his prayers all that god Orono's chief wished to achieve.

Bligh had boats hoisted out and took the shaking high priest and his party along the shores of the bay. It was beginning to blow by the time they had neared the shore, and Koa—no doubt warned by his priests of deteriorating weather—put survival above spiritual matters and insisted on being landed. The storm came up quicker than he, or Bligh, had judged. Other canoes towing behind the *Resolution* and *Discovery* were also departing with some of the girls and heading back to Kealakekua Bay.

The squalls died for a while, but then the storm burst on them. The *Resolution* was brought under the mizzen staysail only, and Cook began to worry about his master's safety. Bligh was all right, but it was blowing hard when he began the passage back to his ship, having satisfied himself that this was not a satisfactory harbour. There were many canoes heading for the shore, and cries of alarm at the rising seas from some of them. Bligh found one small one upturned, an old woman and two men clinging to it, their cries for help quite disregarded by their countrymen who were also rapidly paddling ashore. He got them into the boat, where they collapsed exhausted, and he tried, but failed, to salvage their canoe.

Then it came on to blow very hard for 36 hours. The *Resolution* saved another canoe from destruction and brought on board two men and a boy of four, who were in the last extremes of hunger and exhaustion. There was much seasickness among the Kealakekua women who had not disembarked earlier. But they were better off than those who had left and failed to reach the shore in time, many of whom were drowned.

On 8 February, three years to the day—almost to the hour—since Cook had volunteered at the Admiralty to command this voyage, the *Resolution*'s foremast split. Once again the slackness of Palliser's dockyard men at Deptford had hazarded their voyage. This time the consequences were to be fatal. They could not proceed in this condition, especially as the old leak under the buttock had opened up again like an unhealable wound.

In the storm-swept dawn light, Cook had to make the critical decision on where to put in for repairs. The weariness that increasingly overcame him at times like this, added to the fury that overwhelmed him, left him momentarily exhausted and helpless. Should he continue to Maui and trust that he would find shelter on the west or southerly coast, which he had not yet traced? Or perhaps to another island? Kauai and Niihau had already proved unpromising. In all their sailing among these islands, Kealakekua Bay was the only safe anchorage they had discovered.

To give himself time, Cook sent Bligh across the storm-tossed waters to acquaint Clerke of their situation. Now both ships' companies were conscious of their dilemma. They had already been too long at Kealakekua Bay. They had cleared the whole area of its immediately available food. All those hogs could not have been given to them without depriving the people of supplies. Repairs would take at least a week, probably two weeks.

Cook set himself upon the safer of the two courses open to him, and at 10 a.m. on the morning of 8 February, the two sloops bore away south for their old anchorage, 'all hands much chagrined,' wrote King, 'and damning the foremast.'

The weather teased them all the way: first calm, so that some of the natives ventured ashore or were taken off in the *Resolution*'s pinnace; then squally, a strong gale at night, more squalls, and they found themselves miles south of the bay and once again in danger from breakers. Cook ordered guns to be fired to warn the *Discovery*, and succeeded in hauling off, but only by a narrow margin.

It was not until the morning of 11 February that they managed to get back into the bay, the *Resolution* mooring with her stream anchor in the same place as before. Cook at once ordered the sails unbent and the yards and topmasts to be struck. Then he had the fore and main topmasts unrigged and had the carpenters ashore with a marine guard to set up a repair shop as before.

Everyone noticed the profound change in the atmosphere in the bay, and the contrast with their first arrival. The waters were empty of canoes, the black lowering line of cliff revealed not a single spectator along its crest. Some of Cook's men were uneasy, others, as King observed, felt their vanity hurt that they were so disregarded. Just as they were concluding that the entire population had been evacuated or struck down by some plague, a single canoe put off and headed for the *Discovery*. Up the sloop's gangway there climbed a ferocious looking chief wearing a fine red-feathered cloak. He was the king's nephew, Kamehameha, whose appearance had so alarmed them three weeks earlier when he had introduced himself with Terreeoboo's two sons.

Clerke greeted him with surprise. 'Where are all the people?' he asked.

'My uncle the king is away from Kaawaloa. The priests have tabooed the bay until he returns on the morrow,' the chief explained, taking off his cloak. This sign that he wanted to trade was clear to Clerke. The price was to be nine iron daggers, *pahoas* they called them, nothing else and no less, for the cloak.

Clerke agreed to the transaction. The daggers were brought up and the chief's entourage armed themselves with them, apparently satisfied with the deal. He was watched with suspicion, and also a measure of disgust, for he had a boy with him whom he constantly fondled, exposing without shame what that arch-heterosexual David Samwell called 'a detestable part of his character'.

The sailmakers, carpenters and the marines, with King again in command, found no objection to their reinstalling themselves in the old field with their tents by the *heiau*. Bayly even got his clock and telescopes ashore with his tents. The priests seemed as friendly as before, and were ready to taboo the area again, and the carpenters were able to go about their special craft of cleaning out the mast's heel, dealing with the sprung fishes, shaping new ones from some hard toa wood they had providentially kept from Moorea.

On the following morning King Terreeoboo arrived in the bay as he had before, in great style and at a fine pace. At once the waters of the bay were un-tabooed, and suddenly it was almost as if nothing had changed since those days when there were always numberless canoes plying between shore and ships, and the noise and bustle of trading lasted from dawn to dusk.

But things were not the same. Just below the surface, violence now lurked among these Hawaiians. A great black seam of hostility had been thrust up close to the surface as if Mauna Loa's volcano had erupted again and a lava stream of hatred were about to flow.

King Terreeoboo, shaking and held steady by his sons, came out to the *Resolution*. Why had they returned? What were they doing? How long this time? 'He appeared much dissatisfied,' noted Jem Burney.

Another incident on board the *Resolution* emphasized the contrast. A deal for a hog was being agreed just as Chief Parea was passing by. 'Do not let it go at that price. Ask for more,' he told the native firmly. The sailor who was negotiating the deal swung round on Parea, thrusting him aside and cursing him. The expression on the face of the chief who had been humiliated in front of a commoner was one of terrible fury. He turned and made for the gangway with his entourage. A minute later he was seen being paddled in his double canoe heading towards the *Discovery* and greater mischief.

Clerke had already been visited by the king. Now he was informed in his cabin of Chief Parea's arrival. He wished to see him, and Clerke, who was feeling weak and low that day, agreed. The handsome chief, who had done so much for their comfort and convenience on their last visit, was in an angry mood, unlike the king who had seemed to Clerke to be placatory and had even left him gifts of a cloak and a hog.

'You have beaten one of my men. You will bring violence upon yourself if you beat my king's subjects,' he shouted at Clerke.

Clerke had indeed beaten a native. All that day the thieving had gone on in the *Discovery*, becoming so out of hand that he had had to clear the ship. At one point a native had snatched from the blacksmith's forge a chisel and a pair of tongs. The smith, who was working up long daggers from old iron, for which there seemed to be a sudden and insatiable demand, shouted out and by good fortune the man was caught before he could escape from the ship, although he succeeded in passing on his stolen goods to another, who disappeared in the crowd. To make an example of him, Clerke had ordered him lashed to the shrouds and given forty lashes. He will not be released until the tools are returned, a chief was told. Half an hour later the blacksmith received back his chisel and tongs.

Now, as Clerke wearily argued with Chief Parea in his cabin, there was a shout from above. 'Thief! There he goes!'

Clerke rushed up on deck. 'He just grabbed them and ran, sir,' a sailor told him. 'He was too fast for us.' It seemed that, under the cover of Parea's conversation with Clerke, one of his attendants had climbed up the side of the sloop, raced across the deck, and seized the same chisel and tongs that had been stolen in the morning. He had dived overboard and, with the skill and speed of all these Hawaiians, was swimming towards a waiting canoe — Parea's own canoe — as if unimpeded by the weight of steel.

Marines with muskets were awaiting orders, and Clerke at once told them to open fire. Several volleys rang out, all the shots missing the swimmer. Edgar was already in the small cutter, calling orders for men to man her, and George Vancouver leaped in to join the master. The thief had been hauled into the canoe, and the natives were digging in their paddles, causing the vessel to accelerate at a rate no ship's boat could match, and heading towards the village of Kealakekua.

On board the *Resolution*, John Gore was in command in the absence of his captain ashore. The *Discovery* was barely two cables distant to the east, with the village of Waipunaula beyond, and he could observe, as if momentarily frozen, the crisis at the point it had reached: Figures standing on the *Discovery*'s poop firing at a speeding canoe that was trailing a white wake across the still waters of the bay; a small boat alongside the *Discovery* with four men on board, all dipping their oars for their first stroke in pursuit; the *Resolution*'s pinnace just offshore by the *heiau* turning as if to intercept the canoe that was heading for the north-east corner of the bay where the black cliff arose to its highest point; and distantly on the shore in front of the *heiau* and the tents, a party consisting of the tall figure of Cook himself, King at his side, Gore's friend Corporal Ledyard, and a marine private carrying Cook's double-barrelled gun, all running along the beach to intercept the natives where they would land.

The American concluded in that frozen moment that there could be only abject surrender by the natives, or a clash of arms. In the present mood of the natives he judged violence to be inevitable and ordered his men armed and the gunners to their stations.

Violence had in fact already broken out. Between the two thefts from the *Discovery*, Clerke had ordered a watering party ashore in the sloop's cutter under the command of a steady Londoner, 33-year-old Quartermaster William Hollamby. Hollamby got the casks on shore at the watering place by Kealakekua village, and—as was now the custom here—let it be known that there would be generous payment in iron tools for native labour. He had no difficulty in recruiting these men, and the mixed party for a while worked in harmony rolling the casks up to the rock pool, filling them, and rolling them down to the shore again to parbuckle them into the boats.

There had never before been any difficulty here. In fact it had always previously been a happy business, with women and children watching and laughing, unattached girls flirting with the men and sometimes interfering provocatively with their work. This afternoon it was very different. The women and children disappeared altogether, and before long a murmuring sound arose from the village. Native men wearing protective mats over their torso were seen slipping in and out among the close growing palms, shouting at them, throwing stones from time to time, and making darting assaults on some of the natives working in the party.

A minor chief appeared, to lend authority and a sharper edge to the assaults. The quartermaster, whose party was unarmed—

an indication of their misplaced trust—at length left and ran along the beach to the encampment to appeal to King for help.

King ordered a marine with side arms to accompany Hollamby to the watering place, but within a few minutes the quartermaster was back again.

'The rascals are becoming very insolent, sir, and quite disregard our escort,' he said. 'They seem only to pay regard to a musket.'

King ordered another marine private from his party to accompany him, armed with a musket this time. The three men hastened along the beach. Boldly, King walked into the palm grove, seeking out the chief, and when he found him told him firmly to desist or he would use the musket on him.

The hostilities seemed to cease as quickly as they had flared up. The chief and his warriors dropped the stones in their hands and returned to the village.

'If you have more insults, inform me at once, Mr Hollamby,' King said. He returned along the rocky shore and saw Cook's pinnace heading in. For a moment, King wondered if his captain had come to investigate the trouble, but it seemed that he had merely wished to check on the carpenters' progress.

When King told him what had been occurring up at the watering place, Cook broke into a rage. 'All day we have been troubled with these indian thieves,' he stormed. 'Please instruct Corporal Ledyard to have the muskets loaded with ball instead of shot, and if there is more stone-throwing or insolence, fire upon them.'

Then he stamped off to inspect the mast and talk to the carpenters. He was still dark with fury. King retired to the observatory to acquaint Bayly with recent events. It was at this moment that the trouble on board the *Discovery* merged with the unrest on shore, and the events of the afternoon hastened towards their confused climax. The sharp cracks of musket fire from the sloop brought Cook and King and many of the party from the encampment to the shore. They saw the same scene that Gore had witnessed from a diametrically opposite bearing, with the contestants approaching instead of retreating.

'Come with me, Mr King,' Cook ordered. 'There has clearly

been a serious theft and we must endeavour to recover the article.'

King comfortably outpaced his captain, escorted by Ledyard and a private, but still failed to intercept the canoe in time. The moment its twin prows touched the shore, it was surrounded by a shouting mob of native warriors, all wearing mats and behaving in a threatening manner as they were joined by the crew of the canoe.

King could see the small cutter following in the wake of the canoe, and when he waved towards it, he saw George Vancouver at the prow pointing towards the shore and shouting at the top of his voice. Owing to the noise of the mob, King did not hear a word, and turned to see how far Cook was behind him. To his surprise Cook's tall, stooping figure was striding off in the opposite direction. Uncertain for a moment what he should do, King then decided that his rightful place was beside his captain, so he ran to catch him up.

'Do you have tidings of the thief, sir?' King panted out.

Cook shook his head. He was in a greater rage than ever, the length of his strides in tune with it. King had to trot to keep up with him, and from time to time, Cook himself broke into a run.

They were almost at Kalama when he halted and demanded of a native if the thief was close by, pointing at his big double-barrelled musket in the hands of the marine and threatening to fire it. He appeared so beside himself with rage that King began to doubt whether he knew what he was doing. The frightened native pointed south along the beach, eager to give any information that would rid him of this dangerous party.

A little way farther along the beach, Cook apprehended another group and asked them the same question in his halting Polynesian. Now there were no cries of Orono on his approach, no prostrating; rather the reverse, and King discerned signs that—as he put it—'they were amusing us with false information'.

Several times more the party of four halted, demanding, threatening, the tallest of them gesticulating and shouting, and then proceeding at a trot the way he was directed, always away from Kealakekua. At last Cook turned to his escort and thundered out, 'We shall never apprehend the rascal by this means.'

It was getting dark. Lanterns had been lit in the ships out in the bay. They had come so far that they saw the *Discovery* and *Resolution*, and the black cliff and the promontory and village of Kaawaloa on the other side of the bay all from an entirely fresh, perspective. They had reached Palemano Point, and all four men were weary and discouraged.

'We must return to learn if they have the indian,' said Cook. He was without his jacket and King could see the sweat glistening on his chest. Although the light was fading, the temperature was still in the upper 70s.

By an odd chance, one of so many in this affair, the moment James King turned to pursue his captain, Parea's canoe was launched again, and Parea himself slipped ashore from the *Discovery* in another canoe. The firing from the sloop and the violent reaction to the theft had frightened the natives into returning the chisel and tongs, as well as a tub from the *Resolution* which had been stolen earlier. The canoe bearing these goods came alongside the small cutter, and Vancouver took them thankfully from the natives.

That could have been a satisfactory end to the unhappy affair, but Edgar, seeing the *Resolution*'s pinnace close by and presuming it was carrying arms, called to Cook's cox and told him to come alongside. He and Vancouver transferred into the larger boat, and Edgar directed it ashore and the small cutter to remain. It was their plan to seize the canoe and hold it against the surrender of the thief.

The crowd had dispersed when Edgar jumped ashore and began to push Parea's canoe into the water with the intention of paddling it back to the *Discovery*. But, on being observed, the alarm was raised, a crowd of natives rapidly assembled and charged noisily and aggressively back to the beach, Parea himself at the head.

The chief began to remonstrate with the master, who attempted to shrug him aside and complete the launching with the aid of Vancouver. Parea therefore seized him, pinioning his arms behind his back with one hand, and holding his hair with the other. A seaman responded by leaping out of the pinnace with an oar with which he beat Parea about the head and shoulders until he released Edgar. The fighting now became general, the scene tumultuous. Stones began flying, and a great number of natives closed about the unfortunate crew of the pinnace. Parea demonstrated his frightening strength by seizing the oar out of a seaman's hand and breaking it in two as if it were a twig.

Edgar called for arms, but there were none, and the seamen were reduced to taking the remaining oars and stretchers from the boat, and attempting to beat back the crowd. The stones, launched by slings or thrown with great power and accuracy, were severely bruising the men as they struggled to clear the beach.

Edgar and Vancouver recognized that they had no hope against these numbers, and began to retreat towards the water's edge. There was no chance of getting the pinnace launched again, and now in fear for their lives and a good deal hurt, they leapt into the sea and began to swim out to the small cutter, a perfect fusillade of stones splashing in the water about them, one or two striking their heads.

The master and midshipmen were the last to retreat, and neither could swim. Pursued closely by the sound and fury of the mob, and hit many times with stones, the two men waded out towards a rock offshore. It was not far enough. Some of the natives were already rushing in after them, throwing stones and wielding their spears. One of them carrying half of the broken oar, got close enough to Edgar to swing a blow at him, but slipped in doing so, striking Vancouver a glancing blow instead.

Both men would certainly have been killed if Parea had not intervened. His massive voice carried infinite authority, brought immediate obedience. Instead, the natives turned their attention to the pinnace with the same fury and relish. It was the iron they were after. These people had become iron mad. Not only could it be made into unsurpassed weapons. It was also apparently the currency of these white men. Bolts were knocked out, the gangboard and rudder taken for their iron pieces.

Bleeding and in great pain, Edgar and Vancouver waded back bravely to protest. Vancouver endeavoured again to launch the boat, and was knocked down, losing his hat. Again Parea interceded, fearful of the consequences of a death on his hands. He ordered his people to launch the boat, and indicated to the two men that they should leave in it. Vancouver protested that without oars they were helpless. Parea despatched a warrior to bring them back. One and a second that was broken were recovered. They were enough. Rapidly, before there could be another change in their fortunes, the master and midshipman rowed out into the bay.

It was not quite the end of the affair, for Parea was clearly still fearful of the consequences of the violence. His canoe was launched and he quickly caught up the labouring cutter and handed back Vancouver's hat. Will Orono be angry? he called out to Vancouver, who understood the language. Will he kill me? Will he allow me on his great ship again? I will return all the iron tomorrow.

The midshipman indicated that Orono would not kill him. And he would allow him on board again. On hearing this reassurance, the canoe came close alongside, Parea reached out his arms towards Vancouver as a sign of renewed friendship, and the two young men rubbed noses. Then Parea turned briskly about and his canoe raced away towards the setting sun and Kaawaloa. There would be a full report of the business to King Terreeoboo before darkness set in.

It was nightfall when Cook's party arrived back at the encampment. All were tired, and King was in pain from an abscess on his chest which had been disturbed by the running. The captain's anger still smouldered dangerously, and flamed up again when he heard an account of what had happened. His coxswain took the brunt of it for becoming involved at all, but the whole pinnace crew were severely reprimanded, too, for leaving their station and taking it upon themselves to seek vengeance when they were unarmed and their enterprise certain to fail.

Cook turned to King, who had now applied a poultice to his abscess, which still hurt. He spoke gravely and determindely, and with a note of despair, clearly bent on a line of action he would have wished to avoid.

'I am very sorry, Mr King, but the behaviour of these indians must at last oblige me to use force. They must not,' he continued, 'imagine they have gained an advantage over us by what has occurred today.'

King assured his commander that he would post a double guard for the night, and Cook then ordered him to call at the *Discovery* early the following morning to learn any further details of the affray from Edgar and Vancouver.

This, then, was the situation in Kealakekua Bay at 9 o'clock on the evening of 13 February. The two sloops lay at anchor in the same positions as on their last visit, some 400 yards south of the great black cliff, the *Resolution* to the west of the *Discovery* and therefore closer to the village of Kaawaloa, where the king and his family were residing. The boats, which had been employed so busily during the day, lay moored to a buoy secured to the ships' anchors, and all filled to the gunwales with water.

In a tight shipboard community word travels fast and the climate is mercurial. Details of the thefts, the shooting, the fight on the beach, the abortive hunt by the captain, his demand for violent measures even, all were known within a short time of their occurrence. When Cook returned on board the *Resolution* on that evening, the atmosphere was at once infected by his own mood of angry determination.

There was no need for Bligh to emphasize the need for special alertness by those on watch, though he did so; and Phillips ensured that his men's muskets were loaded with ball and that they did not sleep at their posts, never an easy task.

The mood ashore was similar, although in their much more vulnerable circumstances there was a stronger element of fear among the carpenters, sailmakers, observatory personnel and marines and officers. Ledyard was an exception. The corporal had never been afraid of anything in his life and looked forward cheerfully to a fight and the opportunity of killing a few indians.

An hour later, one of the marines thought he saw some figures—five in all—creeping about the *heiau*, and reported the sighting to King. 'Fire if you see one but only if you are sure of your mark,' said the lieutenant.

At midnight, the same sentry saw another figure advancing, this time towards the observatory. He raised his musket, dropped it clumsily to the ground (was it the rum to keep up his spirits?) and it exploded harmlessly.

After that sudden but ineffectual explosion, the shore party who were not on guard, and perhaps some who were, slept undisturbed.

In the *Discovery*, Jem Burney was keeping the morning watch. The loss of his ship's large cutter may well have occurred on the earlier watch, but it was at first light, with the faint hint of the dawn touching the snowy heights of Mauna Loa, that he noticed the absence of one of the boats. He looked again closely at the water as it was easy to be deceived when so little of a boat showed, but there was no doubt that the mooring from the buoy of the bower anchor lay empty in the sea.

He hastened to Clerke's cabin, confused by a sense of fear and guilt. It was a dreadful loss to his ship which somehow must be remedied, and there could be no doubt now that this day was to be one of violence.

It was close to 5.30 a.m. when Clerke was awakened by Burney and informed of the loss. The captain was feeling poorly, and lapsed into a dreadful fit of coughing as he sat up in his bunk. 'I must inform Captain Cook at once,' he said when he could speak. 'Please call my servant, Mr Burney.'

He dressed rapidly. Burney had already ordered a boat to be made ready, and this was waiting at the gangway with its crew when Clerke appeared on deck. One of them had retrieved the mooring rope from the missing cutter and showed the end to the captain as he embarked. It required only a glance at the four-inch hawser to confirm that it had been cut through, doubtless by some knife forged by one of the ships' blacksmiths.

Cook was warned of the imminent arrival of his second-in-command and was dressed and ready to receive him. 'It is the large cutter,' Clerke told him. 'The indians seized it in the night. This is a serious matter.'

'It is indeed, Charles. They are set upon doing us every injury and we must not allow them to obtain the upper hand.' Cook paused for only a moment. His anger was under control. As Clerke later reported, 'After some conversation upon the subject, Captain Cook proposed that his boats should go to the north-west point of the bay and mine to the south-east point to prevent any canoes going away.'

Cook's proposal was that they should trap in Kealakekua Bay all the canoes, from great double sailing canoes to the little family canoes which could be counted in hundreds at any one time, and hold them to ransom against the return of the cutter. It seemed an eminently sensible proposition.

'You will please instruct your officers to drive any canoes on shore if they should attempt to go away,' Cook instructed Clerke, 'We shall fire our great guns if it should prove necessary.'

Clerke acknowledged these instructions, descended to his boat, and was rowed rapidly back to the *Discovery*. The ship's launch and jolly boat had both been emptied of water and prepared, with crews standing by. Edgar, Burney and Rickman were awaiting his return and Clerke called out his orders before he climbed painfully up the gangway. Already there were signs of movement from both sides of the bay, with canoes being launched as if Cook's blockade had been anticipated.

'Mr Rickman, you will take the launch and this boat with four marines and your own arms,' he called out. 'Mr Peckover, see to it that the guns are primed and all crews standing by.'

The efficient gunner had already taken these precautions, the necessity of which was evidenced when one of the *Resolution*'s four-pounders was fired, the roar echoing from the black cliff. Burney saw the ball send up a tall column of water close to the bows of a sailing canoe that was creeping along the western shore.

Bligh was first away from the *Resolution*. He had no marines, and was thankful for it. He had selected the best crew he could muster in the short time available, every man with a musket loaded with ball. From the stern of the large cutter he could hear a deep humming sound as if from swarming bees emanating from the shore. He did not need the visible evidence of a great gathering of warriors along the cliff top and among the coconut groves back from the shore, with the women and children of Kaawaloa, Kealakekua, Kalama and the other nearby villages trekking inland on a vast exodus.

Bligh had for long advocated a tougher line against thieving natives, and regarded the recent outrages as the inevitable consequence of his captain's softness. The *Resolution*'s master was spoiling for a fight, and there was no doubt in his mind, too, that today there was going to be much spilling of blood. He could see several canoes being launched from Kaawaloa. A large one had set a sail and was speedily making for the point at the entrance to the bay. He set a course to cut it off, and at the same time heard one of his ship's great guns speak. The gunner had aimed well. The white fountain arose a dozen yards ahead of the canoe.

Bligh cursed his own men, who had paused in their rowing in order to turn and witness the fall of shot. 'It'll be a dozen lashes for every man if that canoe escapes, damn your eyes!' he shouted. The canoe had not paused in its flight and was travelling at twice their speed. Bligh waited for another cannon shot from the *Resolution* but none came, the gunner, Anderson, evidently calculating that they were too close to the target. The grunts of Bligh's men in the cutter straining at the oars formed a disparate chorus with the rising drone of anger from the Hawaiian warriors. A seaman turned to spit as a mindless shriek sounded out from Kaawaloa.

Bligh shouted, 'Rest on your oars, prepare to fire!'

The men drew in their oars and reached for the muskets at their feet. They were drifting now 50 yards from the black rock shore upon which the surf broke heavily. The big, high-prowed double canoe was sailing fast towards them before the wind, turning at a slight angle in an attempt to get between the cutter and the rocks.

Bligh's ten men remained seated, holding the muskets to their shoulder awaiting the order. When it came, the noise was appalling, and against the ringing in their ears they could scarcely hear the master's sharp instruction to reload.

The effect of the volley was all that Bligh could have hoped for. Many of the natives leapt into the water. The remainder redoubled their efforts, shrieking words of abuse and fear, and steering their craft for a small inlet among the rocks. There was no need for another volley. In less than a minute the canoe had been abandoned, and the dark figures were pulling themselves out of the water to join the flight of the rest.

Bligh was satisfied, but gave no sign of it.

John Gore, too, witnessed the effect of Bligh's musket fire with satisfaction, and commented on it to his captain. Cook had not spoken since ordering the single cannon shot. Now he said to his servant, 'Fetch my double gun, and look sharp. Mr Gore,' he confided to his first lieutenant, 'I shall proceed ashore with Mr Phillips and bring back with me the king to detain him on board. I believe it necessary to act swiftly against these indians. We have witnessed the effect of musket fire upon them. So also have the indians. They will not stand the fire of a single musket now.'

Gore was greatly troubled when he heard these dangerous words from his commander. There must already be thousands of warriors assembled about the bay. How could Cook hope to bring the old king back to the ship against his will, and the will of these savagely aroused warriors? It was a suicidal plan, and Gore was tempted to say so in the strongest terms. But the expression of determination on Cook's face told the American that any remark contrary to his captain's wishes would only bring forth an angry response.

Gore limited himself to a plea. 'I trust, sir, that you will not proceed without powerful protection. You may be assured that I will keep all our starboard battery trained on the town.'

Cook was loading his gun with steady deliberation, one barrel with shot, the other with ball.

'Mr Phillips will accompany me, with Sergeant Gibson, Corporal Thomas and seven privates. That will be sufficient. Should the king have fled with his family, we shall occupy the morning burning houses and seizing canoes.' Cook turned to the master's mate standing by. 'Hail Mr Williamson and ask him to stand by to support me when I proceed ashore.'

Lieutenant Williamson, commanding the launch, had put off after Bligh in order to seal the gap between the ship and Bligh's more distant cutter. He now rowed back towards the ship in response to Lanyon's call, and Cook, with his servant carrying his musket, followed Phillips and his party down the gangway and into the pinnace. Already waiting to escort his captain wás Lanyon commanding the small cutter, with a crew of four young gentlemen, Trevenen, Ward, Taylor and Charlton.

Gore stood at the head of the gangway, watching his captain settle into the stern of the pinnace as he had so often seen him before, embarking to land on so many islands in the Pacific; but never before under such threatening circumstances, or—as the American believed—with the real prospect of never returning.

James King was equally troubled. He had been the first of the shore party to learn of the theft of the cutter. He had been hailed by Burney as he was rowed close by the *Discovery* en route to the *Resolution*. Clerke had just returned to his ship, and King arrived on board at the critical moment when Cook had decided on the more positive and dangerous action.

When King began to recount the details of the previous evening's occurrences, Cook had interrupted him 'with some eagerness', as King reported. 'It is my intention, Mr King,' Cook had announced grimly, 'to bring on board and detain the king and some of the chiefs as hostages against the return of the cutter.' Cook completed to his satisfaction the loading of his musket. 'Your business is to quiet the minds of the indians on your side of the bay. Inform them that they will not be hurt. And, Mr King, keep your party together and on their guard.'

King stepped into his boat just before his captain embarked in the pinnace. He watched the pinnace, escorted by Williamson in the launch and Lanyon in the small cutter, proceed north from the *Resolution* towards the landing place at Kaawaloa. King landed on the beach by the *heiau* and was met by Bayly, who was anxiously awaiting news. The hostile murmur was scarcely audible here, being carried away on the easterly wind. But there was an atmosphere of tense expectation among the marines, carpenters, sailmakers and others in the encampment, as well as among the natives who stood about uneasily.

Several canoes had been launched, including one under the command of that important and vigorous Chief Kalimu, but had been deterred from paddling far out into the bay by the fate of the canoe from Kaawaloa. King remembered Cook's last words, ordered Ledyard to post his men with muskets loaded with ball, and to open fire under provocation, and then proceeded to High Priest Koa's house.

Koa and his priests were in a nervous condition. 'I explained to them, as well as I could, the object of the hostile preparations,' King wrote in his report. 'I found that they had already heard of the cutter's being stolen, and I assured them that though Captain Cook was resolved to recover it, and to punish the authors of the theft, yet that they and the people of the village on our side need not be under the smallest apprehension of suffering any evil from us.'

Nor was there the smallest risk of Terreeoboo being harmed, King assured Koa in answer to his alarmed enquiry. The high priest appeared a little reassured by King's account, but as the lieutenant returned to the encampment, he heard the boom of cannon again, and saw across the bay puffs of smoke rising from the *Resolution*. It was difficult at this distance to be sure where the shots landed but there appeared to be much activity over at Kaawaloa and there were a number of canoes off the village.

King checked that all the marines were at their posts and retired to the observatory with Bayly. The carpenters were working on the mast in a desultory way that morning, their muskets stacked nearby and guarded by a marine private. Even Ledyard felt unsettled by the events, the rumours of events, the evident arming of the natives, and the concentration of so many of them from more distant parts. The lowering black cliff behind them, the consciousness of an ever-increasing press of numbers, lent an air of claustrophobia to their already very vulnerable circumstances.

From much nearer this time, there was a renewed outburst of musket fire, followed by cries and screams.

*

Jem Burney, standing on the *Discovery*'s forecastle, was too distant to witness the events on shore without his telescope, which he held to his eye almost constantly after Cook had landed at the usual place among the rocks off Kaawaloa. Bligh's cutter was out of sight behind the *Resolution* on its patrol, the *Discovery*'s own two boats on similar patrol to the east, and all were kept busy heading off canoes attempting to leave the bay.

Everything seemed relatively quiet at the *heiau*. He could see between the trees the carpenters beginning their morning's work after finishing their breakfast, and the marines in their red uniform patrolling up and down, one of them right at the water's edge.

Williamson's launch and the *Resolution*'s small cutter were rising and falling in the swell off the landing place, the men from time to time dipping in their oars and pulling to remain on station. Through his glass, Burney could recognize Cook's tall figure with Phillips at his side, walking up the track to the centre of the village. Behind them there marched in their usual ragged formation Sergeant Gibson, Corporal Thomas and the nine privates with muskets sloped. It was the first time Cook had ever gone ashore here with an armed escort. He hoped the captain was right in his firm belief that musket fire would always deter indians, however strong in numbers they might be.

The shore party disappeared from sight among the coconut groves and the outlying houses of the village, and a few minutes later Burney heard and saw the *Resolution*'s great guns firing at a canoe, and Bligh's launch reappeared in pursuit of another big double canoe.

His mind went back to other tense episodes at other anchorages on this voyage—at Nootka Sound when sudden hostility among the natives turned out after all to be inter-tribal; at the Cook islands where the whole male population appeared on the beach flaunting their arms and making hostile gestures behind the surf; at Kauai when Williamson had shot the native dead and had got into trouble for it. Well, it looked now as if that unfortunate lieutenant who so enjoyed showing off his prowess with his musket would before long have more opportunities than he might care for.

But it was from quite another quarter that the next burst of musket fire sounded out. Burney ran the length of the ship to the stern in order to see better what was happening off Waipunaula. Clerke was already at the rails, observing through his telescope the *Discovery*'s launch and small cutter close together, a cloud of smoke from the musket volley drifting away from them on the wind. It was evident that Rickman and his men had been shooting at an escaping double canoe, now stationary, from which loud cries sounded out. Another smaller single canoe in the same area was moving fast towards the *Discovery*.

Burney said to the sentry standing close by, 'Don't fire unless they commit a hostile act.' And Clerke called out, 'Send away the jolly boat to find how matters stand with Mr Rickman, and ask him to bring any seized canoes to the ship.'

The small canoe arrived under the *Discovery*'s stern before the jolly boat had put off. There were four natives in it, all men, and all greatly excited and shouting up at Clerke and Burney.

Although Burney was fluent in Polynesian, it was a while before he could make out the nature of what they were saying, only that the names Kalimu and Orono were frequently repeated. Clerke turned to him. 'What are they saying, Mr Burney?'

'I think Mr Rickman may have shot their chief—Chief Kalimu. You remember him, sir?'

Clerke remembered that first meeting with the chief when he came on board with King Terreeoboo. He had often seen him since and had not much liked the look of the man.

'And now he's off to protest to Captain Cook, I understand?'

Burney nodded. 'I do not think he will find him very readily, sir,' he said wryly.

The canoe was already half way to the *Resolution*, and Burney returned to the bows to watch for some evidence of Cook's progress. The scene was unchanged ashore and Burney could see the small canoe come alongside the *Resolution* and reckoned that it received as dusty a response to the natives' protests as from Clerke and himself. It remained for a very short time, and then steered in towards Kaawaloa, keeping a wide berth from the boats. Burney used his glass to observe the native crew leaping ashore and pulling up their craft. Several more natives greeted them, and the whole party began running towards the village.

Within a short time, Burney heard the rise in volume and note of the murmuring that before had sounded no louder than surf on a distant reef, and became aware for the first time of the haunting, threatening note of many conch-shells being blown.

Only one person witnessed all the events ashore, and that was Lieutenant Molesworth Phillips, an unprejudiced observer whatever might be said of his martial inadequacies. Leaving the body of the marines in the charge of his sergeant, Phillips walked beside Cook over the black lava rocks and onto the track leading towards the centre of Kaawaloa. Being both a brave and an insensitive man, he listened to the hostile hum of the unseen warriors massing inland and upon the cliff top without any special nervousness. He felt confirmed in the power and authority his red-coated marines would impress on any number of these savages when the first whom they met fell to the ground in abasement, just as they always had done at Kaawaloa in the presence of god Orono.

Cook spoke to several of them, ordering them to rise. 'Inform King Terreeoboo and his sons of my arrival and that I wish to speak to him,' he said in his halting Polynesian.

The captain and his lieutenant of marines continued their walk through the village. Some of the citizens offered gifts of breadfruit as well as prostrating themselves. Cook bade several of them good morning as if he had arrived for some entertainment rather than to abduct their monarch.

The princes appeared first, running towards Cook and Phillips, but, as usual, greeting 'Toote' without formality. Everyone in the *Resolution* had conceived a great liking for the lively youngesters, who reminded them of Tiarooa and Koa. They appeared to regard Cook's early arrival and the presence of armed marines, and above all the fact that Cook himself carried his great musket, without alarm.

They led Cook and Phillips straight to Terreeoboo's house, a thatched hut built without ostentation or decoration and little larger than its neighbours. The two officers waited outside for the king to appear, and when he failed to do so after some minutes, Cook said, 'Would you please investigate, Mr Phillips. It would not be suitable for me to do so, and I doubt the old gentleman's being inside.'

Phillips ducked into the house. 'I found the old gentleman just awoke from sleep,' said Phillips later. He then told the king that Cook was outside and wished to see him. Slowly, hesitantly, because of his age and condition, the king arose and put on a cloak. Phillips helped him outside, where Terreeoboo showed every sign of pleasure at seeing god Orono, and betrayed no evidence of guilt.

Cook talked to the king, who sat on his own hands in the usual posture of peace and friendship, and told him of the serious theft but did not allude to the extraordinary gathering of warriors about the village.

He turned to Phillips and said in English, 'He is quite innocent of what has happened, of that I am convinced.' Then he asked the king in Polynesian if he would come on board the *Resolution* with him. King Terreeoboo at once agreed and got to his feet again, with the aid of a son at each elbow, and the party began the walk to the shore.

They had advanced only a few paces, however, when a woman broke out from the crowd that was rapidly gathering about them. Phillips recognized her as Kar'na'cub'ra, one of Terreeoboo's mistresses, and she was in a highly excited state, throwing herself at the king's feet, and with many tears and cries begging him not to go any farther. Two chiefs at the same time laid hold of the king, forcing him to sit down again.

Events now moved forward at an accelerating rate towards a disaster for which only Cook himself appeared unprepared. His first reaction to the detention of the king was one of anger—a fierce outburst which neither the king nor his wife had ever witnessed before. The king himself had in fact suddenly become a pathetic and un-regal figure—'dejected and frightened' were the words Phillips used.

At the same time the news of the death of Chief Kalimu off Waipunaula arrived with the four canoeists who had witnessed the shooting, and spread with the speed of sound through this emotionally charged gathering. They closed in, two or three thousand already, the sound that had once been like a distant murmur now rapidly growing in volume and undisguised hostility, and with a new sharpness now added to it—the mournful shriek of conch-shells being blown. Even Cook could no longer disregard the great press of numbers about them, and their menacing mood. Not one of them even the nearest, was now prostrated. On the contrary, they were waving clubs and spears, and some of them held high the newly-acquired and prized *pahoas* from the ships' forges, some with blades as long as 20 inches.

A priest—'an artful rascal' Phillips called him—made a ridiculous attempt to divert the attention of the two officers by singing and making an elaborate offering of a coconut.

Phillips looked round and saw that his marines were now huddled together surrounded tightly by jeering, menacing warriors. He shouted in Cook's ear, 'Shall I order my men to arrange themselves in order along the rocks by the waterside, sir?'

Cook nodded. 'Yes, do that Mr Phillips. We can never think of compelling the king to go on board without killing a number of these people.'

It appeared from this comment that Cook was about to leave the place and embark in his pinnace. Yet he seemed curiously reluctant to do so as if he either did not care what happened to himself, was not going to lose face by withdrawing at any pace not of his own choosing, or could not make up his mind.

For a period of about a minute the two officers stood side by side, Cook observing the howling, restless natives, challenging them with an expression of the utmost disdain to touch him. He might no longer be god Orono to these people, but as the explorer who had discovered and observed them, charted their islands, shared their food and entertainment, settled their quarrels, granted them gifts and accepted their food, from Easter Island to New Zealand, and now here at the tip of the Polynesian Pacific triangle—James Cook was the undisputed father figure of this remarkable race. Not Orono, but the great 'Toote', in Tongataboo and Queen Charlotte's Sound, Huahiné and Kauai.

And now? Phillips had not spoken since he had given the order to Sergeant Gibson to draw up his men on the rocks. Why did not the captain withdraw? Or give the order to open fire? There were several natives almost within arms' reach of Cook, shrieking and menacing him. One of the them, cutting the air with his *pahoa*, was simulating stone-throwing with his other hand. Cook raised his musket and fired a barrel of small shot at the man's chest. It failed to penetrate the protective shield, or mat, he was wearing and the sound and flash of the musket had no apparent effect on the people.

At the same time another native lunged at Phillips with his *pahoa*, and Phillips struck him hard with the butt end of his musket. Cook fired his other barrel point blank at another advancing native and killed him outright. At once a dozen hands seized the body, another grabbed the *pahoa*. Cook turned and shouted at the top of his voice, 'Open fire!' There were only eight marines still standing, one private having already been felled by a stone. A volley crashed out, and even the worst marksman could not miss.

There were numerous witnesses to what followed, and the accounts differ only in detail. Many were on the *Resolution*'s deck already, alarmed by the sudden rise in the cries of the warriors on shore. At the sound of the muskets, everyone was at the rails or in the rigging—all except a handful of the most faithful girls, who remained below, quite undisturbed, throughout the tumultuous events that followed.

In this ship the naked eye sufficed. From the *Discovery* Burney was still watching through his glass. So were Clerke and several others who had telescopes. The men in the small cutter and the pinnace had the closest view of the fight. They were lying on their oars a mere 50 yards from the shore when Cook's first shot rang out, and the pinnace came in closer to take him off.

Bligh was out of sight round the point and saw nothing. Nor did the *Discovery*'s boats' crews on the east side of the bay. But no one from the two ships failed to note the sound of combat nor experience a sense of imminent doom. Eight bells rang out in both ships simultaneously. 8 o'clock.

The volley did have an effect on the natives, but the brief pause in their advance and evident determination to wipe out every white man on the rocks was caused only by their anxiety to remove the bleeding bodies from sight and opportunity for dread capture, to cover the victims' faces with mats and remove their arms. All this occupied a shorter time than the marines spent in reloading, which was about 20 seconds. And during this time others were pressing forward, stones were thick in the air, and the sound of shrieking and screaming was cacophonous— 'far exceeding all the noise I ever came in the way of', wrote Phillips, who had fired and killed a native and was rapidly reloading as others came in on him, waving their wicked *pahoas*. A stone striking his head felled him just as he was shouting, 'Take to the boats!' Not that anyone would have heard him, and the marines had already turned and, casting aside their muskets, were racing for their lives over the slippery rocks, some stumbling and falling.

A *pahoa* blade sliced deeply into Phillips' shoulder as he lay on his back. He thrust aside his assailant, seized his musket and fired it into the man's body at a range of a yard. Corporal Thomas was another who had succeeded in reloading. Just as he completed the action, a native thrust a blade into his stomach and he fell into a rock pool. He managed to pull the trigger, but must have died soon after as more natives struggled to stab him where he lay.

Other marines were falling on the rocks or as they began to wade out, tantalizingly close to salvation. Private Harrison appeared to the horrified boats' crews to be literally hacked to pieces. Tom Fatchett went down, too, his head as red from gushing blood as his uniform jacket. John Jackson, oldest of the privates and a veteran who had survived a long campaign in Germany, was struck by a spear in the face, just below the eye. Screaming with pain, he attempted to draw it out, and it broke off. With blood pouring from the wound, he waded out, and fell into the sea, unable to swim, with stones tearing up the water all round him. Strong arms held him up, however, and he found himself being hoisted into the pinnace, which was already so crowded that few shots could be fired, and those were reserved for natives who were attempting to drag the boat ashore.

Private Hinks was less fortunate than Jackson. The *pahoas* wielded by a number of raging warriors killed him, some of them stabbing him several times after he was dead.

Phillips was struck on the back of his head by a second stone which almost knocked him out. The stones were thrown either by hand or from a sling. They flew very fast and with great accuracy. Phillips stumbled, nearly fell again on the slippery rocks, threw himself into the surf and swam out to the pinnace. He had just dragged himself over the gunwale, barely conscious, when he saw the wounded Jackson sinking only a few yards away. He at once jumped into the sea, dragged him to the pinnace, and with the help of a sailor got him safely on board. Then, recognizing that the boat was already so overloaded that it might be swamped with his additional weight, he swam off to Lanyon's small cutter.

Another figure left the pinnace at this time—the brown figure of a native. Prince Ka'oo'ah had earlier swum out to the boat in eager expectation of accompanying his father for a happy day on board the *Resolution*. At first puzzled by the preliminaries to the attack, he had looked anxiously for the arrival of his brother and the king. Instead, he had witnessed the swift onset of the fighting and firing, had for a few moments been at the receiving end of the hail of stones, had heard the answering fire of the marines and seen many of his countrymen fall, including the great Chief Kanina. Shocked and terrified at the noise and carnage, the boy now leapt overboard and swam swiftly away, far out into the bay.

By contrast with Lanyon's small cutter, John Williamson with the launch was out of musket range, and the men had given up firing. The crew had seen Cook in the midst of his assailants turn to wave his arm above his head. Everyone except the lieutenant interpreted the sign as an order to come in closer to give support to the pinnace. There could be no doubt that the captain and the marines needed the fire of every musket to give them an edge of a chance to escape. Williamson, however, would have none of this. He interpreted Cook's wave as an order to keep clear. It was the duty of the pinnace to take off the shore party, not his boat.

Shouting to Lanyon to follow him (if the master's mate heard him, he ignored the order), Williamson told his men to bend to their oars. Outraged at this desertion of his captain, many of the men continued to re-load and fire, until Williamson threatened them with a ball from his own musket. Soon the boat was too far out to be of any assistance in the fight, and the crew witnessed the end as they lay on their oars, the launch rising and falling gently on the swell.

From the *Resolution*, Gore saw the blow that felled his senior officer. So did Burney from the distant *Discovery*—'we could see Captain Cook receive a blow from a club and fall off a rock into the water'. Able Seaman William Harvey was among many others who could not understand why Cook 'trifled away his time on the shore', and was agonized to see him struck when he might have made his escape.

David Samwell, with his keen eye and vivid pen, gave the most detailed account. He saw Cook turning at last to walk towards the pinnace, his empty musket under one arm, the other hand holding the back of his head as protection from the stones that flew about him. For a moment it appeared as if he might reach the water's edge, walking with the stately dignity he always assumed among the Polynesians.

Then one native broke from the crowd following him, advanced with a club, withdrew for fear he might turn, advanced again, raised the club and struck him a fearful blow. Cook staggered for several yards, and fell onto a hand and knee, his musket rattling onto the rocks beside him.

The captain was clearly not killed by this blow, though seriously stunned. Another native did the murder. He was recognized by several onlookers. The muscular Chief Ku'a leapt onto the big stooping form, raised his *pahoa*, and plunged it into the back of Cook's neck. Robust to the end, even this did not kill him. The shock of the blow caused him to fall into a rock crevice full of water from the high tide. Ku'a leapt onto him again, stabbing him repeatedly while others who had joined the murderer attempted to hold him down under the water. In one last gesture of defiance, Cook raised his head. Those in the pinnace saw his big craggy face clearly but momentarily. His lips were forming an unheard cry and he was waving an arm feebly towards them. He attempted to rise, received a second fearful club blow. And now it was all over—all finished except for the dreadful performance of mutilation.

Henry Roberts from Shoreham, Sussex, master's mate, was among those who were unwitting eyewitnesses in the pinnace; and the sight would haunt them all for the remainder of their lives. The natives fell on the corpse like wolves upon a fallen moose, stabbing it, grabbing another's *pahoa* and thrusting it in again, stabbing with spears, too, and hitting it with rocks and clubs. At one point a number of them raised his body from the crevice and beat his head repeatedly against the rock face.

Mercifully, the press of numbers became so great that the body was hidden from sight. Roberts ordered the men to the oars, and with difficulty got the pinnace under weigh and his men rowing it back towards the *Resolution*.

It was at this point that the *Resolution* belatedly opened fire, sending balls into the crowd above the beach, and Williamson now gave the order to bring the launch closer to the shore. By the time it was within range, the scene had been transformed by the *Resolution*'s gunfire, which had caused widespread panic. Only a few natives were on the rocks, and they were running off as quickly as they could. Williamson's men took up their muskets and fired at them without effect, and then were astonished to hear Williamson ordering them to put about. They could see Cook's sorely mutilated body on the rocks, and not distant from it the twisted corpses of three of the four dead marines. Surely they could at least land and collect their dead, and save them from further indignity? But Williamson was implacable, and also in an ugly mood. The threat of the lash, or a ball in the back, caused them to raise their oars and row back to their ship.

They were in tears when they came alongside the gangway, several of them crying, 'We have lost our father! Our father is gone!'

The *Resolution*'s men were at the rails, the gunners beside their cannon. It was curiously quiet after the sequence of hysteria they had witnessed—the fire of cannon and muskets, the shrieking and screaming, which had filled the bay during that morning. 'A general silence ensued throughout the ship,' wrote Able Seaman George Gilbert, 'it appearing to us somewhat like a dream that we could not reconcile ourselves to for some time. Grief was visible in every countenance, some expressing it by tears, and other by a kind of gloomy dejection.'

Epilogue

THE CONSEQUENCES OF Captain Cook's murder to both
Hawaiians and the ships' crews were profound. For a short time
after Gore ordered the cease fire, and a silence fell over
Kealakekua Bay, it was as if those many thousands of natives and
that handful of sailors were all suffering from a paralysing
nervous breakdown. 'What have we done?' was the stunning
question the natives asked themselves. It was echoed offshore by
'What has happened to us?' The event was for the present too
overwhelming to attract a positive response.

These sentiments remaining unanswered, they were succeeded by others, fear on shore, anger at sea. Revenge. There
must be terrible retribution. Many in the *Resolution* advocated
warping the ships close inshore and bombarding the villages,
massacring the natives, destroying every house and canoe. Bligh
was the first with this view and other voices were raised in
support, including that of the usually balanced, clever Samwell.
There was no doubt about the feeling of the seamen, either. But
other responsible voices counselled caution. Gore was adamant
that their first priority was to recover their priceless, irreplaceable
possessions ashore, which included the *Resolution*'s chronometer;
to say nothing of their shipmates. Revenge must wait. An even
softer line was advocated—the injury was done, except for this
lapse they had been treated with generosity and kindness here.
The friendship must be reborn. It was a view that was little
supported, and Bligh was outraged by its expression.

The same division was evident in the *Discovery*. Here Clerke insisted upon the postponement of any retribution. His was the ultimate responsibility now. With Cook's death he was supreme commander. The blow had been as shattering for him as for anyone. The two men had been devoted shipmates, a friendship built from three long, dangerous voyages together, and a perfect understanding. Clerke was in no physical condition to stand the blow, or assume the awful duties that lay ahead. He had shrunk to a hollow, bent husk by contrast with the hearty, vigorous officer of the last voyage. For all his determination, his condition was 'so bad as hardly to suffer me to keep the deck'. The considerable qualities of Charles Clerke were never seen better than in those first hours after Cook's murder. There was a new gravity in his demeanour, and no signs now of the old madcap womanizer and boozer. He had not long to live, he knew it, and his sense of duty was rock-fast.

The immediate danger he had to face was the real possibility that the shore party might be overwhelmed before they could be supported. News of the events at Kaawaloa had flashed to the other side of the bay, where the priests now tried in vain to stem the rising tide of hostility among all the villagers along the east coast. The men here were arming themselves, the same rumble of hostility arose from the crowds and was further hardened by the sinister shrieks of the conch-shells. Figures could be seen hurrying over the cliff top to add their strength to the offensive.

Clerke ordered an attack on targets about the *heiau*, not in a spirit of revenge but as a deterrent until he could organize reinforcements. With the help of a spring on the *Discovery*'s cable, the vessel was brought round and fire was opened as he embarked in a boat for the *Resolution* to take up his command. Gore was ordered to replace him as commander of the *Discovery*. Rarely can an officer have taken over his first ship at such a critical time and with a shore bombardment actually in progress.

In the *Resolution*, Clerke found feeling running high against the natives, and almost as strongly against Williamson, who was being widely blamed for Cook's death, as well as for the deaths of the marines. The organizing of a shore party distracted the men from their passions of grief and hatred. Bligh was the obvious choice as commander. He and his men, together with several marines not involved in the fight ashore, armed themselves purposefully with muskets, pistols and hangers, and the launch was cast off and headed for the eastern shore.

The following hours, and days, were filled with inexplicable, paradoxical and fearful events. The first was the arrival alongside the *Discovery* of King in the jolly boat as that ship's guns were firing in his defence. He was in a state of great excitement, and was calling out to halt the bombardment. It was, he claimed, doing more harm than good, inflaming the natives by the destruction of their houses.

'The priests are still friendly to us,' he explained to Gore. 'They are attempting to lower the passions of the indians.' There was another reason for taking a peaceful line, he continued. Now that god Orono had been destroyed, he, Lieutenant James King, was regarded by High Priest Koa and his priests as his successor. Was he not the son of Orono? Orono himself had said so before he died. King was the new Orono. In the eyes of the Hawaiians, this was something to be reckoned with.

Bligh's men, with the support of the few marines guarding the settlement, had meanwhile gone into action against the natives, firing indiscriminately from the *heiau*, and with the utmost satisfaction, killing a number of them and wounding others. This action had been carried out by Bligh against the strong protests of Bayly. King, who was not hastening ashore after silencing the great guns of the *Discovery*, was further outraged at Bligh's independent action. An order for an immediate cease fire was given.

Bligh, who never regretted anything he ever did in all his turbulent life, was certainly quite unrepentant now. He could point to the evidence, which for the present vindicated his action. The natives had fled in confusion. From the more distant coconut groves there came the sound of women lamenting. All threats to the encampment were over for the time being, and the sailmakers and carpenters were able to go about their work of packing up for departure unhindered. The foremast was got down to the shore, and taken off in its half repaired state. Bayly struck his observatory tents and got his instruments into the boats, guarded all the way by Bligh's contingent.

By noon of this day of disaster, not a man, not a possession of the expedition, remained on shore. The *Resolution*'s foremast was alongside, soon to be got on board and placed fore and aft on the forecastle and quarter-deck, like a gravestone to their late commander awaiting erection. The more carefully the carpenters investigated the state of this mast, the more deep-seated they found its rottenness—as rotten as the corrupt dockyard, administration which had allowed it to be stepped. The rot went at least seven feet up from its base, probably much farther. The carpenters dared not cut it down for fear that it would prove impossible to form another step in the rotten timber. The only solution was to shape and drive in an enormous plug, and this the weary carpenters set about doing within the confined space of the *Resolution*'s deck, hemmed in by spars and rigging.

Clerke's next preoccupation was the recovery of the bodies of Cook and the marines. His first move was to send off Burney in a boat from the *Discovery*, and King (now first lieutenant) in another boat from the *Resolution*, both well supported with arms, to parley for the corpses. The natives streamed down to the shore both at Kaawaloa and Waipunaula, casting aside their weapons and extending their arms in gestures of peace and reconciliation. Yes, they indicated, Orono's body would be returned. It had been taken far inland.

Off Waipunaula, High Priest Koa threw himself into the breakers in his eagerness to re-establish a friendship and swam out to Burney's small cutter, holding a white flag in one hand, a remarkable physical achievement for such an old, shaky man. He personally would see to it that god Orono's body would be returned the next day, he told him. Burney thanked him coolly and ordered the boat back to his ship.

High Priest Koa was true to his word, but only in part. The following day, he sent a priest out to the *Resolution* with a parcel. When it was unwrapped in Clerke's cabin, he and his officers present were appalled to discover that it contained only the partly burned flesh cut from the thigh of their late commander. The priest bowed apologetically. The bones, he told the assembled officers, were in the hands of King Terreeoboo. High Priest Koa was endeavouring to recover them

as soon as possible. Only great chiefs—and presumably
gods—were privileged with this ritual.

What could you do with these people? What purpose was
served in punishing these Hawaiians, whose customs and
morality were so completely alien to their own?

Sick at heart, and sick in the stomach, they allowed the priest
to depart unharmed. But the word of what lay in the parcel
flashed about the ship in minutes, and soon reached the
Discovery. Many of the warrant officers, and all the men, were
now hellbent on revenge. Other incidents during the day further
inflamed them. Some of the marines' clothing was used as flags,
flown and waved as messages of mockery. A native put off alone
in a canoe, approached the *Resolution* just beyond musket range,
and stood up to twirl Cook's hat around on the end of a stick.
Then he put it on his head, turned to expose his buttocks and
smacked them, roaring with laughter at the same time. He was
watched admiringly from the shore, where great numbers had
assembled for an obviously prepared performance, and now all
turned their buttocks towards the ships, beating themselves and
setting up a great howl of triumph.

Another native flaunted a hanger indicating it was Cook's, and
that the blood on it was from cutting his body into pieces.

All this was too much for the *Resolution*'s gunners, who opened
fire on the crowd, instantly scattering them screaming into the
woods, and wounding several, including the homosexual Chief
Kamehameha, to the great satisfaction of the entire ship's
company when they heard the news later.

There was more serious provocation and counter-action at
Kealakekua when watering parties commanded by Rickman and
Harvey, now reinstated as lieutenant, went ashore under a strong
escort. They were stoned incessantly and boulders were rolled
down from the cliff-top towards them. Several of the men were
badly cut about and bruised. Here retribution was swift and
savage, so violent that several of the more temperate officers
wrote of it afterwards with shame. But Bligh again commended
Rickman's musketry: 'If this had not been done they would
never have been brought to submission.' Men and women were
shot without compunction. Stone throwers were hunted down

by parties of marines and seamen, brutally beaten and then shot. Several were decapitated, their heads thrust on long poles which were held up on the beach and waved towards the warriors on the cliff tops.

The effect of this demonstration was fearful. There were screams of terror and anguish, and the hordes fled. The Hawaiians also demonstrated fanatical courage. They would brave any fire to recover the body of a compatriot, dipping their mats in water in an effort to quench what they thought was the fire thrown by the white men's weapons.

In order to clear the natives altogether from the watering area, the nearby houses were then set on fire. This fire got out of control, and in a strong wind the flames destroyed hundreds of houses and all the natives' possessions.

During these last days as the carpenters laboured to complete the repairs to the mast, there also occurred many irrelevant or anomalous events, in the best traditions of their experiences in Polynesia. For example, the local girls, the only people on either side during these hostilities to retain a steady eye on priorities, swam out to the ships every evening to join others who had never disembarked. They lay with their sailors when they were off watch, and especially enjoyed and admired the spectacular sight of the villages going up in flames.

At this time, too, while the chiefs were attacking the watering parties with great ferocity, and a general attack on the ships was expected at any time, two boys swam out to the *Discovery* carrying spears. The guard held their fire against such easy targets, and the natives were allowed to swim under the stern of the ship. There they burst into song, a 15-minute lament for the death of the god Orono, to the satisfaction and interest of Jem Burney. They then indicated that they wished to come on board. Here they presented their spears as a gesture of contrition, and dived overboard and swam ashore.

At one hour the whole population ashore appeared intent only on peace and friendship. Flags of truce were flown from the cliff tops. Stacks of provisions appeared on the beach, with every sign that they should be taken. Koa repeatedly came out to the *Discovery* with protestations of good faith. A few believed him.

Most thought he was checking on the state of preparation against an attack, and some of the young gentlemen believed he was the arch plotter of the attack on Cook. One of them pursued him on shore and fired a pistol at his head at point blank range. The spirit of Orono may have intervened because the pistol misfired.

At another hour, there would be further demonstrations of hostility, the ships' boats on guard every night would open musket fire, another half-dozen natives might be shot ashore.

High Priest Koa had been told that he was not to return to the ship without the body of Cook. Several days passed before he fulfilled his promise. From accounts provided by the girls, it appeared that King Terreeoboo and his family and entourage of chiefs had retired to some caves high up in the clifftops. There, the captain's corpse had been shared out among the highest chiefs, the hair to one, the scalp to another, the skull to a third, the hands to another—and the lion's share, so to speak, being retained by Terreeoboo. High Priest 'Bretannee' Koa's difficult task was to extract these prized parts from the chiefs, and arrange for their return in one parcel.

It was not until 19 February that Priest Hiapo sent a message that the body was on shore and awaited collection. Clerke in his pinnace and King in the cutter put off from the *Resolution*, and under strong guard approached the shore at Kaawaloa. Beneath flags of peace, a party of priests and chiefs in solemn and ceremonial state paraded on shore with a massive pile of fruit and hogs from the king.

Clerke refused entreaties to land, and at length Priest Hiapo was prevailed upon to put off and come on board the pinnace while the provisions were loaded into King's boat. Priest Hiapo carried in his hands a large parcel wrapped in plantain leaves and covered with a mourning cloak of black and white feathers.

'On opening it,' wrote King, 'we found the captain's hands (which were well known from a remarkable scar*), the scalp, the skull, wanting the lower jaw, thigh bones and arm bones.' The hands had been pierced and salt rammed in to preserve them.

---

* The consequence of the accidental explosion of a powder horn in August 1764, 'which shattered it in a terrible manner'.

Priest Hiapo and Prince Ka'oo'ah came on board the *Resolution* with several more bones and Cook's shoes and other pieces of his clothing as well as his double-barrelled gun, now mutilated. The party showed every sign of contrition and reported the king to be most desirous of peace between his people and god Orono's people, supporting his wish with a gift of a dozen hogs. As to the bodies of the marines, the king much regretted that, like the other remains of Cook, the bones had been widely dispersed about the island and there was nothing he could do to recover them. Nor were the nine muskets and their bayonets and a number of pistols forthcoming. They would have to be satisfied with what they had.

A week after the murder, its consequences were still being violently felt. The loathing and hatred for Williamson continued unabated, and it seemed at that time unlikely that he would survive the voyage unharmed by his shipmates. The lieutenant demanded a public enquiry into his conduct, and this was held on board the *Resolution*. A number of the men who had been in the launch confirmed that he had threatened them with a shot from his musket if they attempted to row in closer to the fighting. Others, fearful of persecution from the officer who was now second lieutenant and wielded great power, prevaricated. These depositions, and a statement couched in the most condemnatory terms, were circulated among the officers of both ships for judgment.

Questions were also asked about Rickman's shooting of Chief Kalimu, which many believed had led directly to the murder. Had it been necessary? Had the junior lieutenant been influenced, directly or indirectly, by the highly aggressive stance of Bligh, whose own attack had set the precedent and only by chance had failed to cause a chief's death? Bligh denied any link between Chief Kalimu's shooting and the attack on Cook. 'Lieutenant Rickman did fire,' he announced defiantly, 'and it was said killed a man, but the attack was over and past before this was known.' This was not true.

But Rickman was little blamed. It may have been unfortunate, but he was doing his duty, which was more than could be said for Williamson. And Bligh was Bligh.

The launch was never found. Rumour had it that Parea had been behind the theft in revenge for the beating he had received in front of some of his men, and that the boat had been broken up for its iron even before its loss was noticed.

Also on 21 February, Cook's funeral took place on board the *Resolution,* in the presence of the ship's company and the officers of the *Discovery.* The priests were asked to 'taboo' the entire bay, and at 5 p.m. the colours of both ships were hoisted half staff, and the yards crossed in accordance with tradition. In the absence of a chaplain, one of the officers read the service in place of Clerke, who was too weak for the duty. The captain's body was given 'all the attention and honour we could possibly pay it in this part of the world'. The men sang lustily, the sound of their voices reaching out far over the silent and deserted bay. Then the coffin containing the pathetic mutilated remains was lowered over the side under a discharge of ten guns—a disagreeable sound to the natives, reminding them of those recent days of bloodshed, and sending many of them hurrying inland again.

The last hours in Kealakekua Bay reminded everyone of those happier days in January when the seamen and natives alike lived in harmony and trust. Now there was none of the hysteria accompanying their arrival, nor the suspicion which had marked their unhappy return. The women were as many and as willing as at any time. Chiefs and priests and commoners by the hundred roamed the decks freely, yarning and laughing with the sailors, and trading as in the old days.

King Terreeoboo himself at last made a reappearance after receiving assurances that he and his family would be safe and that the quarrel had been buried along with the body of the old god Orono. Clerke was able to receive him briefly. The captain came up on deck as the shaky old man was being helped up the gangway, followed by the princes, a number of chiefs and a final magnificent offering of fruit and vegetables and hogs.

Tears were falling from the bloodshot eyes of the king as he begged to know if they would be friends again when they returned to leave behind, as promised, Lieutenant King, the new god Orono. Clerke reassured him, and as he wrote later, 'he expressed great satisfaction and appeared very happy'.

'And when will Orono return?' asked Terreeoboo.

Lieutenant King replied that he would return before long.

Terreeoboo was not the last to disembark from the *Resolution*. It was only fitting that the girls, who had been among the first on board, and had remained throughout the troubles, should enjoy that privilege.

On 23 February, with the *Resolution*'s patched up foremast stepped and rigged, Clerke gave orders to make sail. At 8 p.m., the small anchors were weighed, and with just a breath of wind from the land to fill the sails, the ships' boats towed the two sloops from their anchorage towards the open sea.

It was a grey, cloudy, dour evening as the black slash of Kealakekua Bay's cliff fell behind them. The weather reflected the mood of the men. One young gentleman wrote of the 'universal gloom and strong sentiments of grief and melancholy' that affected them all. As much as the grief over the loss of their commander was the sense of failure. There was no satisfaction now in having killed so many natives and their chiefs. Even the recovery of the greater part of Cook's body had been only a small satisfaction.

The cause of this black depression was the realization that they had failed in all that they had set out to do. By contrast with the renowned successes and achievements of the past voyages, this one had been fated for disaster from the outset. It had been a tale of continuous losses. They had lost two summer Arctic seasons, they had lost the friendship of many natives, had lost their beloved Scots doctor, many of their shipmates and old man Watman in action or at sea, or from disease, and they had lost their commander—'our greatly loved and admired commander', 'one of the greatest navigators our nation or any nation ever had', as King described him.

Black failure. And now their new commander must die soon, there could be no doubt of that. They all knew that they must venture once more into the Arctic ice before returning home, but not one of them believed there was any likelihood of discovering that passage—not after what they had seen last year, and what

Cook had said about their chances. More bitter cold and suffering, more short hard rations. And few chances of women after they left these islands.

Never on all this long voyage had spirits sunk as low as on this February evening, while the ships picked up the familiar roll of the Pacific and for the second time headed north along the dark volcanic shores of Hawaii.

The dead hand of failure lay over the remainder of the voyage as it had touched it from the beginning. The sharp distinctions and characteristics of the men, their idiosyncrasies and weak spots, their jests and enthusiasms, seemed dulled and then lost in the fogs and blizzards that beset their northern passage again. It was as if with the death of Cook their own personalities had dimmed to the uniform grey of the Siberian coastline along which they groped their way during that summer of 1779, now without the benefit of their Kendall watch, which mysteriously and utterly failed on 26 April.

Only one personality continued to stand out—the contentious, edgy, uneven but highly accomplished William Bligh. As Clerke faded away, Bligh's position as sailing master became even more dominant. Later, he claimed, 'Captain Clerke being very ill in a decline, he could not attend the deck, and thus he publicly gave me the power solely of conducting the ships and moving as I thought proper. His orders were, "You are to explore the [Sandwich] isles as much as you can and from thence carry the ships to Kamchatka, and thence do your utmost endeavours to discover the N.W. passage. . . ." '

Bligh followed out these instructions to the letter. His survey of the Hawaiian islands remains a triumph of cartography, as good as Cook could have accomplished. He navigated the expedition to Kamchatka, through the Bering Strait again at the full height of the summer season this time, probed west and east with no more success than before, and brought the leaking, crank *Resolution* safely back to England by way of the Cape.

On 10 August, Clerke dictated a letter to Joseph Banks, which began:

My ever honoured Friend,
The disorder I was attacked with in the King's bench prison
has proved consumptive, with which I have battled with
varying success, although without one single day's health
since I took leave of you in Burlington Street. It has now so
far got the better of me, that I am not able to turn myself in
my bed, so that my stay in this world must be of very short
duration.

It ended:

Now my dear and honoured friend, I must bid you a final
adieu. May you enjoy many happy years in this world, and in
the end attain that fame your indefatigable industry so richly
deserves. These are the most sincerely and warmest wishes of
your devoted, affectionate and departing servant,

Chas. Clerke.

Twelve days later, the racked captain finally expired, aged 38,
making his final 'escape from the Israelites' on a grey, chill day
off the Siberian coast. After such prolonged sufferings, the
departure was a great relief for this courageous and much-loved
officer.

John Gore took over command and returned to the *Resolution*,
and there were other changes of seniority and responsibility. A
year to the day after Clerke's death, the two ships anchored at
Stromness in the Orkney Islands north of Scotland, having
failed to defeat contrary winds up Channel; they were in the
Thames on 4 October 1780, four years and three months after
the *Resolution*'s departure from Plymouth.

It is no discredit to Gore and his fellow officers that it was
Bligh's voyage after the death of his captain. There is a certain
element of bombast in Bligh's claim of 'sole power', scribbled by
hand in the margin of his copy of the official journal, written
now by King, an officer Bligh despised as effete and futile. Gore
was administrative commander, and was recognized as an able
veteran. But with the loss of both captains, no lieutenant could
claim the absolute authority wielded by Cook. Overall decisions
were made by mutual consent among the officers. Bligh's claim
to 'moving [the ships] as I thought proper' is not an exaggeration.

As navigator throughout the voyage this would be his duty anyway. As Cook's right-hand man for three years, as senior sailing master, as a young man of exceptionally strong personality, his position in the hierarchy was unique. However one judges the personality of the man, Bligh demonstrated unusual powers of leadership of an expedition that had been as demoralized as if defeated in battle.

One last and awful ironical aspect of this voyage of many misfortunes remains to be recounted because it summarizes its futility and waste. All the calculations on which Cook's itinerary was based, in his instructions and in his own decisions on timing, presupposed that the month of June—midsummer—was the ideal time to discover the North-West Passage, when the ice would have receded to its most northerly line. In fact, June is two months early. In June the ice often remains as far south as the Bering Strait. August, the month Cook arrived in the ultimate north, believing he was too late, was in fact the most favourable. He had not missed his second season after all. And he would not have missed his first season if he had followed his instructions and persevered against contrary winds after leaving New Zealand instead of wasting months among the Friendly and Society Islands. He would have arrived in the Arctic at the ideal time.

It is improbable that Cook would have fought his way through to Baffin's Bay and the Atlantic in 1777, even if he had made the attempt in August. But it is worth recalling that when Amundsen finally made it, he never went farther north than 74° and saw no ice at this latitude, such is the unpredictability of the Arctic. Masters of whaling ships at Cook's time frequently sailed up into the 70s. It is also worth remembering, when considering this hypothesis, that Cook had already shown the world that he could accomplish the seemingly impossible.

Pickersgill, whom it was intended by the Admiralty Cook should meet in the passage, was defeated as much by hard liquor as by ice, was away only five and a half months and on his return was court-martialled and dismissed the service. So this unfortunate old shipmate of Cook's provides few clues to the northern conditions in 1777.

The only certain conclusion one can draw from all this speculation is that Cook's luck was out from the moment he arose from that dinner table three years before he died and offered his services as commander of this ill-fated expedition.

As the two sloops worked their way west through the Hawaiian islands, west again before turning north for the Siberian coast, the debate continued, on watch and off watch, on the cause of the catastrophe, the true sequence of events, and the degree of blame attached to those involved, including the captain himself.

The great majority took the simple view that the Hawaiians were all villain—treacherous, thieving and, as the tragic evidence showed, murderous. Never trust an indian. There was a much greater range of opinion among the officers and young gentlemen. Cook's rashness came under severe censure from some. It was asking for trouble to go ashore escorted by armed marines, to abduct the king when so many warriors with such seemingly aggressive intentions had gathered about the bay. There was talk of an unbalanced judgment at work, and none could deny that their commander had, committed misjudgments and indiscretions on this voyage which would never have occurred on earlier expeditions. Had his pride grown too great as a result of the adutlation shown by the indians?

Midshipman Trevenen believed Cook was almost immortal, like the god Orono. Although Trevenen could see the corpses of the marines on the rocks, 'I had been so used to look up to him as our good genius, our safe conductor, and as a kind of superior being, that I could not suffer myself, I did not dare, to think he could fall by the hands of the indians over whose minds and bodies also, he had been accustomed to rule with uncontrolled sway.'

As far as the conduct of the shore party was concerned, there was heavy criticism of the marines and of Molesworth Phillips's tactics, though everyone on record (except Bligh, who thought 'there was not a spark of courage or conduct shown in the whole business') praised the lieutenant's personal courage. Cook himself came in for criticism in this respect. 'It is now the opinion of almost everybody that had we held at first our muskets more sacred,' observed Midshipman John Law, 'and not have fired small shot at a thief, but if necessary have killed him with a ball these people would have dreaded the idea of a musket.'

On the other hand, he believed Cook 'wrongly thought that the flash of a musket would disperse the whole island'. This midshipman was one of the most severe in his condemnation of his commander, hinting at his arrogance—'he hearkened to no advice till it was too late'; and 'he rashly went alone into the middle of the crowd'.

Samwell remained a firm believer in the theory that no native will stand up to musket fire and that they will show courage only against the back of a foe. 'Indians never will, be they ever so numerous, stand before a set of resolute men with firearms who will firmly maintain their ground.' But then the Welsh doctor was not among those marines who stood with a surf behind them and a raging horde of natives advancing upon them. 'No people,' he continued sanctimoniously, 'are quicker to observe or more active in taking advantage of their enemies when that vigour and firmness which ought ever to be kept in full force, begins to relax.'

Bligh's judgments were predictably uncompromising. Although he was not an eyewitness, he was busy as a reporter later that day taking notes from everyone and compiling a dossier of guilt. He was the only one to report Phillip's view of the performance of his own men, and it was not favourable. 'As soon as the muskets were discharged, they ran to the boats.'

Bligh was firmly of the belief that the fleeing of the marines 'occasioned all that followed'. 'Had they fixed their bayonets and not have run, so frightened as they were, they might have drove all before them.' The reason why Phillips had not earlier ordered them to fix bayonets remains a mystery. Perhaps he did and the order was not heard. Perhaps Sergeant Gibson was awaiting the order for which he was not prepared to take the initiative.

Lieutenant King, who was also able to observe the events only distantly, wrote that Cook had 'called [the boat crews] to cease firing and to come in with the boats, intending to embark as soon as possible.' He then speculated whether 'this humanity perhaps proved fatal to him'. But then King was writing the official account and felt the need to show his commander in the most favourable light. No one else, except Williamson defending himself, believed Cook was calling for a ceasefire.

No report, no discussion, no argument that involved Williamson's name contained a word in his favour. The nearest he came to gaining support was in a statement his arch-enemy Phillips made to Cook's first biographer, Kippis, who considered the lieutenant's judgment of the greatest weight. 'It is extremely doubtful whether anything could successfully have been done to preserve the life of Captain Cook, even if no mistake had been committed on the part of the launch.'

The performance of the Royal Marines was in the best traditions of the voyage and the worst traditions of that admirable corps. The consequences of Phillips' slackness, his non-commissioned officers' incompetence, and the privates' poor drill, were all shown up here as a reflection in life-and-death terms of that earlier charade at the Friendly Islands. As an admiral once wrote of his inadequate ships, 'they could neither fight nor run away'.

Accounts of that morning of 14 February and the aftermath to the violence as experienced by the Hawaiians later filtered back from seamen who visited the island after the return of the *Resolution* and *Discovery*, notably George Vancouver, now a captain R.N., and his botanist Archibald Menzies; from the American Nathaniel Portlock, late of the *Discovery*, who was in the first vessel to visit the bay after the departure of the expedition; from David Greene of the American ship *Neptune*; and, best of all, from the first missionaries to the island.

The muscular Chief Ku'a, who had given Cook the *coup de grâce*, was believed to have regretted his act later; but we are here entering a dim world of apocrypha and self-justification. More interesting is a footnote dated seven years later, when one of Portlock's men wrote of their visit to Kealakekua Bay, 'We had the chief on board who killed Captain Cook, for more than three weeks. He was in bad health, and had a smelling bottle with a few drops in it, which he used to smell at. We filled it for him.'

The shattering effect of that battle on the beach was still felt 40·years later when there were few alive who could remember it. There can be no doubt that the attack was unpremeditated, that the gathering of the warriors was defensive, that the dread of losing their king was very great, but the shooting at the boats by Bligh and Rickman, and the killing of Chief Kalimu, catapulted the people from a state of controlled aggression to unrestrained fury.

The hurt pride and fear of the Hawaiians, coupled with the unbalanced state of Cook's judgment, brought on the affray. On the one hand, the natives could claim that they had paid proper obeisance to the god Orono, had presented to this god of abundance and his priests and chiefs such a mass of provisions that their own stocks were becoming seriously depleted. Then Orono had returned, long before his time, his vessel broken, and calling again for the privilege of the *heiau·* and for yet more provisions. This was not the way of a supernatural deity. The natives of Kealakekua Bay were puzzled and vexed. Thieving to these natives was not all covetousness. It was also mischievous, teasing provocation, with a sporting element. When the *Resolution* and *Discovery* reappeared in the bay so soon after the elaborately ceremonious departure, the Hawaiians renewed the thieving on the hysterical scale they had first practised, a sort of testing for a response. Far from protecting the vessels, this time the chiefs organized and encouraged the robberies. And this time the white men responded harshly, publicly beating the great Chief Parea, humiliating the High Priest Koa, killing innocent people, forbidding the free passage of canoes, attempting to abduct their king, and finally killing one of this community's most important chiefs.

This was the Hawaiian view of the events of early February. With the death of Cook, the islanders' attitudes and actions were divided by fear, hysteria, shame and blood lust. Such was the confusion that it becomes impossible to trace clear, single-minded motives. Amidst the terror and anarchy, even the authenticity of god Orono and his disciples, so sedulously advanced by the priesthood, came into doubt.

William Ellis, an early missionary on the island, was of the opinion that when Cook was attacked 'and they saw his blood running, and heard his groans, they said, "No this is not Orono". Some, however, after his death, still supposed him to be Orono, and expected he would appear again.'

For the priesthood, with its vested interest in the gods, Orono's reappearance was manifested in James King. When the new god Orono demanded Cook's bones, High Priest Koa knew that he must comply, in spite of the opposition of the chiefs who were appeased by being allowed to keep some of them, the ribs and breastbone for example. These, according to Ellis, 'were considered sacred, as part of Orono and deposited in a *heiau* dedicated to Orono on the opposite side of the island. There religious homage was paid to them, and from thence they were annually carried in procession to several other *heiaus*, or borne by the priests round the island, to collect the offerings of the people for the support of the worship of the god Orono.'

This yearly parade of the last remains of Cook about the island he had discovered was ended with the suppression of idolatry by the missionaries. But in spite of the most diligent searches and enquiries, these missionaries never found the bones. To maintain this secret was the priesthood's last act of defiance against these heretics, these sponsors of a new religion after they had been shorn of their power and influence.

By a sad irony, the islanders who had most enthusiastically welcomed Cook, and from whom he received the most ardent obeisance, were now taught to vilify his memory. The Hawaiians were informed that Cook was a pagan murderer, and until quite recent times he was seen as an enemy of Hawaii rather than its discoverer. These missionaries were faced with the difficult paradox that the first Christians the islanders had met had not only made a violent and lasting impression on the people, but had actively participated in their pagan rites. Worse, their leader had been welcomed as a pagan god. In traducing Cook, the missionaries were scarcely just, but it was the most effective policy they could pursue.

Poor Cook may not have been an actively practising Christian but he hardly deserved the coals of fire heaped upon his head by his successors at Hawaii. 'We can hardly avoid the conclusion,' wrote one missionary, 'that for the direct encouragement of idolatry, and especially for his audacity in allowing himself like the proud and magisterial Hero to be idolized, he was left to infatuation and died by the visitation of God.'

So much for the good captain's efforts to cultivate a friendship with the natives.

Whether seen through the eyes of a harshly uncompromising missionary, of one of his many admiring officers, or of a historian 200 years later, there is no grand design leading to the death of Captain Cook, as there is, for example, to the death of that other captain-explorer, Scott of the Antarctic, or of officers like Horatio Nelson who died in battle at the height of their fame.

The death of Captain Cook is as melancholy as it is mysterious. How, for example, can we explain all the mis-judgments that led to his death, the lapses in his sense of responsibility which—for example—led to his allowing Gore to persuade him up Cook Inlet in Alaska, to his casual attitude about the timetable that led to his losing two Arctic summers? How can we explain how a navigator of his experience and unsurpassed reputation drew the wrong conclusions from those sightings off Anderson Island, which, among others, Bligh and Gore and Clerke all deduced correctly? What explanation can there be for his sailing straight towards that reef off Bonavista, and those other near-fatal errors of seamanship and navigation?

Is it possible to understand how a man of his notable steadiness and decisiveness could become with increasing frequency vacillating and uncertain of himself? One day the old optimistic and cheerful Cook, the next dour and pessimistic. Vain in London in February 1776 at the beginning in accepting the command; vain again in Hawaii in February 1779 at the end in parading his hollow superiority. But a modest man at heart, as his wife, his patrons, his officers and friends could testify.

Never slow to anger, but never as quick as on this last voyage; quicker still towards the end, and then fatally swift.

Where was the tactful, thoughtful yet firm master of his men? Where was the Cook with the reputation second to none in handling his men? Not force-feeding them stinking walrus flesh in the Arctic, or sugar cane beer off Hawaii. And his treatment of the natives? As a younger man he had spilt blood in exasperation: this incident at Poverty Bay, New Zealand, had scarred him. Never again. His care to avoid bloodshed had been a wonder to his officers, incomprehensible and even outrageous to his seamen. But at Nootka Sound he wounded three or four natives by musket fire on the smallest provocation. Here at Hawaii he shot to kill. The Cook of 1772 would have been appalled at the idea of answering theft with a murderous six dozen lashes, or slicing off ears, or branding an arm with a knife. And the Cook of 1772 would not have recognized the livid commander of 1779, proceeding ashore with murder in his heart and escorted by armed marines, ball in their muskets. 'The behaviour of the indians will at last oblige me to use force.' Instead of marching ahead of a column of armed marines at dawn, he could so easily have proceeded ashore later in the day unescorted, as he had the previous day. But he was seized with a terrible temper—his *heivas*, his Achilles heel.

Then, where was Cook's old burning curiosity on this third voyage? Undoubtedly he was excited by his new discoveries, but they came by chance. With all the days wasted at the Cape, Kerguelen and Adventure Bay, he could have spared a day or two to check Furneaux's contention that Tasmania was a part of mainland Australia. His conclusion would have been a major correction on the maps of the Antipodes. Uneventful weeks passed at the Friendly Islands, to the benefit of no one, and Cook knew all the time that a notable new undiscovered group—the Fijis—lay a day or two north-west.

Then, how to account for the precipitate giving away of much of his livestock at Tonga—the animals he had been at such pains and expense to preserve for their proper destination?

This is not the same man at all. Through his long voyage we see much of the old sturdy, steady, compassionate, brilliant commander and navigator. But as month follows month, so with increasing frequency we catch glimpses of a different man altogether, until at the end we have a virtually total metamorphosis.

Can this transformation, one asks, be ascribed solely to weariness of mind? Of course he was tired out at the end of the second voyage, and he still was at the beginning of his last. Sandwich knew it, Palliser knew it; for all we know, the king recognized his weariness. Certainly, Elizabeth Cook bade goodbye to her beloved husband knowing how tired he was.

But James Cook was also a physically robust and resilient man, with a splendid health record, and at 47—or even 50 when he died—hardly in his declining years. Look what Horatio Nelson, of frail health and physique and dreadfully maimed, could accomplish at 47.

All the evidence points to something graver and more fundamental than mere weariness, or even a mood illness such as depression. There were indeed swings of mood, periods of melancholy or of irritability. But there were also occasions of casualness and carelessness, the unprecedented failure of will, even the emergence of a cruel streak quite foreign to his character. The careless navigation and the many serious errors of judgment suggest an actual decay of his splendid intellect. For such a total transformation we may have to look for the deepest of causes—changes in the organic structure of the brain. Now after 200 years it would be rash to speculate on the nature of the disease, whether tumours or infection or one of the tropical diseases of which we still know too little. But pathology rather than psychology is likely to be our best guide.

Misfortune of one kind or another, severe or mild, touched most of those who sailed on this voyage. Omai's reign of glory and distinction was a brief one. Bligh learned of his fate when he returned to the Pacific on his breadfruit voyage in 1788. For a time Omai enjoyed prestige as a result of his mysterious possessions and from his attempts (surely now more successful) at horseback riding on the beach at Fare: indeed this riding made such an impression on the islanders that it was depicted on the tattooes of several natives, a remote reflection of the Rotten Row morning parade of riders that Omai had so often witnessed.

But it was his armoury that was the real source of Omai's

short-lived prestige. Soon after Cook's departure a conflict arose with Raiatea, in which the warlike Bora-Borans also became involved. Omai was consulted by the Huahiné chiefs, and he gladly offered his services and the use of his muskets. There were only three or four of them, with a limited amount of powder. Moreover, the flints soon gave out and they had to be fired by burning sticks. But, Bligh was informed, they turned the tide of battle.

Did not this give Omai great prestige? Bligh asked. Indeed not, he was told. Omai was always of an inferior class, and remained common in his style to the end. This was brought about by some unnamed fever about two and a half years after he settled at Fare. The New Zealanders, Tiarooa and Koa, had never ceased pining for their homeland, and with the death of their master, they soon expired of broken hearts.

Omai's house and his crops were destroyed immediately after his death. His organ, his electrical machine and many more of his possessions were stolen or destroyed and never seen again. Forty years later, however, one of Huahinés chiefs still proudly possessed several of Omai's trinkets and the serpent Jack-in-the-box. Another chief had preserved his Bible with the coloured engravings, which no doubt gratified the first missionaries when they came to Huahiné. More surprising, at this same date, the house built on the site of Omai's dwelling displayed the helmet and armour suit along with several of his cutlasses, all secured to one of its outside walls.

As for Omai's livestock, his monkey lived to provide amusement for the inhabitants of Fare until it fell from a high tree and was killed. Nothing else survived except for a few pigs and dogs. The livestock at Tahiti suffered the same fate, except apparently for a bull—whether the Spanish bull from Lima or one of George III's, Bligh did not discover—and 'the most beautiful brown heifer that ever trod the earth'.

Of the two best known Americans on the voyage, Gore led the less eventful life after completing his command of the expedition. On his return he was made a post-captain and was offered and accepted the appointment at Greenwich Hospital left vacant by Cook's death. He never went to sea again, and led

a quiet and secure married life with his Nancy until his death on
10 August 1790. His obituary spoke of 'a most experienced
seaman and an honour to his profession. As a practical navigator
he was surpassed by none.'

John Ledyard, by contrast, led a restless existence until his
death a year before his old friend Gore's. He had been among
several of the ships' crews who had purchased furs at Nootka
Sound for a nail or two and sold them later for great sums. On
his return, he refused to fight in the war against his own country
and served two years in barracks in England, nursing all the time
a growing urge to establish a fur trade with the American
north-west. His first attempts to set up a sailing venture from
England failed, so he went to France, made himself known to
John Paul Jones and attempted without success to establish a
similar venture from Paris. He had better luck with Thomas
Jefferson, who was prepared to back Ledyard's astonishing
proposal to walk clear across Siberia, ship to Nootka Sound, and
thence back across the unexplored American continent to
Virginia. This powerful and singular character would no doubt
have succeeded, too, but for Empress Catherine's intervention
when she refused permission for an expedition she reasonably
felt might interfere with the Russian monopoly of the fur trade.

Ignoring this prohibition, and without any financial support,
Ledyard walked 1500 miles to St Petersburg, and thence—
begging for food en route—to Yakutsk, a further 3000 miles or
so, where he met by chance Joseph Billings, late of the *Discovery*,
now a captain in the Russian navy who was commanding an
exploring expedition of the coast of north-eastern parts of Asia
and the Bering Sea. By this time Ledyard believed he must be
close to success. But before he could derive any benefit from this
coincidental meeting, he was arrested on the orders of the
Empress and despatched roughly back to England.

As dogged as ever, Ledyard appealed to Sir Joseph Banks for
support. Banks, now President of the Royal Society, said no to
Nootka Sound and fur-trading, but was so impressed by the
persevering adventurousness of Cook's old sailor that he
appointed him to lead an expedition sponsored by the
Association for Promoting the Discovery of the Interior Parts of

Africa. Ledyard got as far as Cairo, where he fell ill, rashly took a dose of vitriol as a curative but killed himself instead.

James King, like Gore, was appointed post-captain on his return, wrote the last volume of the three-volume official published journal of the voyage, was appointed to command H.M.S. *Resistance* 40 guns, to escort a convoy to the West Indies, picked up consumption and died from it in 1784.

Jem Burney had better fortune. He returned safely to his large and loving family, with his mementoes of his four years' voyaging, his tales of Polynesia, America, the Arctic and Asia, his accounts of curious practices and strange music and musical instruments to fascinate his father. Like many of his shipmates, he had kept a journal, and, learning of the outbreak of war on the way home and fearful of losing this priceless record to the enemy, he copied it out on fine China paper, creating a fascinating document in miniature weighing only a few ounces.

In fact, the *Resolution* and *Discovery* were as carefully protected by the hostile French as by the American revolutionaries, and there was never any risk of interference, let alone capture. Later, however, Burney's earnest wish to do battle with the 'Dons, Monsieurs, and Mynheers' was satisfied, and as a Captain R.N. he was successful in frigate actions against de Suffren.

Burney's health failed after 1784 and he was not employed again. Instead, he turned more seriously to his second talent, authorship, including a book on whist. He mixed freely and was much admired by the poetry establishment of his day, Southey, Hazlitt, Coleridge, and Lamb, who wrote of 'Jem's' death to Wordsworth, 'There's Captain Burney gone! What fun has whist now? What matters it what you lead if you can no longer fancy him looking over you?' But Burney dropped Hazlitt when he ventured to criticize sister Fanny's *Evelina*. Burney was famed less for his poetry, or his book on whist, than for his massive five-volume work, *A Chronological History of the Discoveries in the South Sea or Pacific Ocean*.

Fanny continued to love him through many trials. He increasingly played the part of the bluff sea captain, saying in a loud voice all that came to his mind, in or out of the opera house, and as Fanny had now become the Countess d'Arblay and moved in very grand cultural and social circles, this could be trying, especially as he dressed as if he had just come ashore from a four-year-long cruise. More testing for Fanny was brother Jem's family behaviour. He had 'Sallied forth' (how he loved his puns!) and married Sally Paine, the daughter of his sister's publisher-bookseller, in 1785. Later, he eloped with his half-sister Sarah Harriet Burney, with whom he lived a some-what hole-in-the-corner existence for some five years. 'I have even wished him *dead* ere such an action sullied his fair character,' exploded Fanny. But the breach was healed, partly by the need to show family solidarity in the face of a worse crisis.

Burney had been delighted when his old friend Molesworth Phillips had fallen in love with another of his sisters, Susan, and married her in 1782. But this marriage, too, was a disaster, and to compound the offence he piled up debts to the family, took his wife unwillingly to Ireland, where she contracted a fatal dysentery, dying on her return to England. Fanny never got over her grief for her sister, nor her loathing for Phillips, who remarried, left his second wife, took a mistress, and piled up debts everwhere, yet remained a friend of Jem Burney's to the end. This unreliable, irresponsible and indolent Royal Marines officer rose to the rank of lieutenant-colonel but was captured and detained in France during the Napoleonic Wars from 1802 until 1814.

David Samwell remained in the Royal Navy, at the same time becoming, when on half-pay, a well known member of the Welsh literary circle in London, where he 'was esteemed an elegant poet'. He served as surgeon in James King's ships, and later in 1798 to the British prisoners-of-war at Versailles, dying on his return to London in December of that year.

John Williamson died in the same year after a naval career which showed a continuing talent for survival. No officer spoke to him for a year after Cook's death. But he was never court-martialled on his return for the good reason that the main witnesses refused to testify against him. In the cause of peace, Clerke had disposed of all the testimony. Then, as an ardent Freemason, Williamson had persuaded, bribed or threatened most of those who had been in his launch crew on that critical morning to join his Freemasons' Lodge, which prohibited them from any disloyalty.

He rose to the rank of captain, commanding the *Agincourt* at the Battle of Camperdown in 1797—an engagement in which Bligh served with great courage—when he acted in such a cowardly manner that he was court-martialled and dismissed the service with ignominy.

Sergeant Samuel Gibson, Cook's favourite marine, survived the captain whose life he had once saved by only a year and a half, and was among the few in the ships' companies who never returned to London. During the long period of delay in the Orkneys, Gibson had sensibly married a local girl of Stromness. The sergeant was then unfortunate enough to contract a fatal disease on the last leg, and was buried at sea off the Scottish coast on 22 September 1780.

William Bligh, as all the world knows, was an even better survivor, and for much better reasons, than John Williamson. His character is well known, although it has been subjected to different interpretations over the years. His talents are manifest in his voyages, his weaknesses in his mutinies. Except for Anderson we know of only two officers for whom he entertained any respect on this voyage, Cook and Jem Burney. The officer he despised most was James King.

Of the two men on the voyage who served under Bligh in the *Bounty*, Nelson the gardener survived the open boat voyage after the mutiny but died in Coupang, Timor, on 20 June 1789; while the gunner, William Peckover, continued to prove indestructible and returned with Bligh to England.

As for the three men who had sent Cook on this fatal voyage, Stephens continued in his post and was deservedly knighted. Palliser was replaced as Comptroller of the Navy while Cook was struggling to find the North-West Passage. His successor was Charles Middleton, who was to become a notable naval reformer and administrator, later, as Lord Barham, First Sea Lord during Nelson's greatest years. He found chaos and corruption everywhere at the Admiralty, and not only at the dockyards. Palliser had been an excellent officer up to that time, a first class commander-in-chief and Governor of Newfoundland, discerning the true quality of Cook and becoming his patron.

While Cook was in the Pacific and war broke out again with France, Palliser was made third-in-command of the Channel Fleet under Admiral Augustus Keppel. It was an unhappy appointment, Palliser being a strong Tory, Keppel a convinced Whig. At the Battle of Ushant in 1778 Palliser failed to support his commander-in-chief as strongly as he could have done, there were hints of cowardice, and both admirals were court-martialled. Although both were acquitted, Keppel's reputation suffered no damage, while Palliser was discredited in the eyes of the public and the navy.

Lord Sandwich's reputation suffered a less abrupt decline than Palliser's, but it was deeper and even more damaging. As right-hand man to the Prime Minister, Lord North, during the American War of Independence, he was inevitably and rightly associated with all the naval and some of the military disasters of that campaign.

The Royal Navy was better for the loss of both these men; and there is a certain measure of tidiness and justice in the fact that their period of success and public esteem ended with their despatch of Cook on his third fatal voyage.

The ships fared no better than the men. The *Resolution* suffered the shame of capture by the French soon after she was made fit for service again, and is believed to have foundered almost at once. The *Discovery* ended her days near Deptford as a convict hulk.

The name Cook, which had risen rapidly from such North Yorkshire obscurity, disappeared almost completely after the body of James was lowered into the waters of Kealakekua Bay in 1779. His eldest son, James, became a naval officer like his father but was killed in 1794, probably at the hands of robbers. The second son, Nathaniel, followed his father and brother into the navy, and went down in his ship a year after his father's murder but before Mrs Cook had learned of it. Three more children had already died at ages between four months and four years. Finally, the youngest son, destined for the church, succumbed to a fever in 1793, leaving Elizabeth Cook a childless widow.

She lived for 56 years after the death of her husband, a stalwart, determined old lady of 93, always eager to talk about 'poor, dear Mr Cook' and to protest, when proper, that 'poor dear Mr Cook would never have done that'. She was left well-off, with a generous pension and a half-share of the proceeds of the expensive and wide-selling published journal.

The last confirmed knowledge of the family that had grown up under such severe moral control and had become synonymous with heroism and adventure was in 1801. Cook's sister Margaret appealed to Banks for some support for herself and her husband, 'a poor fisherman' now advanced in years and 'thereby reduced to a state of great distress'. Banks referred her to her sister-in-law, and Elizabeth Cook sent her £10 and arranged for an annuity of £20 a year. Alas for her generosity! The local justice of the peace later reported that, 'It appears she is addicted to insobriety and I have much reason to apprehend that what is given in a pecuniary way is converted to improper purposes.'

The supposed site of Cook's murder has been visited by countless people over the years, among them souvenir hunters who have hacked at the volcanic rocks, and an enterprising Frenchman who dynamited and took away more than a ton of them, so that it is no longer possible to stand on this shore and say, 'This is where he fell.'

Otherwise Kealakekua Bay is little changed from the time when Cook first anchored here in January 1779. The population is much reduced, but dwellings are scattered on the sites of the old villages, and a few tourists' sailing boats ply across the water that was once filled with high-prowed double canoes. Mauna Loa has erupted many times, and one suspects that the vegetation is sparser than in the days of King Terreeoboo. Certainly the rich coconut palm groves have long since disappeared, and today Cook would have found the anchorage a less attractive place than 200 years ago, although just as sheltered.

At Hawaii a monument marks the man and his murder, one of so many that have been set up across the Pacific, whose waters he explored more fully and boldly than any other commander—

at Adventure Bay, Queen Charlotte's Sound, Point Venus, Tahiti and elsewhere. It is appropriate that 250 years after his birth a replica of the statue that depicts the great explorer-scientist looking out over Whitby Bay in Yorkshire, where he first went to sea, has been erected at Anchorage, Alaska, the place where he was beguiled into believing that he might have found the North-West Passage.

A note on longitude

JAMES COOK HAD the good fortune to be an accomplished navigator at a time of unprecedented advances in navigational skills and instruments. While working as a young sailor out of Whitby, he had relied upon the primitive but satisfactory back-staff for ascertaining *latitude*. He would take the altitude of the sun, its angle of elevation above the horizon, make several simple calculations, and there it was. In 1731 John Hadley had refined the backstaff with a mirror arrangement, which made for much greater accuracy, 'though the ship rolls ever so much'. Later, another John, John Campbell, a contemporary of Cook's, who had also left the coal trade for the lower deck of the navy, developed Hadley's quadrant into the sextant.

So, on all Cook's three great Pacific voyages, there was no trouble about latitude. And he had the compass for his direction, and the lead line, as old as the seagoing ship, for ascertaining the depth of water—the shape of the seabed.

Longitude was something entirely different, and for centuries very intractable. In other words, it was easy enough to find your way from side to side across the globe, but something altogether different to know where you were going up and down. On his numerous Atlantic passages, Cook (to put it crudely again) got himself on the right latitude, and sailed east or west. He was by no means navigating blindfold. He used dead reckoning. He was able to measure the speed of his ship from his log, he knew his direction, he knew a little about the tides and currents and more about the winds. But it was hit-or-miss navigation—a good deal more hit than miss in his case.

So important was it considered for a ship at sea to know its longitude, that a Board of Longitude was set up as early as 1714, and later a considerable prize of £20,000 was offered to a successful inventor. Nothing very significant emerged for several decades. A specialized form of lunar observation—taking the angular distance between the moon and the sun or one of a number of fixed stars—was devised. It was accurate, and was used on Cook's first Pacific voyage, on which he made some of his most brilliant running surveys. But you had to have a mathematician on board to make your calculations. And even then it might take four hours.

For many years it had been known that an accurate means of telling the time would provide the answer, time being a function of longitude. If you could take a standard point of departure—like Greenwich—and compare *accurately* the time there with wherever you were east or west, your longitude could readily be calculated, even by the simplest merchantman skipper.

Upon this sea of blind uncertainty there now appears a man who never sailed in a ship, a man of a calibre dire necessity occasionally throws up, John Harrison, a humble village carpenter and clockmaker—yet another John and another Yorkshireman genius. In 1735, John and his brother James constructed their first timekeeper, with new features, which showed unprecedented accuracy. Two more followed over the years, all completed with a certain amount of outside aid and much outside encouragement. Harrison completed his first 'nautical watch', or 'watch machine' or 'chronometer' (twice the size of a big pocket watch) in 1759. On a 156-day voyage to the West Indies a Harrison remained correct within eight seconds.

These Harrisons, which were eventually to win the award, were masterpieces of fine horology. One of their most important innovations was an arrangement by which power continued to be transmitted through the train to the escapement while the mechanism was being wound.

Cook took a Harrison 'copy' by the London watchmaker Larcum Kendall on his second voyage. After completing his circumnavigation, the longitude error was just eight miles at Plymouth. The watch's steady tick can be heard at Greenwich naval museum today.

These 'watch machines' were as expensive as they were accurate, and took years to make. So the ready calculation of longitude remained unresolved for many decades, until the first cheap chronometers, which are still carried in ships today, although largely superseded since the advent of reliable international radio, which 'pips' out Greenwich time.

Select bibliography

J. Banks: *Journals*, ed. J. Hooker (London, 1896)

J. C. Beaglehole: *The Life of Captain James Cook* (London, 1974)

Bering Sea and Strait Pilot (1920)

W. Besant: *Captain Cook* (London and New York, 1890)

H. Bingham: *A Residence of 21 Years in the Sandwich Islands* (Hartford, 1849)

H. Carrington: *Life of Captain Cook* (London, 1939)

J. Cook: *The Journals of Captain James Cook R.N. on his Voyages of Discovery*, ed. J. C. Beaglehole, 4 vols. and portfolio of charts (Cambridge, 1955–69)

W. Ellis: *Narrative of a Voyage through Hawaii* (London, 1828)

J. R. Forster: *History of the Voyages and Discoveries made in the North* (London, 1786)

R. Y. Gould: *Captain Cook* (London, 1935)

W. Heberden: *Commentaries on the History and Cure of Disease* (London, 1767)

J. Hemlow: *The History of Fanny Burney* (London, 1958)

R. Hough: *Captain Bligh and Mr Christian* (London, 1972)

A. Kippis: *The Life of Captain James Cook* (London, 1788)

A. Kitson: *Captain James Cook* (London, 1907)

J. Sparke: *Memoirs of the Life and Travels of John Ledyard* (London, 1828)

J. P. L. Thomas: *Admiralty House, Whitehall* (London, 1960)

J. Trevenen: *The Memoirs of James Trevenen*, ed. C. Lloyd and R. C. Anderson (London, 1959)

G. Young: *The Life and Voyages of Captain James Cook* (London, 1836)

Gentleman's Magazine   *Mariners Mirror*

Cook's Earlier Voyages

James Cook was late going to sea at 18 by comparison with most naval officers, and he did not in fact transfer to the Royal Navy until he was 27, in 1755. His experience at that time was limited mainly to home waters and the Baltic, but he was already a highly competent seaman and navigator. His promotion in the navy was rapid and he was a ship's master two years later, sailing across the Atlantic many times, first in connection with the war against the French in Canada, and subsequently as his own commander in his surveys of Nova Scotia and Newfoundland.

Cook's exceptional scientific, hydrographical and astronomical talent became known to the Admiralty, and his observations of an eclipse of the sun from Newfoundland in 1766 drew the attention of the Royal Society. When the civilian, Alexander Dalrymple, proved unacceptable to the Admiralty as commander of the scientific expedition to the Pacific to observe the transit of the planet Venus across the face of the sun, Cook was recommended to lead the enterprise.

The Whitby-built ex-collier *Endeavour*, a type of ship which Cook had sailed for many years, was chosen and fitted out for the long voyage with elaborate scientific equipment and supplies of anti-scorbutic articles of diet, including pickled cabbage, dried soup, malt and citrus fruit. The talented and colourful scientific personnel included Joseph Banks, the Swedish naturalist, Daniel Carl Solander and his assistant, and the astronomer Charles Green.

The *Endeavour* sailed from Plymouth 25 August 1768 and returned 12 July 1771. The health of the crew was preserved to an unprecedented degree until the ship called at Batavia on the way home, when dysentery and malaria carried away a number of the company.

The voyage, which included charting parts of Tierra del Fuego, a great part of New Zealand's coastline, proving that it was not a northern promontory of the fabled *Terra Australis Incognita*, and the east coast of Australia, was a triumph of exploration. The astronomical observations on Tahiti and Cook's experiences in the Society Islands were to have a crucial influence on further Pacific exploration, which was not long delayed.

The absence of a second vessel had proved disadvantageous on the first circumnavigation, and Cook took two sloops on his second epochal voyage, upon which he sailed one year after his return. The first purpose was to prove or disprove the existence of the great southern continent for reasons of national power as well as for the advancement of science and discovery. The track of Cook's *Resolution* (unfortunately the *Adventure* became separated) on the three-year-long voyage makes great whorls and sweeps on a map of the world, from England to Cape Town to New Zealand, a vast circle of discovery about the Pacific and back circuitously by way of Cape Horn. The voyage included three penetrations into the Antarctic, proving to all but the most gullible or obstinate that no southern continent existed.

This second voyage showed the world that James Cook was the greatest navigator-explorer of his day, and his use of the chronometer for the first time, and the good health of his men, were to have a marked influence on all future long voyages in the age of sail.

Index